REA's Test Prep Books Are The Best!
(a sample of the hundreds of letters REA receives each year)

" Your book was such a better value and was so much more complete than anything your competition has produced — and I have them all! "
Teacher, Virginia Beach, VA

" Compared to the other books that my fellow students had, your book was the most useful in helping me get a great score. "
Student, North Hollywood, CA

" Your book was responsible for my success on the exam, which helped me get into the college of my choice... I will look for REA the next time I need help. "
Student, Chesterfield, MO

" Just a short note to say thanks for the great support your book gave me in helping me pass the test... I'm on my way to a B.S. degree because of you! "
Student, Orlando, FL

" I really appreciate the help from your excellent book. Please keep up the great work. "
Student, Albuquerque, NM

" This book was right on target with what was on the [CLEP Introductory Sociology] test. I highly advise studying it before you take the exam. "
Student, Washington, DC

(more on next page)

(continued from front page)

" I just wanted to thank you for helping me get a great score
on the AP U.S. History exam... Thank you for making great test preps! "
Student, Los Angeles, CA

" Your *Fundamentals of Engineering Exam* book was the absolute best
preparation I could have had for the exam, and it is one of the major
reasons I did so well and passed the FE on my first try. "
Student, Sweetwater, TN

" I used your book to prepare for the test and found that the advice and the
sample tests were highly relevant... Without using any other material, I earned
very high scores and will be going to the graduate school of my choice. "
Student, New Orleans, LA

" What I found in your book was a wealth of information sufficient to shore up
my basic skills in math and verbal... The section on analytical ability was
excellent. The practice tests were challenging and the answer explanations most
helpful. It certainly is the *Best Test Prep for the GRE!* "
Student, Pullman, WA

" I studied this guide exclusively and passed the [CLEP Introductory Sociology]
test with 12 points to spare. "
Student, Dallas, TX

" I am writing to thank you for your test preparation... your book helped me
immeasurably and I have nothing but praise for your *GRE* preparation."
Student, Benton Harbor, MI

THE BEST TEST PREPARATION FOR THE

CLEP
American
Government

With REA's TestWare® on CD-ROM

Preston Jones, Ph.D.
Associate Professor of History
John Brown University
Siloam Springs, Arkansas

Research & Education Association
Visit our website at
www.rea.com

Planet Friendly Publishing
✔ Made in the United States
✔ Printed on Recycled Paper
  Text: 10%   Cover: 10%
  Learn more: www.greenedition.org

GREEN EDITION

At REA we're committed to producing books in an Earth-friendly manner and to helping our customers make greener choices.

Manufacturing books in the United States ensures compliance with strict environmental laws and eliminates the need for international freight shipping, a major contributor to global air pollution.

And printing on recycled paper helps minimize our consumption of trees, water and fossil fuels. This book was printed on paper made with **10% post-consumer waste**. According to Environmental Defense's Paper Calculator, by using this innovative paper instead of conventional papers, we achieved the following environmental benefits:

**Trees Saved: 4 • Air Emissions Eliminated: 642 pounds
Water Saved: 658 gallons • Solid Waste Eliminated: 198 pounds**

For more information on our environmental practices, please visit us online at **www.rea.com/green**

Research & Education Association
61 Ethel Road West
Piscataway, New Jersey 08854
E-mail: info@rea.com

The Best Test Preparation for the
CLEP AMERICAN GOVERNMENT EXAM
With TestWare® on CD-ROM

Published 2011

Printed in the United States of America

Library of Congress Control Number 2009922320

ISBN 13: 978-0-7386-0306-3
ISBN 10: 0-7386-0306-6

Windows® is a registered trademark of Microsoft Corporation.

REA® and TestWare® are registered trademarks of Research & Education Association, Inc.

CONTENTS

Chapter 4   Congress: Powers and Organization

Chapter 5   Congress: Rules, Lobbyists, Taxes, the Budget, and Operations

Chapter 6   The Presidency

About Our Author

Dr. Preston Jones has been a Fulbright scholar and a fellow of the Pew Program in Religion and American History. He received his doctorate in History from the University of Ottawa (Canada) in 1999 and an M.A. in History from California State University at Sonoma in 1995. Dr. Jones has taught courses in European, American, and world history at the secondary and university levels. He also teaches Latin. He has published over 200 articles in scholarly journals, magazines, and newspapers. Currently he teaches at John Brown University in Arkansas.

Author's Acknowledgments

The following students of mine lent this project small but significant assistance: James Cooke, Chris Cox, Brianna Knott, Michael Morriss, Kelsey Norbash, Emily Nuss, Abigail Roth, Karissa Schmoe, and Kristen Starkey.

Jacob Little and Abigail Jeppsen provided more substantial help.

Most of all, I am grateful for the work of Kelly Neighbors, my teacher's assistant, and the patience and goodwill of Diane Goldschmidt, my editor at REA.

Inevitably, this book is a synthesis of syntheses. I relied very much on the following excellent textbooks and am grateful to these scholars for their labors:

Barbara Bardes et al., *American Government and Politics Today* (Belmont, CA: Cengage Higher Education, 2009);

Kenneth Dautrich and David A. Yalof, *American Government: Historical, Popular and Global Perspectives* (Belmont, CA: Cengage Higher Education, 2009);

Kenneth Janda et al., *The Challenge of Democracy: Government in America* (New York: Houghton Mifflin, 2008);

David M. Kennedy et al., *American Pageant* (New York: Houghton Mifflin, 2002); and

Peverill Squire, et al., *Dynamics of Democracy* (Cincinnati: Atomic Dog Publishing, 2001).

About Research & Education Association

Founded in 1959, Research & Education Association (REA) is dedicated to publishing the finest and most effective educational materials—including software, study guides, and test preps—for students in elementary school, middle school, high school, college, graduate school, and beyond.

Today, REA's wide-ranging catalog is a leading resource for teachers, students, and professionals.

We invite you to visit us at *www.rea.com* to find out how "REA is making the world smarter."

Acknowledgments

In addition to our author, we would like to thank Larry B. Kling, Vice President, Editorial, for his overall guidance, which brought this publication to completion; Pam Weston, Vice President, Publishing, for setting the quality standards for production integrity and managing the publication to completion; John Cording, Vice President, Technology, for coordinating the design and development of REA's TestWare®; Diane Goldschmidt, Senior Editor, for project management; Alice Leonard and Mike Reynolds, Senior Editors, for preflight editorial review; Heena Patel and Amy Jamison, Technology Project Managers, for their design contributions and software testing efforts; Jeff LoBalbo, Senior Graphic Designer, for coordinating pre-press electronic file mapping; and Christine Saul, Senior Graphic Designer, for designing our cover.

We also gratefully acknowledge Dr. Paul Babbitt of Southern Arkansas University for his technical review of the manuscript, Mary O'Briant and Caroline Duffy for copyediting, Marianne L'Abbate and Ellen Gong for proofreading, Terry Casey for indexing, and Kathy Caratozzolo of Caragraphics for typesetting this edition.

CLEP AMERICAN GOVERNMENT
Independent Study Schedule

The following study schedule allows for thorough preparation for the CLEP American Government exam. Although it is designed for four weeks, it can be condensed to a two-week course by collapsing each two-week period into one. Be sure to set aside enough time—at least two hours each day— study. No matter which study schedule works best for you, the more time spend studying, the more prepared and relaxed you will feel on the day of exam.

Week	Activity
1	Read and study Chapter 1 of this book, which will introduce you to the CLEP American Government exam. Take Practice Test 1 on CD-ROM to determine your strengths and weaknesses. Assess your results by using our raw score conversion table. You can then determine the areas in which you need to strengthen your skills.
2 and 3	Carefully read and study the CLEP American Government review material included in Chapters 2 through 10 in this book.
4	Take Practice Test 2 on CD-ROM and carefully review the explanations for all incorrect answers. If there are any types of questions or particular subjects that seem difficult to you, review those subjects by again studying the appropriate sections of the CLEP American Government review chapters.

Note: If you care to, and time allows, retake Practice Tests 1 and 2 printed in this book. This will help strengthen the areas in which your performance may still be lagging and build your overall confidence.

Chapter 1

Passing the CLEP American Government Exam

ABOUT THIS BOOK AND TESTWARE®

This book provides you with complete preparation for the CLEP American Government exam. Inside you will find a targeted review of the subject matter, as well as tips and strategies for test taking. We also give you two practice tests, featuring content and formatting based on the official CLEP American Government exam. Our practice tests contain every type of question that you can expect to encounter on the actual exam. Following each practice test you will find an answer key with detailed explanations designed to help you more completely understand the test material.

The practice exams in this book and software package are included in two formats: in printed format in this book, and in TestWare® format on the enclosed CD. **We strongly recommend that you begin your preparation with the TestWare® practice exams.** The software provides the added benefits of instant scoring and enforced time conditions.

All CLEP exams are computer-based. As you can see, the practice tests in our book are presented as paper-and-pencil exams. The content and format of the actual CLEP subject exams are faithfully mirrored. Later in this chapter you'll find a detailed outline of the format and content of the CLEP American Government exam.

ABOUT THE EXAM

Who takes CLEP exams and what are they used for?

CLEP examinations are typically taken by people who have acquired knowledge outside the classroom and wish to bypass certain college courses and earn college credit. The CLEP is designed to reward students for learning—no matter where or how that knowledge was acquired. The CLEP is the most widely accepted credit-by-examination program in the country, with more than 2,900 colleges and universities granting credit for satisfactory scores on CLEP exams.

Although most CLEP examinees are adults returning to college, many graduating high school seniors, enrolled college students, military personnel, and international students also take the exams to earn college credit or to demonstrate their ability to perform at the college level. There are no prerequisites, such as age or educational status, for taking CLEP examinations. However, because policies on granting credits vary among colleges, you should contact the particular institution from which you wish to receive CLEP credit.

There are two categories of CLEP examinations:

1. **CLEP General Examinations**, which are five separate tests that cover material usually taken as requirements during the first two years of college. CLEP General Examinations are available for English Composition (with or without essay), Humanities, College Mathematics, Natural Sciences, and Social Sciences and History.

2. **CLEP Subject Examinations** include material usually covered in an undergraduate course with a similar title. For a complete list of the subject examinations offered, visit the College Board website.

Who administers the exam?

The CLEP exams are developed by the College Board, administered by Educational Testing Service (ETS), and involve the assistance of educators throughout the United States. The test development process is designed and implemented to ensure that the content and difficulty level of the test are appropriate.

When and where is the exam given?

CLEP exams are administered each month throughout the year at more than 1,300 test centers in the United States and can be arranged for candidates abroad on request. To find the test center nearest you and to register for the exam, you should obtain a copy of the free booklets *CLEP Colleges* and *CLEP Information for Candidates and Registration Form*. They are available at most colleges where CLEP credit is granted, or by contacting:

CLEP Services
P.O. Box 6600
Princeton, NJ 08541-6600
Phone: (800) 257-9558 (8 A.M. to 6 P.M. ET)
Fax: (609) 771-7088
Website: *www.collegeboard.com/clep*

CLEP Options for Military Personnel and Veterans

CLEP exams are available free of charge to eligible military personnel and eligible civilian employees. All the CLEP exams are available at test centers on college campuses and military bases. In addition, the College Board has developed a paper-based version of 14 high-volume/high-pass-rate CLEP tests for DANTES Test Centers. Contact the Educational Services Officer or Navy College Education Specialist for more information. Visit the College Board website for details about CLEP opportunities for military personnel.

Eligible U.S. veterans can claim reimbursement for CLEP exams and administration fees pursuant to provisions of the Veterans Benefits Improvement Act of 2004. For details on eligibility and submitting a claim for reimbursement, visit the U.S. Department of Veterans Affairs website at *www.gibill.va.gov/pamphlets/testing.htm*.

SSD Accommodations for Students with Disabilities

Many students qualify for extra time to take the CLEP American Government exam, but you must make these arrangements in advance. For information, contact:

College Board Services for Students with Disabilities
P.O. Box 6226
Princeton, NJ 08541-6226
Phone: (609) 771-7137 (Monday through Friday, 8 A.M. to 6 P.M. ET)
TTY: (609) 882-4118
Fax: (609) 771-7944
E-mail: ssd@info.collegeboard.org

Our TestWare® can be adapted to accommodate your time extension. This allows you to practice under the same extended-time accommodations that you will receive on the actual test day. To customize your TestWare® to suit the most common extensions, visit our website at *http://www.rea.com/ssd*.

HOW TO USE THIS BOOK AND TESTWARE®

What do I study first?

To begin your studies, read over the introduction and the suggestions for test taking. Take Practice Exam 1 on CD-ROM to determine your strengths and weaknesses, and then study the course review material, focusing on your specific problem areas. The course review includes the information you need to know when taking the exam. Make sure to follow up your diagnostic work by taking the remaining practice exam on CD-ROM to become familiar with the format and feel of the CLEP American Government exam.

To best utilize your study time, follow our Independent Study Schedule, which you'll find in the front of this book. The schedule is based on a four-week program, but can be condensed to two weeks if necessary by collapsing each two-week period into one.

When should I start studying?

It is never too early to start studying for the CLEP American Government exam. The earlier you begin, the more time you will have to sharpen your skills. Do not procrastinate! Cramming is not an effective way to study, since it does not allow you the time needed to learn the test material. The sooner you learn the format of the exam, the more time you will have to familiarize yourself with it.

FORMAT AND CONTENT OF THE EXAM

The CLEP American Government exam covers the material one would find in an introductory college-level American government and politics class. The exam covers topics such as the institutions and policy processes of the federal government, the federal courts and civil liberties, political parties and interest groups, political beliefs and behavior, and the content and history of the Constitution.

The exam consists of 100 multiple-choice questions, each with five possible answer choices, to be answered in 90 minutes.

The approximate breakdown of topics is as follows:

30–35%	Institutions and policy processes: presidency, bureaucracy, and Congress
15–20%	Federal courts, civil liberties, and civil rights
15–20%	Political parties and interest groups

10–15%	Political beliefs and behavior
15–20%	Constitutional underpinnings of American democracy

ABOUT OUR COURSE REVIEW

The review in this book provides you with a complete background of all the important American government topics relevant to the exam. It will help reinforce the facts you have already learned while better shaping your understanding of the discipline as a whole. By using the review in conjunction with the practice tests, you should be well prepared to take the CLEP American Government exam.

SCORING YOUR PRACTICE TESTS

How do I score my practice tests?

The CLEP American Government exam is scored on a scale of 20 to 80. To score your practice tests, count up the number of correct answers. This is your total raw score. Convert your raw score to a scaled score using the conversion table on page 6. (**Note:** The conversion table provides only an *estimate* of your scaled score. Scaled scores can and do vary over time, and in no case should a sample test be taken as a precise predictor of test performance. Nonetheless, our scoring table allows you to judge your level of performance within a reasonable scoring range.)

When will I receive my score report?

The test administrator will print out a full Candidate Score Report for you immediately upon your completion of the exam (except for CLEP English Composition with Essay). Your scores are reported only to you, unless you ask to have them sent elsewhere. If you want your scores reported to a college or other institution, you must say so when you take the examination. Since your scores are kept on file for 20 years, you can also request transcripts from Educational Testing Service at a later date.

STUDYING FOR THE EXAM

It is very important for you to choose the time and place for studying that works best for you. Some students may set aside a certain number of hours every morning, while others may choose to study at night before going to sleep.

PRACTICE-TEST RAW SCORE CONVERSION TABLE*

Raw Score	Scaled Score	Course Grade	Raw Score	Scaled Score	Course Grade
100	80	A	50	50	C
99	80	A	49	50	C
98	80	A	48	49	C
97	80	A	47	49	C
96	79	A	46	48	C
95	79	A	45	48	C
94	79	A	44	47	C
93	78	A	43	47	C
92	78	A	42	47	C
91	77	A	41	47	C
90	77	A	40	46	D
89	76	A	39	46	D
88	75	A	38	45	D
87	74	A	37	45	D
86	73	A	36	44	D
85	72	A	35	44	D
84	71	A	34	43	D
83	70	A	33	43	D
82	70	A	32	42	D
81	69	A	31	41	D
80	69	A	30	40	D
79	68	A	29	39	D
78	67	A	28	38	D
77	66	A	27	37	D
76	66	A	26	36	D
75	65	A	25	35	D
74	64	B	24	34	F
73	63	B	23	34	F
72	63	B	22	33	F
71	62	B	21	33	F
70	61	B	20	32	F
69	61	B	19	32	F
68	60	B	18	31	F
67	59	B	17	31	F
66	59	B	16	30	F
65	58	B	15	29	F
64	57	B	14	28	F
63	57	B	13	28	F
62	56	B	12	27	F
61	56	B	11	27	F
60	55	B	10	26	F
59	54	B	9	25	F
58	54	B	8	24	F
57	53	B	7	23	F
56	53	B	6	22	F
55	52	B	5	21	F
54	52	B	4	20	F
53	51	B	3	20	F
52	51	C	2	20	F
51	50	C	1	20	F
			0	20	F

* This table is provided for scoring REA practice tests only. The American Council on Education recommends that colleges use a single across-the-board credit-granting score of 50 for all CLEP computer-based exams. Nonetheless, on account of the different skills being measured and the unique content requirements of each test, the actual number of correct answers needed to reach 50 will vary. A 50 is calibrated to equate with performance that would warrant the grade C in the corresponding introductory college course.

Other students may study during the day, while waiting on a line, or even while eating lunch. Only you can determine when and where your study time will be most effective. But be consistent and use your time wisely. Work out a study routine and stick to it!

When you take the practice tests, try to make your testing conditions as much like the actual test as possible. Turn your television and radio off, and sit down at a quiet table free from distraction. Make sure to time yourself. Start off by setting a timer for the time that is allotted for each section, and be sure to reset the timer for the appropriate amount of time when you start a new section.

As you complete each practice test, score your test and thoroughly review the explanations to the questions you answered incorrectly; however, do not review too much at one time. Concentrate on one problem area at a time by reviewing the question and explanation, and by studying our review until you are confident that you completely understand the material.

TEST-TAKING TIPS

Although you may not be familiar with computer-based standardized tests such as the CLEP American Government exam, there are many ways to acquaint yourself with this type of examination and to help alleviate your test-taking anxieties. Listed below are ways to help you become accustomed to the CLEP, some of which may be applied to other standardized tests as well.

Know the format of the test. CLEP tests are not adaptive but rather fixed-length tests. In a sense, this makes them kin to the familiar paper-and-pencil exam in that you have the same flexibility to go back and review your work in each section. Moreover, the format isn't a great deal different from the paper-and-pencil CLEP.

Read all of the possible answers. Just because you think you have found the correct response, do not automatically assume that it is the best answer. Read through each choice to be sure that you are not making a mistake by jumping to conclusions.

Use the process of elimination. Go through each answer to a question and eliminate as many of the answer choices as possible. By eliminating just two answer choices, you give yourself a better chance of getting the item correct because there will be only three choices left from which to make your guess. Remember, your score is based only on the number of questions you answer correctly.

Work quickly and steadily. You will have only 90 minutes to work on 100 questions, so work quickly and steadily to avoid focusing on any one question too long. Taking the practice tests in this book will help you learn to budget your time.

Acquaint yourself with the computer screen. Familiarize yourself with the CLEP computer screen beforehand by logging on to the College Board website. Waiting until test day to see what it looks like in the pretest tutorial risks injecting needless anxiety into your testing experience. Also, familiarizing yourself with the directions and format of the exam will save you valuable time on the day of the actual test.

Be sure that your answer registers before you go to the next item. Look at the screen to see that your mouse-click causes the pointer to darken the proper oval. This takes less effort than darkening an oval on paper, but don't lull yourself into taking less care!

THE DAY OF THE EXAM

On the day of the test, you should wake up early (hopefully after a decent night's rest) and have a good breakfast. Make sure to dress comfortably, so that you are not distracted by being too hot or too cold while taking the test. Also plan to arrive at the test center early. This will allow you to collect your thoughts and relax before the test, and will also spare you the anxiety that comes with being late. As an added incentive to make sure you arrive early, keep in mind that no one will be allowed into the test session after the test has begun.

Before you leave for the test center, make sure that you have your admission form and another form of identification, which must contain a recent photograph, your name, and signature (i.e., driver's license, student identification card, or current alien registration card). You will not be admitted to the test center if you do not have proper identification.

If you would like, you may wear a watch to the test center. However, you may not wear one that makes noise because it may disturb the other test-takers. No dictionaries, textbooks, notebooks, briefcases, or packages will be permitted and drinking, smoking, and eating are prohibited.

Good luck on the CLEP American Government exam!

Chapter 2

Background to American Government

The Constitution of the United States, which was written in 1787, begins with the words "We the people of the United States." These words point to the idea, as Abraham Lincoln would say in his Gettysburg Address in 1863, that the United States is a nation governed "by the people, for the people. . . ." In other words, the United States is a **democracy**.

WHAT *DEMOCRACY* MEANS

What, exactly, does *democracy* mean? In the United States, France, Japan, South Korea, and New Zealand, for example, democracy means freedom: freedom of speech, freedom of religion, and freedom to protest nonviolently against government. It also means the freedom to be uninvolved (though in Australia, people are legally required to vote). However, these freedoms do not exist in the Democratic People's Republic of Korea (North Korea), which is probably the most politically repressed country in the world. North Korea's government is a democracy in name only.

The word *democracy,* according to the authors of *Dynamics of Democracy,* means "a form of government in which the people (defined broadly to include all adults or narrowly to exclude women and slaves, for example) are the ultimate political authority."[1] In the United States today, every citizen who is eighteen years of age, is not a felon serving time in prison, or has not, by reason of insanity, been placed under the supervision of another person has suffrage—the right to vote. Citizens can elect mayors, city council and school board members, state and federal legislators, U.S. presidents (indirectly), and so on. "The people"—in this case, most adults—have the freedom to decide who will govern them.

Before 1870, however, only white men had the right to vote nationwide. In that year, African American men were given the right to vote, though it wasn't until the mid-1960s that blacks could vote without facing intimidation in the South and parts of the Midwest. Women did not receive the vote nationwide until 1920 (though they did have suffrage in several states before then). So even though fewer *classes* of people could vote in 1860 than can do so today, the United States was still a democracy because its government leaders were chosen by the nation's people.

But what *kind* of democracy is the United States? For the most part, the United States is a **representative democracy**, meaning that voters elect the people who represent them in governmental bodies. For example, citizens elect members of the U.S. House of Representatives, and they, in turn, vote on legislation, tax bills, and so on.

Of course, not every voter gets the representation he or she wants. For example, even though many votes might be cast for a Democrat or for a candidate from the Green Party, a Republican might ultimately win the election because one feature of American democracy is that the majority rules—that is, if more Americans vote for Republicans than for candidates from other parties, the Republicans will govern because they represent the majority. (As we will see, things are really more complicated than this, but we're just getting started.)

In some instances, though, Americans exercise **direct democracy**. In other words, they vote directly on political issues, and the majority wins. The first direct democracy we know of was in the Greek city-state of **Athens**, where free male citizens debated and voted on every law.

Direct democracy in the United States today can be seen in **New England town meetings**, where citizen-residents of a town make decisions about local matters. The state most associated with direct democracy is California. In 2003, for example, the right of the people to **recall** political figures was exercised at the expense of Governor Gray Davis, a Democrat. Before his term ended, Davis was voted out of office as the result of direct voter action. In his place, the Austrian-born actor and moderate Republican, Arnold Schwarzenegger, became governor.

Other manifestations of direct democracy come in the form of **initiatives** (also known as propositions) and **referenda** (the plural of *referendum*). In 2006, voters in Michigan voted on an initiative to eliminate **affirmative action** programs in public universities and in state employment. (Affirmative action programs seek to compensate for past discrimination by giving special attention in hiring and college or university admissions to people from the groups discriminated against.) In a referendum, a piece of legislation (intended or actual) is submitted directly to the people for approval. In Canada, for example, in 1995 the residents of the province of Quebec narrowly voted, in a referendum, *not* to empower the province's government to negotiate independence from Canada. In the United States today, direct democracy in the form of initiative, recall, and referendum is most common in the Western states, with the exception of Texas.

THEORIES OF DEMOCRACY

The framers of the U.S. Constitution were opposed to direct democracy, however. Support for direct democracy in the United States didn't become strong until the late nineteenth and early twentieth centuries. As we saw earlier, the Constitution's framers put in place a representative democracy. They worried that the "passions" of the people, which sometimes were driven by political fads, could derail good government.

The framers were also committed to republican democracy. Simply put, a **republic** is a political system without a monarch. It is a political system in which the people have political power—that is, they exercise **popular sovereignty**. (The United States is a **democratic republic**.)

But in the United States, who *really* governs? According to the theory of **majoritarianism**, the government should do what most people in the country want it to do, and in the United States, majorities do get their way, generally speaking. But this reference is to majorities of people *who actually vote*. Since 1945, only about 42 percent of eligible Americans have voted for members of Congress in years when there was no presidential election. So representatives can be sent to Congress with only about 22 percent of eligible voters explicitly supporting them.

Why don't people vote? One reason they give is that they think that no matter how the vote turns out, a small group of elites will do what they want to do. People who believe this are proponents of **elite theory**. According to this idea, elites run for office, pay for campaigns, scratch their friends' backs, and accumulate power—all while singing the praises of popular sovereignty. People who see American democracy in this light really see democracy as a kind of elaborate political fraud.

We said earlier that the framers of the Constitution were opposed to direct democracy; we can now add that the framers seemed to advocate a form of elite theory. Even after the American Revolution, most of the new country's leaders argued that only men who owned a certain amount of property should have the vote.

Others see the United States as operating on the theory of political **pluralism**, meaning that different **interest groups** argue for different things; they are then willing to make political compromises and accommodations, which is considered the art of politics. A potential problem here is that interest groups can be led and financed by elites. Another problem is, as **James Madison** wrote during debates about how to frame the Constitution, that *factions* (his word for interest groups) could put their own causes ahead of the national good.

HISTORICAL BACKGROUND OF THE CONSTITUTION

When the framers of the U.S. Constitution did their work in Philadelphia in the summer of 1787, they could not have known how successful the document they signed would be. Taking up only about nine pages in a textbook, the Constitution is much shorter than the constitutions of the individual American states, and since the time it was written, it has been changed (amended) just twenty-seven times. Why were the Constitution's writers so successful?

One reason for the Constitution's success is that, by 1787, Americans had behind them long experience in self-government. They had experienced both governmental success and failure: they had successfully emerged from dependence on the British Empire and become self-governing, but they failed to avoid a bloody war in the process.

Emergence from the British Empire: U.S. Self-Government

The United States emerged from the British Empire, of which America had been a part. From the British point of view, however, America was secondary in importance to other parts of the empire, such as Barbados and India. This meant that, generally speaking, the colonial Americans were allowed substantial self-government. Sometimes this permissiveness was intentional on the British government's part, such as when the English king empowered the settlers in the colony of tobacco-growing Virginia to establish a **representative assembly** in Jamestown for the purpose of promoting the general good. Members of this assembly were men who owned large amounts of property, but nonetheless the principle of self-government was put in place.

In New England, a form of self-government came about accidentally. The Puritans aboard the *Mayflower* intended to land in territory under the Virginia Company's jurisdiction but instead came ashore at Plymouth in Massachusetts. Being outside the Virginia Company's jurisdiction, the Puritans drew up their own governing document called the **Mayflower Compact**. In this compact, the signers agreed to live under the colony's recognized authority and wait for a royal charter similar to Virginia's. In the Mayflower Compact, we see the emergence of two important concepts: (1) government by consent and (2) a willingness to live under the rule of law.

Ironically, a third way in which Americans learned to be self-governing was by breaking laws. In an effort to keep the wealth of the British Empire within the empire, the British government passed navigation laws that sharply restricted American trade with the Dutch, French, and Spanish. The restrictions of the **Navigation Acts**, which aimed to keep as much wealth as possible in British hands, favored Britain but were not so beneficial to American merchants. Many Americans either ignored the laws or did not comply with them completely. Because Britain had a global empire on its hands by the mid-1700s, the Americans were, in effect, left alone. They learned to manage their own affairs, and they grew accustomed to doing so. The Americans benefited from Britain's **salutary neglect**.

Prelude to the Revolutionary War: The End of Salutary Neglect

Following the costly French and Indian War in America (1754–1763), however, the era of salutary neglect was over. Britain wanted the Americans to become more obedient to the mother country and better contributors to the empire. Between 1764 and 1774, the British government passed a series of laws against which Americans protested. Ultimately, American protest led to the first American civil war, usually called the Revolutionary War. This conflict really was a civil war, however, because it pitted **Tories** (Loyalists living in America who did not see that revolution was justified) against others who wanted to achieve independence from Britain.

Some of the British laws that brought on the revolution were the following:

- **Sugar Act** (1764): A tax designed to help pay the costs of the French and Indian War and to fund the British government's operations. It also established **admiralty courts,** in which smugglers would be tried without the benefit of a jury of their peers.

- **Stamp Act** (1765): A tax on many paper goods, such as newspapers, marriage announcements, playing cards, and so on. Against this tax, colonists raised the slogan "no taxation without representation." The British response was that the colonists enjoyed **virtual representation** in the Parliament in London. Every member of Parliament had the empire's interest in mind—or so these Britons said. In the face of great opposition, this law was repealed.

Boston Tea Party: Colonists dumped British tea into Boston Harbor because they were angry with the British government for taxing the colonies.

- **Townshend Acts**, sometimes called the **Townshend Duties** (1767): These taxed goods directly imported from England, such as tea.

- **Coercive Acts**, sometimes called the **Intolerable Acts** (1774): These acts were passed in response to the **Boston Tea Party**, in which a protesting colonial mob cast British tea into Boston Harbor. The acts called for greater British control of the government of Massachusetts and prevented colonials from trying British officials. They also provided for the housing of British soldiers in private homes.

The argument over taxation was about more than money: real principles were involved. One of the key principles was that a government should govern only if it has the consent of the people. The tax laws passed by the British Parliament had not been voted on by American representatives, for there were no Americans in Parliament. Therefore, the tax laws passed without the Americans' consent were, according to the leaders of the revolution, illegitimate.

PHILOSOPHICAL BACKGROUND OF THE CONSTITUTION

Although Americans had long practical experience with self-government, by the time shooting started at Lexington and Concord, Massachusetts, in 1775,

American leaders also were drawing on a long political and philosophical history. Greek and Roman ideas were important to them; they were well aware of the democracy that had existed in ancient Athens.

But the greatest philosophical legacy came from England itself. In the twelfth century, the Englishman **John of Salisbury** (1115–1176) argued that law was a gift from God and that if a monarch placed himself above the God-given law, then his subjects could revolt against him—even kill him. The American revolutionaries did not call for the execution of England's **George III**, but they did suggest that the king of England had placed himself above the "Laws of Nature and of Nature's God," to use the words of the **Declaration of Independence**. Another important step on the road to American democracy came in the thirteenth century, when, in the famous **Magna Carta**, England's nobles put some limitations on the English monarch's powers. This document enunciated three important principles: (1) the king could not levy taxes without the consent of his councilmen, (2) a person could be imprisoned only after being tried by a jury via the due process of law, and (3) the king himself was under the law. In other words, a nation's true monarch was the law.

Also highly significant to the framers of the American Constitution was the **English Bill of Rights** (1688), which, among other things, required that "freedom of speech" be allowed in parliamentary proceedings and that "excessive bail ought not to be required nor excessive fines imposed nor cruel and unusual punishments inflicted." These ideas would make their way into the **American Bill of Rights** (Bill of Rights is the name given to the first ten amendments to the U.S. Constitution).

Probably the greatest single philosophical influence on the leaders who would advocate the break with England was the work of English philosopher **John Locke** (1632–1704). In his ***Second Treatise on Civil Government,*** Locke argued that

- everyone should be held accountable to just laws, including rulers;
- the purpose of laws was to promote "the good of the people";
- the people's property and wealth should not be taken from them, chiefly through taxation, without their consent;
- the people possessed an inherent right to "life, liberty, and property";
- the people possessed the right to overthrow a government that held itself above the law, that passed unjust laws, or that confiscated people's property without their consent.

We can see the influence Locke had on America's leaders by comparing his words with some lines in the Declaration of Independence. The quotations are

John Trumbull's painting *The Declaration of Independence* (1817) depicts the committee that drafted the Declaration of Independence presenting the document to John Hancock, President of the Continental Congress.

expressions of a people who have grown exasperated with a tyrannical government and have decided to revolt:

> But if a long train of abuses, prevarications [lies], and artifices [tricks], all tending the same way, make the design visible to the people, and they cannot but feel what they lie under, and see whither they are going, it is not to be wondered that they should then rouse themselves, and endeavour to put the rule into such hands which may secure to them the ends for which government was at first erected . . .[2]

> But when a long train of abuses and usurpations, pursuing invariably the same Object, evinces a Design to reduce them under absolute Despotism, it is their right, it is their duty, to throw off such Government, and to provide new Guards for their future security. (Declaration of Independence)

BEGINNINGS OF A NATIONAL GOVERNMENT

In 1774, the year before war began, twelve of the thirteen revolutionary colonies sent delegates to meet in Philadelphia (Georgia was the exception). This meeting came in response to the Intolerable Acts. Among the delegates were some of the names most associated with the nation's formation: Samuel Adams,

John Adams, George Washington, and Patrick Henry. This **First Continental Congress** met through September and October. Some at this convention argued for greater home rule in the American colonies rather than for independence. Others, John Adams prominent among them, argued for a more revolutionary course, though he did not yet advocate outright independence. The Congress appealed to the British crown to repeal its tax laws, and it created **The Association**, which called for a complete boycott of British goods. But the British king was not interested in compromise.

In June of 1776, after British troops and colonists had been engaged in hostilities, the **Second Continental Congress** (convened in 1775) adopted a resolution penned by Richard Henry Lee of Virginia. The resolution called on the Congress to determine that "these United Colonies are, and of right ought to be, free and independent states." The Congress did adopt this resolution on July 2, 1776. An additional document was not needed, but some in the Congress wanted a document that would evoke inspiration. The result was the Declaration of Independence, penned primarily by Thomas Jefferson.

The Continental Congress soon called on the newly declared states to write their own constitutions. Among the more important of the states' innovations was Massachusetts's determination that, after ratification, its constitution could be amended only by a convention called together for that purpose. This idea would find its way into the U.S. Constitution. In addition, most of these new state constitutions included bills of rights, and the influence of everyday Americans was symbolized by the movement of the capitals of New Hampshire, New York, the Carolinas, and Georgia further west, where there was less wealth.

Articles of Confederation

Before independence had been formally declared, the Congress had formed a committee to write a national constitution. The result was the **Articles of Confederation**. These were adopted by the Congress in 1777 and ratified by all the states by 1781—the same year the Americans, with much help from France, won the Revolutionary War.

A challenge the new country faced was widespread suspicion of centralized power. After all, the revolution had been spurred by the colonists' resistance to a distant power. This suspicion manifested itself in the Articles, which made the central government weak and reserved all but a few powers to the governments of the states. This is pointed to in the very name of the document, for a **confederation** is a form of government in which the confederating parties retain their **sovereignty** in all matters not directly delegated to the national government.

The new government's Congress was **unicameral**, meaning that it had one house, unlike the later **bicameral** Congress, which comprises two houses: a House of Representatives and a Senate. Each state had more than one member representing it in the federal government (between two and seven), but each state had only one vote. For laws to be passed by the **Congress of the Confederation**, nine of the thirteen states had to agree. In other words, a **super-majority** was needed. For the Articles to be amended, each state had to agree. Each year, members of Congress selected a member to be its president, or presiding officer. (This is a **weak executive** model.)

Though the form of government called for under the Articles failed and was superseded in eight years, it did get some important work done. Most important were the **Land Ordinance of 1785** and the **Northwest Ordinance of 1787**. Both involved the land that would become the states of Ohio, Indiana, Wisconsin, and Illinois. The first of these two laws called for the land to be sold and for the funds gained by the sale to help pay off the national debt. This law also provided for the organization of townships in the territory. Among other things, it required that a portion of each township be set aside for a school. The second law pertained to how the territory would be governed. If a territory had sixty thousand residents, it would be under the control of the central government; a territory with more residents could be admitted as a state. This 1787 ordinance also forbade slavery in the territories.

The central government, under the Articles of Confederation, had the power to do the following:

- Declare war and arrive at peace treaties
- Form alliances and make treaties with other nations
- Maintain a national military force
- Regulate coinage
- Regulate Indian affairs
- Create a postal system
- Decide arguments between the states

The Congress of the Confederation did *not* have the power to do the following:

- Ensure that states would abide by treaties with foreign powers
- Draft soldiers (therefore, it could not force states to supply troops needed in case of emergency)
- Prevent states from setting up interstate tariffs—that is, taxes on goods moving from one state to another

- Raise taxes directly (it had to rely on the states to raise taxes for the central government, and the states were often reluctant to do this)

- Regulate currency (therefore, monies circulated in different states differed dramatically in value)

These lists show that the central government was weak, and weakness prevented it from responding firmly to many serious problems such as the British remaining in forts in the present-day upper Midwest, the Spaniards' control of and closure of the Mississippi River in 1784 (a threat to American trade), and pirates off the coast of North Africa kidnapping and enslaving American sailors. Meanwhile, states argued about interstate trade and boundary lines, and some of the states refused to send any tax revenue to the central government.

Shays' Rebellion of 1786, in western Massachusetts, sent home the message that the Articles of Confederation needed serious reform. Taking part in the rebellion were farmers who demanded fewer taxes and other economic reforms; they wanted to end the loss of their properties as a result of debt. The rebellion was put down by a small state army, but the threat it represented made national leaders realize that a stronger central government was needed to contain events like it in the future. Also critical was the central government's need to control commerce. Though opinions about the Articles varied, most agreed that reform was needed.

Compromises and the U.S. Constitution

In May of 1787, delegates from all the states but Rhode Island gathered in Philadelphia for the purpose of amending the Articles of Confederation. George Washington presided as chairman. Instead of simply revising the Articles, however, the delegates were determined to scrap them. Delegates disagreed about most other things as well, including representation in Congress, the balance of states' power, how to count slaves, the design of the executive, and how much to remove government from the people.

Representation in Congress

One point of disagreement was how to (and whether to) balance the power of the states. The **Virginia Plan**, or **large state plan**, called for a bicameral legislature, with the number of representatives based on population: the more populous the state, the more representatives it would have. New Jersey countered with its **small state plan**, which called for a unicameral Congress and equal representation for all the states. This seemed unfair to the large states, and the small states feared the power of the big states. The **Great Compromise** provided for a House of Representatives to be based on population and a Senate in which each state would be equal. This compromise set the stage for other compromises to come, and the willingness to compromise set the stage for the Constitution's passage and its future success.

How to Count Slaves; Whether to End Slavery

Some of the compromises built into the Constitution are unattractive. Southerners wanted their slaves (who could not be citizens because they were property) to count for purposes of representation in the House of Representatives. Some Northerners retorted that, by light of that logic, horses should also count for representation. In the end, the slaves were neither fully counted nor fully left out. The **three-fifths compromise** counted each slave as three-fifths of a person—that is, every five slaves counted as three people.

Another compromise involving slavery allowed the Congress to end the slave trade—the buying and selling of slaves imported from Africa—beginning in 1808. Most states wanted to end this trade immediately, but South Carolina and Georgia opposed that reform.

Design of the Executive

Unlike the Articles of Confederation, this new national document called for a **strong executive**—that is, a figure at the center of the government whose power would be great, though fairly easily checked by other entities in the government. In the United States, this strong executive is the president. The Constitution provided for the president to be elected by the people, but indirectly. The actual votes for a president would be cast by an **Electoral College**, and each state's representation in the college was the equivalent of the number of the state's Senate and House members.

Removal of Government from the People

The Electoral College is one example of the way the United States functions like an indirect democracy. Another example is the people's indirect election of senators. Until the World War I era, during which the direct election of senators began, they were chosen by state legislatures. Still another way the Constitution's framers distanced the government from the people was by giving federal judges their jobs for life (barring behavior meriting impeachment). This meant that federal judges would not need to fear the ill will of the people; they could make unpopular decisions but maintain their positions. As the original Constitution envisioned it, only members of the House of Representatives were directly elected by the people.

Why this desire to distance government from the people? The Constitution's framers feared **"mobocracy"**—government by the mob. They knew that political fads and passions come and go. The framers did not want the government to be blown about by every political wind. Better to distance some of the decision makers from the passions of the crowd.

RATIFICATION OF THE CONSTITUTION

The compromises needed to write a constitution suggest that few were fully happy with the final product of the convention at Philadelphia. This unhappiness became clearer as the Constitution was sent to the various state legislatures for their approval. Delaware was the first state to ratify the Constitution, and it did so unanimously. Pennsylvania was the first large state to ratify.

According to an agreement reached in Philadelphia, once nine states had ratified the Constitution, it would go into effect *in the ratifying states,* leaving those that had not ratified the Constitution outside the new nation's fold. The last four states to ratify were Virginia, New York, North Carolina, and Rhode Island. Except in North Carolina, the votes in these state conventions were close.

The pro-Constitution vote in New York had been helped along primarily by the writings of Alexander Hamilton and James Madison, with some help from John Jay. These three men wrote under the pen name **Publius,** and their eighty-five articles appeared in New York newspapers, primarily the *Independent Journal* and the *New York Packet.* Taken together in one volume, the articles comprise the **Federalist Papers** (or, simply, *The Federalist*)—a volume some historians consider the most penetrating commentary ever written on the Constitution. The **Anti-Federalists** also wrote essays in defense of the Articles of Confederation. They feared a strong central government. Because the Anti-Federalists lost the argument, and because their arguments were not as strong as those presented by Hamilton and Madison, their written works are much less known.

The Federalist Paper most cited is **Federalist No. 10**, written by Madison. In this essay, Madison takes up the topic of factions, which today we call interest groups. He was particularly concerned about groups that pushed their own interests to the detriment of the nation as a whole. A nation with a weak central government is less likely to be able to control such groups, but in a country as diverse as the United States, different regional groups and interests, along with different levels of wealth in various parts of the country, would balance one another out. In such a country, Madison noted, it was unlikely that one faction could impose its will on the country as a whole. People would indirectly select their leaders and, ideally, the leaders would govern with their own **constituencies** in mind—but also with the interests of the entire nation in mind. The

The Federalist Papers: A series of 85 articles advocating the ratification of the
U.S. Constitution. Written by Alexander Hamilton, James Madison, and John
Jay, the articles were published between October 1787 and August 1788.

Constitution as devised would prevent the **tyranny of the majority**; the rights
of minorities would be protected.

Madison furthered this theme in **Federalist No. 51**, arguing that in the nation envisioned by the framers of the Constitution, "ambition must be made to
counteract ambition"—that is, competing interests would prevent groups from
trampling on the rights of others.

When New Hampshire ratified the Constitution in June 1788, the document
went into effect nationwide. The four remaining states faced the choice of joining the United States or, in effect, becoming independent nations. The last state
to come into the Union, in May 1790, was Rhode Island, which feared the
power and influence of the big states. The vote in Rhode Island's convention
was close: 34 to 32.

ALTERATION OF THE CONSTITUTION

A final item of constitutional history to note pertains to the alteration of the
U.S. Constitution. Since the ratification of the Constitution and Bill of Rights,
the Constitution has been amended only seventeen times, resulting in a to-

tal of twenty-seven amendments. The most recent amendment was ratified in 1992, though it was first submitted for consideration in 1789! This amendment says that no pay raise, or any change in compensation for senators or House members will go into effect until "an election of representatives shall have intervened." One purpose of this amendment was to let the people express their opinion about congressional pay via the ballot.

What is the process for amending the Constitution? There are two basic ways to do that, and both require the involvement of a super-majority of the states. One way to amend the Constitution is for three-fourths of the state legislatures to vote in favor of an amendment proposed by Congress. The second way, which was used to repeal the Eighteenth Amendment mandating prohibition, is for the states to call constitutional conventions and then for three-quarters of them to vote in favor of the proposed amendment. Notice that, although the federal Congress can propose a constitutional amendment (by two-thirds votes in both chambers), a super-majority of the states must consent for the amendment to be ratified.

Amendment of the Constitution is rare. Some eleven thousand proposed amendments have been considered by Congress, but only seventeen amendments have found their way into the Constitution since the 1790s. Since 1919, most amendments have been given a time period of seven years to fail or to be ratified.

References

[1] Peverill Squire, et al., *Dynamics of Democracy* (Cincinnati: Atomic Dog Publishing, 2001), 723.

[2] John Locke, *Concerning Civil Government,* 1690, Chapter XIX, para. 225.

Chapter 3

Political Parties and Voting Patterns

The U.S. Constitution says nothing about political parties. The Constitution's framers hoped the country they had helped create could avoid political parties. This ideal lasted only through the presidency of George Washington, although he favored the policies of the Federalist Party. This was the party designation of the second American president, John Adams. The Federalists advocated a relatively strong central government. In opposition was the Democratic Republican Party, which favored strong state governments.

The first Democratic Republican president was Thomas Jefferson. In the decades before the American Civil War, these two parties, plus the Whigs, National Republicans, Anti-Masonics, Free Soilers, and Democrats, offered voters candidates for president. The first Republican president was Abraham Lincoln. Since the Civil War, no party has seriously challenged the dominance of the Republican and Democratic parties. Essentially, American political life operates within a two-party system.

THE ROLE AND NATURE OF THIRD PARTIES

Though they have had little formal political power, **third parties** (also called **minor parties**) have played an important role in American politics. A question to ask about third parties is, "Why do they form?" We can answer this question, partly, by saying something about third parties themselves. **Economic protest parties** focus on some aspect of the economy, whether the monetization of silver or the national budget. **Ideological parties** express views that go beyond mainstream opinion. The 2008 platform of the **Libertarian Party**, for example, calls for the replacement of the "government-sponsored Social Security system with a private voluntary system. The proper source of help for the poor is the voluntary efforts of private groups and individuals." Although many Republicans would agree with the gist of the Libertarian statement, any effort to eliminate taxpayer-funded Social Security for the elderly would gain little traction on **Capitol Hill**, where Congress meets.

Issue parties—third parties that focus on one topic—tend to be small, and they are usually short-lived. Perhaps the best example of an issue party is the Prohibition Party (discussed later in the chapter). **Factional parties**, meantime, break away from other parties and often center on an individual who has left a major party. In 2006, Senator Joseph Lieberman of Connecticut lost the Democratic **primary election** in his state, so he ran as an Independent Democrat and was reelected to the Senate.

In sum, third parties form because their leaders and supporters feel that the major parties are not attentive to their concerns. During the 2008 presidential election season, the **Green Party** announced that the policies of Barack Obama (Democrat) and John McCain (Republican) on energy and global warming amounted to "a capitulation to corporate lobbies." Whereas most Americans saw substantial differences between Obama and McCain, the Greens, who are well to the political **left** and focus on environmental issues, felt that neither candidate was willing to confront big business. (From the time of the French Revolution, the "left" has referred to political liberalism, and the "right" has referred to political conservatism.)

In the presidential election of 2000, the Green candidate, **Ralph Nader,** won 2.7 percent of the national vote, including about 100,000 votes in Florida, where the election was the most closely contested. Many observers think that, had Nader not run, most of his votes would have been cast for the Democratic candidate, Al Gore, who lost the election by four **electoral votes**. Thus the outcome of an election may have been shaped by a third party, whose leader the Democrats called a **spoiler** because their chances for electoral victory were spoiled. (In 2008, Nader ran for president again, as an Independent.)

As noted earlier, sometimes minority parties form around personalities. In the early 1900s, some Republicans were angered by President William Taft's backing away from a promise to reduce **tariffs** and his seeming lack of commitment to environmental conservation. Arguments within the Republican Party contributed to landslide congressional losses for Republicans in the elections of 1910. The next year the **National Progressive Republican League** was formed, and disaffected members of the **Grand Old Party** gathered around the reform-minded former Republican president, Theodore Roosevelt. The Republican Party's leaders refused to grant the presidential nomination of 1912 to Roosevelt, so he and his followers formed the **Progressive "Bull Moose" Party**—a classic example of a **splinter party**, so called because it splintered the Republican vote, handing the presidential election of that year to the Democrat, Woodrow Wilson.

A purer example of a presidential campaign stemming from personality comes from the election of 1992, when **Ross Perot** ran as an Independent, gaining more than 19 million votes. Perot's appeal was his emphasis on **anti-incumbency** and his charge that the government needed to deal with the federal budget deficit. Perot's candidacy showed that third parties can provide dissatisfied or **dissident** voters with a political outlet, thus perhaps preventing violent confrontation. It is also important to know that the key issue of Perot's campaign was adopted by the candidates of the major parties. Indeed, one of Democrat Bill Clinton's priorities was tackling the problem of the federal budget deficit. Third parties often raise issues that are adopted by candidates of the major parties. If nothing else, third parties serve as a platform for ideas that are not expressed in the major parties.

THE MAJOR THIRD PARTIES

Let's look briefly at some of the major third parties.

Nineteenth-Century Third Parties

The **Greenback Labor Party** found support primarily in rural parts of the country and ran presidential candidates in the elections of 1880 and 1884. The Greenbacks gained no **electoral votes** in either election, but their key issues were important. As the party's name suggests, it wanted the federal government to continue to allow paper dollars (called greenbacks) to circulate as currency, as they had done during the Civil War and in the years immediately following. In order to handle rising debt, the Greenback Labor Party demanded that the government print more money. The party also called for government regulation of railroads and corporations, political reform that would end rampant corruption, and environmental conservation.

Greenback Labor was one of several reformist parties that began in the late nineteenth century. James Weaver, who ran as a Greenback Labor candidate in 1880, ran as the candidate of the **People's Party** (also called the **Populist Party**) in 1892. Whereas Greenback Labor won no electoral votes in 1888, four years later the Populists gained twenty-two. To complicate things a little, the best-known Populist candidate to run for president, **William Jennings Bryan**, actually ran on the Democratic Party ticket in the elections of 1896 and 1900. In giving the nomination to the Populist, the Democratic Party hoped to win more votes—and it did get many Populist votes. But Bryan scared away many conservative Democrats who, like the **Reagan Democrats** of the 1980 and 1984 elections, voted for the Republican candidate.

Having much in common with Greenback Labor, the Populist movement drew support primarily from the South and West, and the party railed against large "plutocratic" institutions—those run by and for the wealthy—that seemed increasingly to control the nation: banks, railroads, corporations, and corrupt **political machines**. The Populists called for federal government control of railroads, as well as telegraph and telephone wires; they advocated a graduated income tax; they demanded government-operated warehouses for their crops; and they called for the unrestricted coinage of silver—the "poor man's currency." The Populists' key issue of the election of 1896 was taken up by William Jennings Bryan, who opposed the country's adherence to the **gold standard**.

Twentieth-Century Third Parties

Although the **Prohibition Party** continued to exist in the early twenty-first century, the number of votes for its presidential candidates did not even come close to one thousand. In the early *twentieth* century, however, Prohibition candidates made a fairly respectable showing, though they never came close to a million votes. As the party's name suggests, its primary concern was the prohibition of alcohol for beverage purposes. This concern found its expression in the ratification of the Eighteenth Amendment in 1919 (repealed in 1933). The reason the Prohibition Party never garnered much support was that many Democrats and some Republicans shared their primary concern and felt no need to cast their votes for a party they knew could not win an election.

The American **Socialist Party** was founded in 1901 and disbanded in 1972. The Socialist presidential candidate with the greatest drawing power was **Eugene Debs**, who ran in the elections of 1904, 1908, 1912, and 1920. Debs never received a single electoral vote, but he did receive enough popular votes to gain attention and a place in American history textbooks. In 1912 he received almost 901,000 votes. (The winner, Woodrow Wilson, received 6.3 million votes.) Largely because individualism is an important part of American intellectual history, **socialism**, which emphasizes government-directed equalization of wealth and government control of industry, never appealed to many Americans. The fact that socialism, as people talked about it, was sometimes indistinguishable from **communism** (which looks for the abolition of private property) also ensured that its roots would never go deep into American soil. In the late twentieth and early twenty-first centuries, the most prominent socialist in national political life was **Bernie Sanders**, who represented Vermont in the House of Representatives. Avoiding the word *socialism,* Sanders adopted the political label **"progressive"** and founded the House Progressive Caucus. Early in his career, Sanders had run as a member of the Liberty Union Party, which bills itself as a "nonviolent socialist party." In the Senate, Sanders served as an **Independent**.

The last party to be mentioned here—the **States' Rights Democratic Party**—ran a presidential candidate in the election of 1948. The candidate, Strom Thurmond, opposed the Democratic Party's nomination of Harry Truman for president. Called a **Dixiecrat**, Thurmond won four states—South Carolina (his home state), Alabama, Louisiana, and Mississippi—and thirty-nine electoral votes. The Dixiecrats opposed desegregation and favored states' rights. Its **platform**, adopted in Oklahoma City in 1948, declared:

> We stand for the segregation of the races and the racial integrity of each race; the constitutional right to choose one's associates; to accept private employment without governmental interference, and to earn one's living in any lawful way. We oppose the elimination of segregation. . . . We favor home-rule, local self-government and a minimum interference with individual rights.

From 1954 to 1964, Thurmond served in the U.S. Senate as a Democrat and then switched to the Republican Party. He served in the Senate until the age of one hundred. Thurmond is also remembered for delivering the longest filibuster speech in American history (see Chapter 4).

BENEFITS OF A TWO-PARTY SYSTEM

Most Western democracies are **multiparty systems**. In Canada, for example, the Liberal, Conservative, Bloc Québécois, and New Democratic parties vie for federal votes. Why does the United States have just two dominant parties? For one thing, the **Electoral College** heavily favors a two-party system: the winning presidential candidate must gain a majority of electoral votes. (In other democracies, chief executives usually are required to gain a **plurality** of votes—that is, more than any other candidate.) Because a majority of votes would be unlikely in a system with more than two major parties, the system is biased in favor of a two-party system. To be sure, voters can vote for third parties and, in doing so, send a message to the political establishment, register a protest, or simply stay true to their own principles. But there's a political cost to voting for third-party candidates—namely, they have no serious chance of winning a presidential election. In the 1992 election, Ross Perot won more than 19 million votes but not a single electoral vote.

Another thing that contributes to the strength of the two parties is the **winner-take-all** system that prevails in Congress. Whereas a majority of electoral votes is needed to elect a president, members of Congress can be elected via a plurality. In other words, if a Democratic candidate gets 47 percent of the vote, and the rest is divided between two other parties, the Democrat wins the seat. Other countries provide for proportional representation. In Israel, for instance, a party that gets 10 percent of the vote is entitled to about 10 percent of the seats in the Knesset (Israel's parliament), so Israeli voters have some incentive to vote for minor parties. The American system provides no such incentive.

Finally, we should note that American political opinion is, on the whole, centrist and pragmatic. Truly radical political ideologies have never acquired much traction in the United States. Because the Democratic and Republican parties are so large and comprise so many interest groups (some in opposition to one another on certain issues), both parties tend to legislate from the political center—the Republicans a little to the right, the Democrats a little to the left.

Finally, **campaign finance** laws favor the two parties, which shouldn't surprise us because they were written by members of the major parties! To receive federal funds for elections, parties must receive at least 5 percent of the popular vote nationally, and they must appear on at least ten state ballots. Notice that these goals must be met *prior* to getting the funding. This means that the first time around, a third party must *fund itself*, not an easy thing to do because elections are so expensive.

DISSENSION WITHIN PARTIES

Because two parties dominate American politics, political victories usually go to candidates with a clear majority of votes. To be sure, this is not always the case. Because presidential victories are determined by electoral and not popular votes, Rutherford B. Hayes (1876), Benjamin Harrison (1888), and George W. Bush (2000) received fewer popular votes than their chief competitors. Most of the time, however, elected presidents can say that they enter office with a popular **mandate**, that is, a majority of the popular vote. But then, because the parties must appeal to so many different people in so many different regions and subcultures, and because the political interests of people are so different, it can be difficult to know just what the major parties stand for.

As a general rule, for example, Republicans oppose marriage rights for homosexuals, but the **Log Cabin Republicans** favor such rights; the Republican Party is generally **pro-life** (or anti-abortion), but the **Republicans for Choice** are not. On the other hand, the Democratic Party favors abortion rights, but in 2008, Democrat Harry Reid, the Senate majority leader, had a pro-life voting record (though his Senate Web site did not make this clear). While, generally speaking, Democrats favor government spending on social programs more than Republicans do, the **Blue Dog Democrats** advocate fiscal restraint. Both parties comprise conservative and liberal wings; some conservative Democrats are more conservative than some liberal Republicans. Such is the nature of parties that dominate political life in a country as large and varied as the United States.

Democrats and Republicans first competed against one another in the election of 1856. Since that year, except for Theodore Roosevelt's second-place finish as a Progressive "Bull Moose" Party candidate in the election of 1912, candidates from no other party have been serious contenders for the presidency. In the election of 1860, the Republican candidate, Abraham Lincoln, advocated a relatively strong central government, whereas Democrats favored states' rights. This political disagreement helped to push the nation into civil war. The election of 1860 is sometimes referred to as a **critical election**, meaning that it is associated with a major political realignment in the United States that persists through subsequent elections, thus leading to what political scientists call **electoral realignment**. Whereas the Democratic Party had been strong in urban areas in the North and South before the election of 1860, after the election the Republicans came to be associated primarily with the North, while the Democrats came to be associated largely with the "**solid South**." Whereas Republicans won the large majority of presidential elections between 1860 and 1932, congressional delegations from the South were solidly Democratic. The South remained solidly Democratic until 1964, when five Southern states voted for the Republican candidate, Barry Goldwater. In the next election, five Southern states gave their electoral votes to George C. Wallace. Southern voters were responding, in part, to the dramatic change they were experiencing as a result of the civil rights movement. As of the 1980s, the Southern electoral votes have generally gone Republican.

The Democrat Woodrow Wilson won the election of 1912, but the most powerful Democratic president was **Franklin D. Roosevelt**—the only American president to be sent to the White House four times, beginning in 1932. Roosevelt's presidency and his New Deal programs that sought to address the Great Depression inspired a powerful coalition of groups that have remained loyal Democratic voters: African Americans, Jews, union members, city dwellers, and intellectuals. (Roosevelt also attracted the votes of most white Southerners but, as we have noted, most of those votes began working against the Democrats in the 1960s.) Whereas Republicans were reluctant to have government shape the economy during the Depression's early years, Roosevelt argued for **activist government**—a government that created work, employed people, and provided tax-funded benefits such as **Social Security**.

From the election of 1932 to the election of 1968, Democrats dominated the White House. Since 1968, both parties have shared the presidency, though the

Republicans have been more successful. While the South has become increasingly Republican, the Northeast has become increasingly Democratic.

It is also true, however, that the late twentieth and early twenty-first centuries have been periods of political **dealignment**—that is, more and more citizens have become disenchanted with the major parties. This has led to an increasing desire for **bipartisanship** (cooperation among politicians in the major parties). Although large majorities of voters remained affiliated with parties, a growing minority declared themselves to be **Independents**. In California in 2008, for example, almost 15 percent of voters were Independents, and these were seen as **swing voters**—that is, as voters who could "swing" the presidential election one way or another. Both major political parties saw winning these Independent voters as crucial to gaining the presidency. This led aspiring politicians to speak well of the ideal of bipartisanship.

CAMPAIGN FINANCE

The primary purpose of political parties is to gain political power for the sake of promoting the party's agenda and shaping public policy. In the American republic, the formal way to gain political power is to win elections. To win elections, parties must be well organized at the local, state, and national levels. Parties also must be well financed, especially since the late twentieth century when elections began to cost enormous sums. Parties need money to pay for (1) full-time campaign advisors; (2) the services of pollsters; (3) radio, TV, and print advertisements; (4) bumper stickers, yard signs, and e-mail and telephone outreach; (5) travel expenses; (6) campaign literature; (7) office space in various campaign headquarters; and (8) staff salaries.

The **Federal Election Commission** (FEC), a government agency, oversees campaign financing. The FEC ensures that financial contributions to candidates stay within legal limits. When we speak of campaign contributions, we first must distinguish between **hard money** and **soft money**. Hard money is given directly to a candidate, whereas soft money is given to party committees to be used more generally. The relationship between money and politics is often troubled and corrupting. A recent attempt to control money's influence on political campaigns for federal offices comes in the form of a law passed in 2002. Called the **Bipartisan Campaign Reform Act** (BCRA), but better known simply as McCain-Feingold (the last names of its original sponsors), this law was fiercely challenged in court, though it was upheld by the Supreme Court in 2003 and went into effect the following year. Some had challenged BCRA because they believed its limitations on gifts to **political action committees**, or PACs (which pool funds and donate them to candidates), amounted to an abridgement of free speech. The giving limits of individuals that BCRA put in place for 2005–2006 were as follows:

- $2,100 to a candidate in a two-year period
- $10,000 in a year to a state party or political committee
- $26,700 to a national party committee

McCain-Feingold prohibited political parties' committees from raising or spending funds beyond federal limits, whether the elections in question were at the national, state, or local levels. Also, as a result of a "stand by your ad" provision in McCain-Feingold, politicians are required to tell viewers of political messages that they "approve this message."

One result of BCRA is that parties and candidates have increasingly appealed to voters for small donations. The Internet has been quite useful here. In the presidential election of 2008, the official Web sites of both the Obama and McCain campaigns prominently featured appeals to donors, most of whom would give $20 or less.

Another unforeseen consequence of BCRA was the increased importance of **527 committees**, named after code 527 of the Internal Revenue Code. So long as these committees are not formally affiliated with a political party and do not specifically endorse a candidate, their political advertisements are not taxed. So instead of attacking a candidate specifically, the 527 committees promote certain issues. The best-known 527 group of the 2004 presidential election called itself Swift Boat Veterans for Truth. In the committee's advertisements, the patriotism of Democratic candidate and Vietnam veteran John Kerry was thrown into question. After his service in Vietnam, Kerry had protested the war. Now, during the campaign of 2004, he referred to his wartime experience in an attempt to attract votes. In one advertisement, as a camera showed the faces of some forty Vietnam veterans, a voice said:

> They're his entire chain of command, most of the officers in Kerry's unit. Even the gunner from his own boat.

> And they're the men who spent years in North Vietnamese prison camps.

> Tortured for refusing to confess what John Kerry accused them of . . . being war criminals.

The swift boat advertisements did not explicitly discourage people from voting for John Kerry; they only raised the "issue" of Kerry's credibility. There's no question that they helped George W. Bush win a close election. The swift boat ads also led to a new political verb: *swift boating.*

One effort to control presidential campaign costs has come in the form of **public financing**. If a candidate qualifies for public financing by raising $5,000 in twenty different states in donations of less than $250, then that candidate qualifies for government funding for his or her campaign. However, there is a limit placed on how much public funding a candidate can receive, so successful candidates often decline public financing so as not to tie themselves to its limits. In the presidential election of 2000, Republicans Steve Forbes and George W. Bush declined public financing, as did the Democrats Howard Dean and John Kerry in 2004.

Of course, to succeed in elections, parties must find candidates who are attractive and well qualified. Successful candidates have often worked their way up, beginning with political volunteer work in localities. Sometimes these locals are asked to stand for local offices, such as on city councils. From there, they may run for state office, and from there they may try for national office. Consider the case of Sarah Palin, the 2008 Republican vice-presidential candidate: she began as a local volunteer, became mayor of a small town; then, while serving as governor of Alaska, she became John McCain's running mate.

WHAT PARTY IDENTITY MEANS

The major political parties provide voters with a general outlook. Citizens often vote according to this outlook, often not knowing much about the candidates themselves. If I strongly favor abortion rights, then I will be much more likely to vote for a Democrat than for a Republican. If I favor a strong military and dislike the United Nations, I am much more likely to vote for a Republican, even if I know very little about the candidate. Political scientists refer to this as **political identification**: people tend to adopt a certain political identity fairly young and stick with it through life. This is because party identification is linked to other elements of a person's identity—church life, the views of parents and teachers, the temperament of the subculture a person grew up in, and so on. This may help to explain why Blue Dog Democrats stick with the Democratic Party, even though they often vote with Republicans.

Sometimes Democrats will vote for Republicans, and vice versa, but this is rarer than one might think. In the 2004 election, for example, just 7 percent of Democrats voted for the Republican candidate, and just 8 percent of Republicans voted for the Democrat. This stability—or **normal vote**—allows political observers to reliably predict the number of voters who will vote Democratic and Republican. Because identification with the two parties has been about equal since the late 1900s, the relatively small number of Independent voters receives a great deal of attention from the parties.

Having said this, we also need to know that often the American electorate opts for **divided government**: presidents of one party often face one or two congressional houses in the hands of the other party. The benefit of divided government is that it provides a check on one party's ambitions. The downside is occasional **gridlock** (when government can't get things done) and interparty bickering and finger-pointing. As an example of divided government, consider the years of George W. Bush's presidency, 2000–2008. In Bush's first six months in office, Republicans held a majority in the House, while the Senate was evenly divided, giving the tie-breaking vote to Vice President Dick Cheney. The next year, James Jeffords, a senator from Vermont, left the Republican Party and gave the Democrats a one-vote majority. The following year, in 2002, the Republicans retook the Senate and held the House, but in 2006 the Democrats took both houses of Congress. Divided government can be seen as the electorate expressing its desire for change or simply expressing its fatigue with the party in power. In the 2008 presidential campaign, Republican John McCain ran as a Republican "maverick" who often bucked his own party. The claim was useful, for fatigue with the Republican Party (particularly with President George W. Bush) was deep.

During political campaigns, nominees make political promises. Their goal, once they enter office, is to keep these promises. Otherwise, they will face pointed criticism from opponents come the next election. Usually, the promises candidates make are in line with what their party would favor. This contributes to **party unity**—to politicians voting the **party line**—a phenomenon that has increased over the years. In 1964 fewer than 70 percent of Congress members consistently voted with their party; in 1999 that figure had risen to 85 percent.

HOW CANDIDATES ARE SELECTED

To be elected, however, candidates must often win **primary elections** (often simply called primaries). Primary elections come from reforms instituted in the 1960s and 1970s, and they place more power in the hands of the voters. In earlier times, party nominees were selected by party officials, sometimes in "smoke-filled rooms"—a term that refers to the behind-the-scenes orchestrations of political powerbrokers. Every four years, at party conventions, presidential nominees were chosen and weren't always the candidates who had won the most votes in primaries.

In recent decades, voters themselves have decided which Democrat or which Republican or Libertarian (and so on) will run in a district or state, or nationally. In the Democratic presidential nominating primaries of 2008, Barack Obama and Hillary Clinton were the last candidates standing, and Obama won the nomination. The last two Republicans were John McCain and Mike Huckabee, with McCain winning the nomination. Until Obama and McCain were formally nominated by their parties, they were called **presumptive nominees**, the recognition being that the parties would not cross the will of primary voters.

Some states, such as Louisiana, Maine, and Nevada, have **closed primaries**, meaning that party members can vote only for candidates from their own party. Other states, like North Dakota, South Carolina, and Wisconsin, have **open primaries**, meaning that Republicans can vote for Democratic candidates, and vice versa.

Even though nominations are now decided by voters, candidate delegates from the American states and territories still go to their nominating conventions. Most Democratic primaries allot delegates proportionally. In other words, if a candidate gets 35 percent of a state's vote in its primary, that nominee will receive 35 percent of the state's delegates to the convention. (Most Republican primaries are winner-takes-all). Some states use **caucuses** instead of primaries. In caucuses, locals select delegates to county meetings, and the delegates back a certain candidate. These county delegates then select delegates to represent them at a higher level, and the nominee with the most delegates wins the caucus. In the end, the state party caucus selects delegates to the national convention. Delegates at the party conventions are grouped by state, which is why we see convention banners with slogans like "Iowa for Obama."

WHO VOTES—AND WHY

Who turns out to vote—or, more formally, who exercises **the franchise** or **suffrage** (synonyms for the right to vote)? The Constitution grants states the power to determine who has the vote. Consequently, **voter registration** has been left primarily to the states. A basic point of voter registration is to prevent fraud. A system might work this way: when voters appear at a **polling place**—a school, church, home garage, or some other place—their names are on a list because they've registered to vote. Once their name is checked, they cannot vote again, and because they must vote at that polling place, they are ineligible to vote elsewhere. As of 2008, North Dakota was the only state not to require registration. Just three states—Maine, Minnesota, and Wisconsin—allowed people to register to vote on Election Day.

Though citizens who are at least eighteen have the right to vote, many Americans do not do so. In the presidential election of 1996, just over 49 percent of **the electorate** (eligible voters) turned out to vote. In the congressional elections of 2006, only 41 percent of eligible voters went to the polls. There are many reasons people don't vote, among them a lack of interest; perhaps work or family responsibilities don't allow them to get to the polls (traditionally, most elections are held on Tuesdays). Some voters feel that their single vote doesn't matter. The political scientist Robert Putnam claims that, on the whole, Americans are less involved in their community's public lives than they used to be. They do not join clubs and civic organizations as much, and they do less volunteer work. Americans thus have less **social capital** to work with because fewer people are involved in their communities and more involved in their own lives, or they are just sitting in front of televisions and computers. With a decline of social capital, the theory says, comes a decline in political interest and involvement.

Some political scientists, drawing on **rational choice theory**, say that people decide not to vote because the costs of doing so—learning about the candidates, driving to the polls, standing in line, and so on—are greater than the perceived benefits of voting. Rational choice theory may also explain why uninformed people simply vote for candidates of their party. In addition, there are many elections in the United States, and sometimes a kind of voters' fatigue sets in. Citizens may vote in well-advertised elections (such as for president) but forgo voting for local school board members. Observers refer to **high-stimulus elections**—that is, elections for influential offices or on important issues that get substantial media coverage and that feature attractive candidates and stiff competition. When presidential candidate John McCain selected Sarah Palin as his running mate in 2008, for example, many voters who had been apathetic about McCain suddenly took an intense interest in the election: they saw Palin as a "breath of fresh air."

Though some argue that democracy is better off if poorly informed people do not cast ignorant votes, the fact that many Americans do not vote is often seen as a sign that American democracy is marked by apathy and thus isn't healthy. A low voter turnout seems to suggest a low sense of *political efficacy*—that is, the sense that one's vote matters in political life of the town, county, state, and nation. Also, when only half of the country's eligible voters participate in elections, victorious presidents are placed in office with perhaps as little as 25 percent of the eligible vote behind them. Various concerned groups and the government itself encourage citizens to vote. A well-known example of this is MTV's **Rock the Vote** campaign, which was designed to get young people interested in the country's political life.

But to return to our original question: Who actually votes? Obviously, people who have a keen interest in politics are more likely to show up at the polls than others who have little or no interest. Some vote out of a sense of **civic duty**, whether or not they are personally interested in politics or in a particular election. Some vote because they are committed to a particular issue—say, abortion—and they vote mainly with that in mind. And when it seems that election results will be very close, people can be motivated to vote because they feel that their vote may really count. In the presidential election of 2000, about 55 million votes were cast, but the difference in the popular vote between the Republican and Democratic candidates was just about 500,000 in the Democrat's favor (though he, Al Gore, lost the election by four electoral votes). Sometimes people have strong feelings against a candidate and vote with the primary aim of *preventing* that candidate from winning.

As a general rule, middle-aged and elderly citizens vote more regularly than eligible voters in their late teens and twenties. Young people tend to be more on the move—attending college, serving in the military, or getting started on a career or family. Younger people have fewer children and sometimes tend to think less about a future beyond their own. Citizens with children tend to think more about what the country will be like for their children and grandchildren. And the more educated and wealthy a person is, the more likely it is that he or she will vote. High levels of education and the accumulation of wealth (whether a comfortable middle-class life or real riches) require investments of time and energy. People who invest a lot in their lives want the society they live in to function well so their investments will pay off. Thus they are more interested in their nation's political life, and they are more likely to vote.

Some citizens are **sociotropic voters**, meaning that they vote based on general economic conditions rather than on their own or their family's economic condition. As suggested already, some vote in response to **easy issues**—that is, issues that are easily stated and often linked to high emotions (such as abortion). If I know nothing about candidates but am pro-life, and I know that Republicans are more pro-life than Democrats, then I will vote Republican. Sometimes voters base their vote on **valence issues**, or issues that are universally disliked, such as corruption. If the electorate is angry about corruption, the party most associated with it will pay at the polls. Complicated **hard issues**—for example, how best to ensure that the United States has good relations with China ten years from now—do not play a large role in elections, though aspiring politicians' positions on such topics help to reveal their **candidate characteristics**. Most voters want to know if a candidate is knowledgeable, serious, and trustworthy.

The Role of Image in Voters' Decisions

So there you are at the polling booth. We'll make our original question more personal: For whom will you vote and why? As we know, you may vote the simple party line. Perhaps you are a pro-choice Democrat and the House candidate you're voting for is pro-life, but you know that, overall, the Democratic candidate represents your views more than the Republican or Libertarian does. If you are fairly well informed, you will probably also do some **retrospective voting**, meaning that your decision about who should have political power in the future will be based on what you know about the candidates' acts in the past. (Retrospective voting can also refer to how one feels about the past, and if the incumbent's party has done well, that party will get a vote—or vice versa.) If you are a "fiscal hawk" Republican, and a candidate from your party seems to be no different from a "tax-and-spend liberal," you may opt to vote for a Libertarian. **Prospective voters** make their decisions based on what candidates say they will do in the future, but political scientists have found that voting decisions are much more influenced by the past than by the future.

Or perhaps you will base your vote on the candidate's **name recognition** or on the image of the candidate you have in mind. Perhaps one candidate is a better speaker or seems healthier than the other, so you vote for her. Or maybe a candidate has cultivated an image as a person who is strong on defense, as opposed to his supposedly weak counterpart, so you vote for the strong candidate. In the age of TV, the Internet, and short attention spans, image means a great deal, as do **sound bites**—the short and snappy phrases candidates use, hoping the phrases will get into the TV and radio news, even if the candidates know that it isn't possible to convey serious ideas with phrases supplied by political campaign professionals.

Because image means so much in the age of twenty-four-hour news channels and the Internet, candidates do well to pay attention to how they look on camera and to what they sound like on tape. **Gaffes**—mistakes, careless statements, or remarks that are easy to take out of context—on the campaign trail can be very costly. In the Democratic presidential nomination campaign of 2003, Vermont's governor, Howard Dean, let loose a little scream that, played over and over, made him seem unbalanced. Oftentimes, campaign assistants and candidates will have to engage in "**spin**" to win the battles of words—that is, they will have to shape the meaning of a candidate's words and try to make that meaning stick in voters' minds.

As you linger in the voting booth, perhaps your decision will be shaped by the **attack ads** on TV, radio, and the Internet that are designed to create negative feelings about a candidate's opponent. The **contrast ads** you saw, on the other hand, drew distinctions between opponents. The presidential campaign of 2008 was about "change" in Washington, D.C. Republican John McCain advertised his previous efforts to reform Washington, contrasting his record with that of the Democrat, Barack Obama.

Types of Ballots

Once people decide to vote, actually go to the polls, and make a final decision about whom to vote for, what kinds of **ballots** do they use? The answer to

A mechanical lever voting machine: Voting booths provide privacy for voters while they mark their ballot papers or use a voting machine, many of which are now electronic.

this question depends on where voters live. There are about ten thousand voting jurisdictions in the country, and they operate in various ways. One thing all jurisdictions have in common is that voting is done privately: no one must know how anyone else votes. This follows the model first introduced in Australia in the late 1800s, thus the term *Australian secret ballot*.

A small number of jurisdictions rely on **paper ballots**. Using a pen or pencil, a voter marks the candidate of her choice and drops the ballot into a box; later, these votes are hand counted. A little less than one-quarter of voting jurisdictions rely on **lever voting machines**. Ballots in the forms of **punch cards** were made famous by the 2000 presidential election in Florida. As votes were being counted in the very close election, some **chads** next to candidates' names weren't completely punched through—these were called hanging chads—and other chads were only dimpled. There was debate over how these votes should be counted. About 37 percent of voting jurisdictions use punch cards.

One-quarter of jurisdictions use **optical scan ballots**: voters fill in bubbles next to candidates' names, and a computer reads and counts the votes. Some jurisdictions use paper-free **electronic voting**. Instead of punching a chad or filling in a bubble on a piece of paper, voters may press a button or touch a choice on a computer screen. **Internet voting** is currently being considered, though it would be difficult to ensure privacy and voter authenticity.

THE ELECTORAL COLLEGE VOTE

So now you've voted, and you go home to see what the election results are. If you voted in a **general election** you probably cast votes for national, state, county, and local officials. (If you wondered whether voters in other democracies vote as often and for as many things as American voters do, the answer is no.) Let's say you voted for one of three candidates for a seat in the House of Representatives. In **first-past-the-post elections** such as American congressional races, your candidate may win with less than 50 percent of the vote. At the same time, your presidential candidate may also end up with less than 50 percent of the vote, but if he or she has less than 50 percent of the **Electoral College** vote, the election is lost.

The Constitution never refers to an electoral college, though it does call on each state to "appoint . . . a Number of Electors" equal to the number of a state's U.S. senators and House members for the purposes of selecting presidents. So when you vote for a presidential candidate, you're not exactly voting for that candidate. Rather, you're voting for an elector who is pledged to vote for that candidate. (Very rarely, a **faithless elector** will vote for a person other than the one he or she is pledged to, and no election result has been changed as a result of this.) Because there are 435 members of the House of Representatives and 100 members of the U.S. Senate, plus three electoral votes for the District of Columbia (that is, Washington, D.C.), the number needed to get a majority of electoral votes is 270. According to the Constitution, if no candidate gets a majority of electoral votes, the election goes to the House of Representatives, where each state's delegation will count as one vote. No election has gone to the House since 1824. Except for the states of Maine and Nebraska, which award electoral votes based on which candidate wins a district, the electoral vote is **winner-take-all**. In other words, in forty-eight of the states, just over 50 percent of the vote leads to all of that state's electoral votes.

After the election of 2000, which was the first election since 1888 in which the candidate who won the most votes did not win the election, many people called for reform of the electoral system. To many voters, the issue seemed simple: the person who wins the most votes nationally should win the election. But others defend the Electoral College system. For one thing, the defenders say, the Electoral College gives states with small populations an electoral voice. In a very close race, Alaska's 600,000 voters are unlikely to make a difference, but its three electoral votes could. For a similar reason, the electoral system gives rural voters more say than they would have in a direct vote, in which large cities would have even greater influence than they do already. In addition, consider the problem of conducting a nationwide recount. Citizens who remember the intense recounting of votes in Florida following the very close election of 2000 will shudder at the possibility of a nationwide recount in a close election.

So now you've voted and let's say that your preferred candidates for the House, Senate, and presidency have all won their elections. What will they do when they show up in Washington? In the next chapter, we begin examining what members of Congress do.

Chapter 4

Congress:
Powers and Organization

Ideally, everything that happens in the American government can be explained by reference to the U.S. Constitution. Some cases are clear. Members of the House of Representatives have to stand (or run) for election every two years because the Constitution explicitly says so: "The House of Representatives shall be composed of Members chosen every second year by the People of the several states" (Article I, Section 2). Also, perhaps you have lived in different states during elections and have noticed that they are conducted somewhat differently. This is because the Constitution says, "The Times, Places and Manner of holding elections for Senators and Representatives, shall be prescribed in each State by the legislature thereof" (Article I, Section 4).

Most of the time, state elections closely resemble each other, but there can be substantial variation. Since the late 1990s, for example, the state of Oregon has emphasized **mail-in voting**. This comes as an effort to raise the level of voter participation, and it seems to have succeeded. In a **special election** for a seat in the U.S. Senate in 1996, about 65 percent of registered voters returned ballots that had been mailed to them. Potential problems, however, can come with the loss of the more controlled environment of the **polling place**, such as the selling of votes, the coercion of voters, or the marking and returning of ballots without the knowledge of the voter. So what if a state's voting practices are clearly problematic, but the state legislature seems unwilling to fix the problem? The Constitution empowers the Congress to alter a state's voting practices (Article I, Section 4).

CONGRESS AND THE UNWRITTEN CONSTITUTION

A simple reading of the Constitution makes all of this, along with many other things, rather clear. But what about the federal government's Department of Health, Education, and Welfare, founded in 1953, and renamed the Department of Health and Human Services in 1979? The Constitution mentions no such entity. The Constitution is silent about a Department of Energy (established in 1977) and a Department of Education (1979). Surely, the writers of the Constitution never envisioned a Department of Veterans Affairs (1989). Such entities are manifestations of what we might call the country's **unwritten constitution**—they are certainly not called for in the Constitution, but they are not seen as being at odds with it either, at least by a majority of Americans.

The existence of such institutions (and much else) is substantially founded in the Constitution's **necessary and proper clause**, also called the **elastic clause**. According to this flexible part of the Constitution, Congress has the power to "make all Laws which shall be necessary and proper for carrying into Execution the foregoing Powers, and all other Powers vested by this Constitution in the Government of the United States, or in any Department or Officer thereof" (Article I, Section 8).

Embedded within this clause are Congress's **implied powers** (as opposed to the Constitution's explicitly stated **enumerated powers**). The perceived power that Congress has to carry out its responsibilities has sometimes conflicted with another part of the Constitution—the Tenth Amendment, which reads as follows: "The powers not delegated to the United States by the Constitution, nor prohibited by it to the States, are reserved to the States respectively, or to the people."

As the United States grew and developed, and reforms and new institutions were needed, questions about which governmental bodies had the power to act arose. People like Alexander Hamilton, who advocated a strong central government, read much into the elastic clause. Others, who advocated a weaker central government and stronger state governments, emphasized the Tenth Amendment.

The Supreme Court has often decided arguments between Americans who take these two approaches. In 1819 the Supreme Court handed down its decision in an important case, *McCulloch v. Maryland*. Congress had passed a law establishing a national bank—an institution not mentioned in the Constitution. Federalists supported this idea; Democratic Republicans and many state legislatures opposed it, seeing this expansion of federal power as an intrusion into affairs that should be reserved to the states. Maryland attempted to diminish the influence of the bank by taxing its operations. With Chief Justice John Marshall at the helm, the Supreme Court ruled that Maryland's tax was unconstitutional because state governments could not pass laws that were at cross-purposes with legitimate federal laws. Of course, this decision depended on the Court's finding that the federal Congress possessed the power to establish a national bank. Constitutionally, this power derived from the necessary and proper (elastic)

The Capitol Building in Washington, D.C., has housed the meeting chambers of the House of Representatives and the Senate for two centuries.

clause. *McCulloch v. Maryland* established the principle of **national supremacy**, though it did not end the underlying philosophical debate that led to it.

The basic point is that, while much that is in the Constitution is fairly straightforward, some of the Constitution's language is rather vague and open to interpretation.

STATED POWERS OF CONGRESS

Now, let's return to what the elastic clause refers to as government's stated powers. According to the Constitution, what powers does government have or not have? Which branch of government has what powers? This chapter and the next focus on Congress.

Article I, Sections 1–9 of the Constitution states what powers Congress does and does not have. Article I is the longest and most detailed portion of the Constitution. The Constitution's framers put Congress's powers first because they saw that law making is a government's most important function.

Power to Legislate

Section 1 of Article I says that the Congress of the United States must be **bicameral**, that is, composed of two bodies—a House of Representatives and a Senate. So, like the British Parliament, with its House of Commons and House of Lords, the American Congress is composed of two bodies—that is, it is bicameral. Unlike the British Parliament, however, both American congressional bodies wield substantial power. One body can check the power of the other.

Section 1 also states that "All legislative Powers" reside in Congress. Presidents and candidates for the presidency often speak of passing legislation related to federal matters. What they actually mean is that they *will propose* legislation to the Congress. But one doesn't need to interact long with government agencies to know that government departments set up policies that are legally binding on citizens.

Use of Administrative Discretion

If Congress alone has the power to legislate, how is it that government agencies can wield so much power? The answer lies in what can be called **administrative discretion**. Congress passes legislation that provides government with agencies that have guidelines to follow. In following these guidelines, the government bodies set policy. For example, in 2008 the Department of Veterans Affairs received a mandate from Congress to provide certain military veterans with service dogs. Immediately, questions arose. What kind of dogs can be used? What kind of training should they have? What kind of certification should their trainers have? Obviously, Congress cannot get into this kind of detail. So it is left to the Department of Veterans Affairs to set up policy consistent with the congressional mandate. To the dog trainers involved, the policies will feel like laws.

Critics of this state of affairs deny that government always protects the "public interest," as it is charged to do. Critics also point out that congressional directives frequently are too vague. The Federal Communications Commission (FCC), for example, has been charged with combating indecency, as understood within the context of "community standards." One doesn't need to watch much TV from the 1950s to see that community standards have changed over the decades. In the 1960s, some worried that the now seemingly tame show *Star Trek* was too violent. Some cases are fairly straightforward, such as when a celebrity singer bared a breast during the 2004 Super Bowl halftime show. Congress fined CBS (the TV network airing the Super Bowl) and, worrying that Congress might tighten decency rules, the National Cable and Telecommunications Association sponsored a campaign to educate parents about TV channel-blocking devices for the protection of children (which, actually, would have done nothing to prevent children from seeing the bare-breasted singer). Here is an example of a business interest acting to prevent Congress from acting—and thus spurring the FCC to act.

HOW LEGISLATION WORKS

But how do laws get passed in the first place? To return to the example mentioned earlier, when an official with the Department of Veterans Affairs was asked by a C-SPAN interviewer about the department's service dog program, the official said, "An interest group put some pressure on some Congressmen, so Congress passed a bill, and now we have to figure out how to make it work." In a few words, the Veterans Affairs official summarized a long and complicated process.

Let's take the official's words one clause at a time. First, an **interest group** or an interested person—for example, the U.S. president, a civic club, a newspaper editor, a business interest, or a church group—perceives a problem. Some advocates of legislation who don't hold formal political power can channel their energies through formalized institutions, such as the Children's Defense Fund and the Family Research Council. Other interest groups are less formal and spur ad hoc letter-writing, e-mailing, and telephone-calling campaigns. Interest groups bring issues to legislators' attention. Of course, sometimes issues do not need to be brought to legislators' attention. In the immediate wake of the terrorist attacks on the United States in 2001 or of a bridge collapse in Minnesota in 2007, it is clear that something needs to be done, and legislators act, usually, at the behest of the U.S. president.

The Path of a Bill Through Congress

Once a legislator (or a group of legislators) has been made aware of an issue and has determined to try to do something about it, the legislature introduces a **bill**. Members of the House do this by dropping their bill in a box, called the hopper, which is near the House Speaker's seat. Senators hand a bill to the Senate clerk or introduce the bill themselves on the Senate floor. In doing this, the bill becomes part of the congressional agenda. But bills are like newly hatched salmon; not many survive into adulthood—that is, into law.

In both houses of Congress, bills go through defined steps. First, bills are referred to appropriate committees, which then often refer them to subcommittees. Hearings on the subject of the bill may be held, and congressional staffers will do research into the substance of the bill. Sometimes a bill is revised during this process, and many bills do not survive.

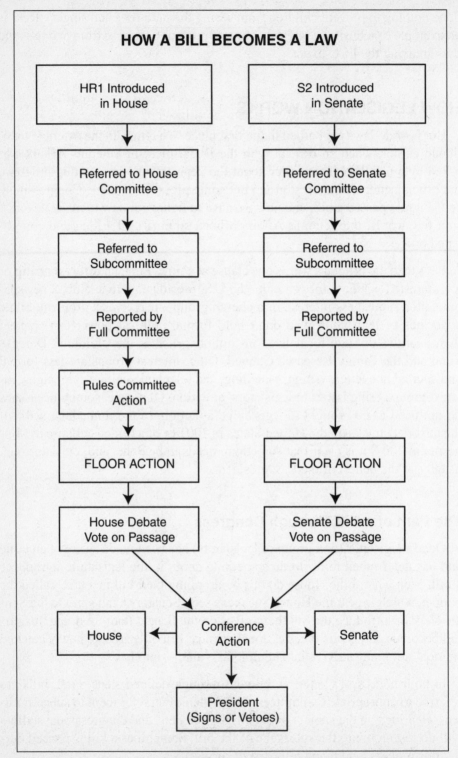

HOW A BILL BECOMES A LAW

HR1 Introduced in House	S2 Introduced in Senate
Referred to House Committee	Referred to Senate Committee
Referred to Subcommittee	Referred to Subcommittee
Reported by Full Committee	Reported by Full Committee
Rules Committee Action	
FLOOR ACTION	FLOOR ACTION
House Debate Vote on Passage	Senate Debate Vote on Passage

House ← Conference Action → Senate

President (Signs or Vetoes)

Source: *http://www.lexisnexis.com/help/cu/The_Legislative_Process/How_a_Bill_Becomes_Law.htm.*

If the subcommittee passes a bill, it then goes to the full committee. Some bills that survive the subcommittee process will not survive the full committee's treatment. If the full committee does approve the bill, it is sent to the House or Senate for consideration by the entire chamber.

Bills reported to the House first pass through the **Rules Committee**, which determines the length of debate that will be allowed on the bill and the kind of amendments that may be offered. Debate in the Senate is much less restricted, though senators usually limit debate on bills via **unanimous consent agreements**. A single senator can derail a consent agreement, but it usually isn't in his or her own interest to do so. Senators make reputations for themselves by getting bills passed; obstructionist senators will find their own projects obstructed.

The Filibuster

Another way a senator can end the life of a bill is to talk on the floor until the time allotted to debate the bill has expired. Whereas members of the House do not speak longer than an hour without unanimous consent from the chamber, senators usually speak for as long as they like. When senators seek to talk a bill to death, they are employing the **filibuster**. The country saw this for the first time in 1790, when a proposal to move the U.S. capital from New York to Philadelphia was debated into oblivion. The record-setting filibuster, however, was offered by Strom Thurmond, a Democrat (at the time) from South Carolina, in 1957. Opposing civil rights legislation, Thurmond spoke for twenty-four hours and eighteen minutes. If at least sixteen senators want to check a filibuster, they can sign a petition initiating **cloture** for debate. For cloture to go into effect, two days must have passed since the petition was offered, and sixty senators must vote for it. After this, each senator is restricted to one hour of debate.

It is easy to see that a relatively small number of senators can derail legislation via filibuster. In 2005, after Senate Democrats had regularly filibustered debate over President Bush's judicial nominees, Republicans in that chamber threatened to pass a rule (called the nuclear option) that would disallow filibustering of judicial nominations. A compromise was worked out between the two parties.

The Veto

Now, let us suppose that a bill has survived a subcommittee and a full committee, and has received majority votes in the House and Senate. Now what? Here enters part of Section 7 of Article I of the Constitution. According to Article I, Section 7, if a bill passes with a majority of votes in both houses of Congress, it goes to the president, and if the president approves the bill, it becomes law. If the president does not approve the bill, however, he returns it to the House where the bill originated, with a statement of objections to the bill. If the president does this, he or she has exercised the power of **veto**. The president's veto of a bill **may be overridden by a two-thirds majority in both houses**. This is one of many instances of the checks and balances built into the Constitution. We also need to know that if the president neither signs the bill nor returns it to Congress within ten days, the bill becomes law, just as though he had signed it.

But what if the president doesn't sign a bill, and Congress adjourns within ten days of the president's receiving it? Then the president is said to have exercised a **pocket veto**.

Relatively few bills survive the long legislative process. Very few of the ones that do survive make it through the process unchanged. To gain majorities in both chambers, compromises have to be struck, and the interests of various constituencies have to be tended to. This is even truer if a presidential veto has to be overcome with two-thirds majorities in the House and Senate. In order to make bills more attractive to **constituents** (the citizens they represent) and fellow politicians, members of Congress attach amendments to them. House rules require amendments to bills to be directly relevant to the purpose of the bill. In the Senate, however, amendments to bills can involve purposes far removed from the bills' original concerns. One often hears senators and House members saying that they voted for a bill that they felt was not ideal but was still useful.

Pork and Earmarks

One perceived problem that comes with amending government appropriation bills is **pork barrel spending** or the securing of **earmarks**—that is, federal funds being designated for specific purposes that assist Congress members' constituencies. In 1987, President Ronald Reagan vetoed a bill that had 121 earmarks. In 2006, Congress passed bills that included some 14,000 earmarks. In early 2007, when the Democrats took control of the House, efforts to curb earmarks were put in place, but within a few months billions of earmark dollars were attached to a spending bill designed to fund the conflict in Iraq; those earmarks had nothing whatsoever to do with the bill's purpose. One of the projects funded helped peanut farmers in Georgia with storage.

Why are earmarks and pork an issue? Let's read the words of one congressman who, as of 2008, excelled at bringing home the bacon to his constituency of Alaska, Representative Don Young. Facing a challenger for his seat in the House, Young was asked by Alaska's largest newspaper how he responded to his opponent's call for a one-year moratorium on earmarks. Young responded:

I hope he continues [to call for a moratorium]. It may be very attractive to those who don't understand the process. But there's never been an earmark for Alaska that has not been asked for by a city, a person, a community activist group. They've all been requested. . . . I hope that, Mr. Whoever He Is keeps saying [that earmarks should be ended or curbed]. I can guarantee that if he was . . . to win this primary you can just about be assured he won't be (re-elected) and back in Washington, D.C.[1]

Young's ability, like the ability of Ted Stevens, Alaska's senior senator (as of 2008), to bring pork home to Alaska is one thing that partly accounts for his being elected to serve eighteen terms in the House. Earmarks have become a problem because constituents want them, and meeting these requests is essential to a politician's keeping his or her job. What Young might have added is that earmarks help to bring in political donations.

Critics of the relatively new phenomenon of earmarking see it as a process that is inevitably corrupting: people with power and ability to fund elections want goodies from congressmen; Congress members oblige and get reelected. Observers on the other side of the debate say that Congress cannot debate the merits of every single thing Congress spends money on—and, anyway, pork accounts for only about 1 percent of the federal government's budget.

ELECTION OF MEMBERS OF CONGRESS

In the previous chapter we learned about elections. Here we'll focus on congressional elections.

The relevant portion of the Constitution is Article I, Section 2. The Constitution requires members of the House of Representatives to face elections every two years and to be elected directly by the people. Whereas members of the Senate are elected every six years, members of the House must stand for election every two years. Also, if a seat in the House comes open when an election is not under way, the seat must be filled via a **special election**. A vacant seat in the Senate can be filled (until the next election) via appointment.

Power of Incumbency

In the minds of the Constitution's framers, frequent elections would provide for **turnover**—that is, a relatively quick change in House membership. The reality is that **incumbents**—politicians who run for reelection—don't often lose elections. Most surprising is that this seems to be *especially* true for members of the House. Since 1946, incumbent representatives have won about 92 percent of the elections they have contested, whereas incumbent senators have won about 78 percent of their elections. The Constitution writers' theory and modern practice have diverged. Why?

One answer is that, in fact, there *is* a fairly high level of turnover because members of Congress retire, return to the private sector, or run for other offices. But as we have seen, members who run for reelection usually get reelected. Let's first focus on the House. One reason incumbency is so powerful is that state legislatures determine congressional districts, and districts can be drawn in such a way as to favor candidates from particular parties. As a result of laws passed in Congress and a Supreme Court decision in the 1960s, districts must include a roughly proportionate number of residents, and each district can be represented by only one House member (thus the term **single-member districts**). In Alaska, which has only one representative, these issues are irrelevant, but in states with large populations and many representatives (California has fifty-two), districts can be drawn that favor Republicans or Democrats. (The other states with just one member in the House are Delaware, Montana, North Dakota, South Dakota, Vermont, and Wyoming.) Sometimes district designers engage in "**packing**"—that is, they pack members of the opposite party into as few districts as possible, and sometimes they opt for "**cracking**"—or breaking opposition party votes into as many districts as possible.

Role of Gerrymandering

When districting for the purposes of making districts politically "safe" is done intentionally, it is called **gerrymandering**. In 1986 the Supreme Court determined that gerrymandering—the intentional rigging of districts to favor one or another party—was unlawful, but the ruling supplied no definition of *gerrymandering*. In 2004 the Supreme Court declined to get involved in cases of alleged gerrymandering. The phenomenon continues and has created some bizarrely shaped districts.

Some districts have been drawn to increase the number of minorities in Congress. Their twists and turns include African American or Hispanic neighborhoods. This was encouraged by Congress itself when it passed an updated **Voting Rights Act** in 1982. But at what point does the desire for diverse representation in Washington, D.C., become mere gerrymandering? In 1995 the Supreme Court ruled, in a case involving a district in Georgia, that race could not be a "predominant factor" in the drawing of districts. Around the same time, districts in Texas and in North Carolina that seemed to have been racially gerrymandered were nullified. But then, in 1999, the Court allowed judges discretion to delve into the motivations behind redistricting, and two years later the Court determined that race could be one factor in redistricting but not the primary factor. Thus a weirdly shaped and racially solid district might stand if its reason for being serves a perceived public interest and it seems to have been put together for reasons not having to do *primarily* with race. If this seems a little confusing, that's because it *is* a little confusing, and staying within these fuzzy boundaries can make redistricting into a kind of political game.

But districting and gerrymandering by themselves do not explain a lot; those maneuvers have no bearing at all on senators who are elected by entire state electorates, though they probably do help explain why incumbency is a greater predictor of reelection in the House than in the Senate. What other factors are involved?

Home Style and Other Advantages

One factor is what some political scientists call **home style**. The two senators from Florida, for example, know how to make a pitch to Floridians, and they (like House members) know how to appeal to subcultures within a state. Obviously, a politician's home style in very liberal San Francisco would be quite different from another's style in very conservative rural Utah. Another factor, as we saw earlier, is the federal money an incumbent can say he or she brought to the district or state. Thus, incumbents can usually point to accomplishments—bills or amendments proposed or passed—and they can trumpet the amount of pork (sometimes euphemized as investments) for the local economy, and so on. Representative Don Young of Alaska, mentioned earlier, was able to brag that he had brought home the federal bacon, and he derided a primary opponent as a legislative "zero." Voters may not necessarily like their incumbent, but sometimes they will take the devil they know rather than a person they don't know at all.

Because they already hold office, incumbents more easily attract media attention. Their **press releases** are likely to gain more notice than statements of lesser-known aspirants to office. Incumbents also have the great advantage of an organized, paid staff that has engaged in **constituent service**. For example, their staff members may have helped veteran constituents get help from the Bureau of Veterans Affairs or provided constituents with information about federal education-assistance programs. Incumbents also have the advantage of **franking privileges**, which refers to the freedom that members of Congress have to deliver official mail at government expense. Restrictions placed on the frank by Congress, along with e-mail, have diminished the amount of mail a congressional member sends, but the costs of the resources that make the e-mail possible are still covered by his or her privileges. The frank is a clear advantage for the incumbent, for people running for office must pay mailing costs themselves or with the help of donors and political parties.

In addition, whereas challengers for office must pay their own travel costs, members of Congress have substantial **travel budgets**. These funds allow congresspersons to return to their states or districts to meet with constituents, give speeches, and hear from lobbyists. These activities are often difficult to distinguish from campaigning, but because House members must stand for election every two years, they are usually in campaign mode. Challengers must find other ways of paying for all such expenses.

Challengers must also be willing to take a risk to run for office. Most often, serious challengers have political experience and hold political office—say, a city council seat or a position as mayor—or a challenger might have served as a representative in a state legislature. The rigors of political campaigning or the campaign rules themselves may require these candidates to surrender their current positions. Thus, unless they have a good chance of winning, potentially strong challengers are unlikely to risk running for a job when the odds are stacked against them.

All these advantages give incumbents the further advantage of being able to raise campaign funds. The help they have provided to constituents, the **name recognition** they have gained, and the record they have compiled make raising funds easier. And political campaigns are expensive. In the election of 2000, House incumbents spent an average of nearly $880,000 on elections. In the Senate election of that year, an open seat for New York cost about $70 million. Donors know that incumbents usually win, and they have good reason to think that donations will put them in good stead with the incumbent. Donors want the goodwill of incumbents who can get things done for them, and incumbents need donors.

Of course, all this assumes that voters *like* their members of Congress. In fact, only about 40 percent of Americans can even recall the name of their representative in the House, and only about 60 percent can recall the name of one of their U.S. senators! Fewer can speak with confidence about their legislators' actual records. But in the voting booth, people tend to vote for names they recognize, and even though opinions of Congress are generally low—as of October 2008 only about 13 percent of Americans approved of Congress's work—views on *my* congressman are generally high. An Alaskan may be tired of a pork-addicted Congress while seeing his own pork-laden representative as a great fighter for the good of Alaska. Generally speaking, as with public schools, so it is with congresspersons. The institution as a whole is a mess, but *my* congressperson (or school) is OK.

The writers of the Constitution required members of the House to run every two years with the hope that this would lead to high turnover. For all the reasons listed here, this hope has not been borne out.

APPORTIONMENT OF HOUSE SEATS

Article I, Section 2 states that to be eligible for service in the House of Representatives, candidates (1) must be at least twenty-five years old, (2) must have been a U.S. citizen for at least seven years by the time of their seating in the House, and (3) must reside in the state they wish to represent. The framers of the Constitution intended the House of Representatives to be the federal government body that is closest to the people. The framers attempted to ensure this by requiring members of the House to stand for **election every two years**.

Another way the framers did this was by making more people eligible for membership in the House. As we see next, U.S. senators must be at least thirty years old, and they must have been a citizen of the United States for at least nine years.

The Constitution says that the number of representatives a state has in the House of Representatives depends on the number of people living in the state, though every state will have at least one representative. Whereas every state has two senators, regardless of population, seats in the House are based on population. There are 435 seats in the House. These seats are divided among the states, based on population. To determine how House seats should be proportioned, a **census** is taken every ten years, as called for in Article I, Section 2 of the Constitution. As population shifts, such as when the population of the West grew dramatically after World War II, seats are **reapportioned**. In 1980 California was represented by forty-three seats in the House, whereas South Dakota had two seats. In 2004 California's number of seats in the House had grown to fifty-three, representing the great population growth of that state, while South Dakota's number of seats had fallen to the minimum of one seat.

The Constitution requires that the number of people living in the states be determined every ten years. This is accomplished via the **census,** administered by the U.S. Census Bureau every ten years. In addition to providing population information for the purposes of congressional reapportionment, some people use information gained from the census about the racial and ethnic makeup of the United States to argue for **descriptive representation**—the belief that Congress should resemble the nation in terms of gender and ethnicity. This, following the census of 1990, is what led to the districts (described earlier) that were redrawn to make it very likely that minorities would be elected to office.

Gender is a more difficult issue. Women make up just over 50 percent of the population, but in 2006 only sixteen of the one hundred U.S. senators (just over 6 percent) were women; the number of women in the House in 2002 stood at 14 percent. Relative to Sweden's legislators (almost 43 percent women) this was quite low, but relative to France (11 percent) and Brazil (just under 7 percent), it was higher. Obviously, districts cannot be gerrymandered to include only women.

Wealth is another way in which Congress does not really represent the American population. In 2002, over 40 percent of U.S. senators and representatives were millionaires. But again, it is difficult to see how to ensure that people who represent economically middle-class America can get a majority of congressional seats.

ORGANIZATION OF THE HOUSE AND POWER OF IMPEACHMENT

The Constitution grants members of the House of Representatives the power to choose their own leadership. As we know, the Constitution's writers were silent on the question of political parties. Some hoped that American politics would rise above the interests of party. Leadership in the Congress, therefore, soon became a party issue. Whatever party holds a majority in the House or Senate will make up the chamber's leadership.

In both chambers, Democrats and Republicans elect their leaders. In the lower chamber, the leadership is made up of a **Speaker of the House**, a **majority leader**, and a **whip**. The Speaker, or the person who sits in his or her stead, presides over House sessions. This is why debaters in the House address themselves to "Mr. Speaker" or, after the Democrats chose Nancy Pelosi of California as Speaker in 2006, "Madame Speaker." The primary task of the majority leader is to guide the majority party's agenda through the legislative agenda. The whip keeps count of votes—who is for, against, or undecided on a piece of legislation—and drums up support for his or her party's agenda.

The minority party has its own **minority leader,** who should be prepared to step into the Speaker's position should his or her party gain a majority in an election. The minority party also has a whip.

The Constitution grants the power of **impeachment** to the House alone. An impeachment is a kind of political accusation. It is roughly akin to an indictment in the criminal legal system: a person can be indicted for a crime but found not guilty. As of 2008, two U.S. presidents had been impeached by the House, though neither was removed from office because the vote in favor of removal in the Senate fell short of the two-thirds vote called for in Section 3, Article I of the Constitution. To discuss impeachment, we also need to cite Article II, Section 4 of the Constitution, which says, "The President, Vice President and all civil Officers of the United States, shall be removed from Office on Impeachment for, and Conviction of, Treason, Bribery, or other high Crimes and Misdemeanors."

In America, two presidents have been impeached. In 1868, President **Andrew Johnson** was impeached for acting against the Tenure in Office Act. This act required the president to get Senate approval before getting rid of cabinet members. This act was later found to be unconstitutional, but Johnson's presidency was saved at the time by a single vote in the Senate; the episode critically weakened Johnson who, in any case, has been numbered among the worst of the U.S. presidents.

The second president to be impeached was **Bill Clinton**. In 1998, the House impeached Clinton on two counts: (1) lying to a grand jury about an affair he had with an intern and (2) obstruction of justice. In this case, the Senate vote did not come close to the two-thirds required by the Constitution. Much of the debate during this process centered on whether lying about an extramarital affair "rises to the level" of "high crimes and misdemeanors." Some said questions about this private matter should not have been raised in the first place; others said that, whatever the circumstances, a president must not lie while under oath in the course of a legal proceeding.

In 1974 President **Richard Nixon** resigned from office before articles of impeachment could be voted on in the House. (They had already been approved by the House Judiciary Committee.) Nixon had been involved in the coverup of a politically motivated break-in of the Democratic Party's office at the **Watergate Hotel** in Washington in 1972. Nixon is the only U.S. president to resign from office. (As of 2008, eight presidents had died in office.) Had Nixon not resigned, he almost certainly would not have survived an impeachment trial in the Senate.

ORGANIZATION OF THE SENATE

Article III of the Constitution says that each state must have two members in the U.S. Senate, regardless of the state's population. As we learned in Chapter 2, the writers of the Constitution gave every state two senators, regardless of population, to provide some protection to states with relatively small populations and thus little representation in the House. To flesh this out a little, let's look briefly at a historical case. The crisis that led to the **Compromise of 1820** (also called the Missouri Compromise) involved representation in the Senate. By 1820 the Northern and Western states were growing at a faster pace than the Southern states. In 1819 Southern (that is, pro-slave states) and non-Southern states could be grouped into an equal number of states; thus representation in the Senate was equal. The South could not do anything about the increasing influence of the non-slave states in the House, but equality in the Senate was essential. For our purposes, we can simply say that the crisis was resolved when Missouri entered the Union as a slave state, Maine entered the Union as a free state, and equality was maintained in the Senate.

Senators are elected every six years. The Constitution writers' goal here was to distance senators from the "passions" of the people and from political fads. House members, who stand for election every two years, must (in theory, at least) stay close to the sentiments of the people they represent. This is good for representative democracy. But at the same time, some legislators should be distanced from the temporary whims of the people. The Constitution originally called for senators to be elected by state legislators and thus only indirectly chosen by the people. As a result of reforms associated with the Progressive movement of the early twentieth century, this was changed by the **Seventeenth Amendment** and ratified in 1913, which provided for the **direct of election of senators**.

As noted earlier, to be eligible for service in the Senate, a candidate must (1) be at least thirty years old, (2) have been a U.S. citizen for at least nine years, and (3) reside in the state he or she wishes to represent. Recall that House members must be twenty-five and must have been citizens for seven years. Eligibility for a seat in the Senate is more restricted—another indication that the Senate was designed to be a "higher" house—meaning, in this case, more difficult to get into.

The **vice president of the United States is president of the Senate** but has a vote only in the case of a tie. In Senate debates, for example, senators address themselves to "Mr. President," pointing to the vice president's position as president of the Senate. In reality, the vice president is rarely in the Senate, presiding only when there may be a tie vote, in which case the vice president has the power to cast the deciding vote. In the Senate, the vice president's place is taken by a **president pro tempore** (*pro tempore* is Latin for "president for the time"). The president pro tem, as he or she is frequently called, is usually the member of the majority party who has served the longest in the Senate. But, of course, the president pro tem has plenty of work to do, so Senate proceedings are most often presided over by junior senators selected for that purpose.

The last point to be made in this chapter is that the Constitution requires Congress to assemble at least once a year. Aside from this requirement, the amount of time Congress spends in session is its own decision to make.

Of course, members of Congress have to account to constituents for how they spend their time. In the 1960s and 1970s, Congress was usually in session for about 320 days. The 109th Congress of 2006 was in session for fewer than

250 days. Even when in session, Congress members did the bulk of their work only when they were physically present in Congress on Tuesdays, Wednesdays, and Thursdays. This Congress came under criticism for working less than the so-called Do-Nothing Congress of 1947–1948. In response, Congress members say that they must spend time back home, among constituents—doing the things necessary to serve constituents and to ensure reelection.

References

[1] Sean Cockerham, "Young Sets Sights on 19th Term," *Anchorage Daily News*, June 13, 2008.

Chapter 5

Congress:
Rules, Lobbyists, Taxes,
the Budget, and Operations

The previous chapter discussed Sections 1 through 4 of Article I of the Constitution, which focuses on the U.S. Congress. This chapter continues the discussion of Congress, focusing on Sections 5 through 9 of Article I.

CONGRESSIONAL RULES AND COMMITTEES

Section 5 of Article I states that each house of Congress "may determine the Rules of its Proceedings, punish its Members for disorderly Behavior, and, with the Concurrence of two thirds, expel a Member." This statement is about organization. Congress is empowered to organize itself and to police itself. We learned about congressional leadership in the previous chapter. Now let's focus on the primary way Congress gets work done: via committees. Then we will look at ways Congress polices itself.

Congressional committees are a little like academic departments in schools and universities. On matters pertaining to biology, for example, one expects the professors of biology to have the most insightful things to say. So suppose a career military man enters one of the congressional chambers. It would make sense for him to serve on a committee having to do with military matters. Or if a doctor enters Congress, it would make sense for her to serve on a committee having to do with medical and health topics. It isn't possible for all members of Congress to become experts on the subject matter of every bill they have to vote on; they must rely on the competence and expertise of their colleagues.

Committees themselves are usually organized into subcommittees. Consider our career military man. Let's say that he spent most of his career in the Pacific. Then it might be best for him to serve not only on the Foreign Relations

Committee (Senate) or Foreign Affairs Committee (House), but to place him on a subcommittee concerned with Asia.

Standing Committees

The most basic kind of congressional committee is the **standing committee**. A standing committee is permanent, whereas a **select committee** is organized to deal with a temporary matter and is disbanded once its purpose has been served. (In other contexts, a select committee may be called an **ad hoc committee**—*ad hoc* being Latin for "toward this thing.") Thus an ad hoc committee is organized to deal with a particular, temporary matter. Both chambers have **appropriations committees,** which are concerned with the spending of federal dollars. Both chambers have armed services committees, judiciary committees, and veterans' affairs committees. Some of the two chambers' standing committees have similar names—for example, in the Congress of 2007–2009, the House had a Homeland Security Committee, whereas the Senate had a Homeland Security and Government Affairs Committee.

Altogether, both chambers have about twenty standing committees, and it is in these committees that most of Congress's work gets done. Usually, about forty-two House members serve on a committee, as compared to about eighteen senators. The majority party in a chamber determines how many seats the minority party gets on a committee. Ideally, the number of committee seats represents the proportion the minority party holds in Congress, but the majority party will ensure that it has a sufficient number of seats in each committee to control the committee.

Other Important Committees

Most of Congress's work gets done in standing committees, but there are other important committees. **Joint committees** comprise members of both houses and are primarily responsible for fact finding and for raising awareness of particular problems and issues; they rarely report bills to the House or Senate. **Conference committees**, like select committees, are temporary and are put together to work out differences between Senate and House versions of a bill. Before a bill can go to the president for his (or her) signature, both congressional chambers must pass identical bills. A conference committee will iron out differences between the chambers' bills. Given the power that conference committees have, some have called them the "third house of Congress."

The **House Rules Committee** is a uniquely powerful institution. (Because there are many fewer restrictions on debate in the Senate, that chamber has no such committee.) For example, this committee has the power to bring a certain bill immediately to the floor for debate rather than place the bill on a calendar, where it may languish. In 1994 Speaker of the House Newt Gingrich (R-Georgia) published a **Contract with America**, in which he promised "a detailed agenda for national renewal, a written commitment with no fine print." This promise was predicated on the Republican-controlled Rules Committee moving bills quickly through the House.

Committees also determine who sits on which committees. Each party has a **Steering Committee**. Usually, the member of the majority party with the longest service on a committee will be named that committee's chairperson. Generally, Congress relies on a **seniority system** to determine who committee leaders will be. This is not failsafe. In the 1970s a secret ballot was instituted in House committee leadership selection, so it is possible that the chairperson will not have seniority. In the 1970s the Democrats, and in the 1990s the Republicans, passed over ranking members for chair positions because the senior members did not share the views of the most powerful elements within their party. The highest-ranking member of the minority party is called the **ranking committee member**.

In response to a general desire in the 1990s to place **term limits** on how long politicians could hold power—term limits seek to restrict how long a person can serve in a certain office—the House Republicans determined that a person could be a committee chairperson for up to six years. Because conservatives are generally more suspicious of government than liberals are, and because there are more conservatives in the Republican Party, the idea of term limits is more popular among Republicans and was an area of intense interest in the 1990s.

LOBBYISTS AND DISCIPLINE

Section 5 of Article I also empowers Congress to police itself. Many Americans might wish that Congress did a better job of this, which is why some of them are interested in term limits—that is, in limiting the amount of time politicians can serve in particular offices. In recent decades, many Americans seem to have taken for granted the idea that "power corrupts." In 1989 a **Gallup poll** showed that 39 percent of Americans had a high level of confidence in Congress. As it comes in well below 50 percent, that seems low. But a similar poll in 2007 showed that just 14 percent of Americans had high confidence in Congress. (Compare that to 69 percent for the U.S. military and 46 percent for organized religion.) Between 2003 and 2008, there was a lot of commentary on the growing unpopularity of President George W. Bush. In May 2006, for example, a **poll** showed his approval rating at 31 percent. That is low, but it was high compared to approval of Congress.

Why do Americans have such a low opinion of Congress, and what has Congress, using its self-policing powers, done to try and improve its image? How does Congress police itself and discipline its own members? To answer these questions, we must digress and take up the issue of **lobbying.**

The general answer to the question about Congress's low standing in public approval polls is that members of Congress are perceived as pursuing their own interests at the expense of the public interest. The widespread perception of how things run is as follows: the primary interest of politicians is to keep power, and keeping power takes money, which means that politicians need to court people and groups that have money to spend. **Interest groups**, or **lobbies**, on the other side, want to influence public policy, which means that they must influence politicians, which means, in turn, that they must do things that make politicians feel good about them and thus their causes.

In a sense, anyone who cares at all about the political life of the nation is part of an interest group, insofar as others share one's views. But most Americans aren't organized into lobbies, and most Americans do not have the kind of resources that get a congressperson's attention. **Lobbyists**—formal representatives of interest groups—often do have such resources available to them. Early in the twenty-first century, Jack Abramoff, a now notorious lobbyist who ended up in jail, illegally paid almost $7,000 for Speaker of the House Tom DeLay to play golf in Scotland and to stay at an expensive London hotel. It's difficult to believe that Abramoff did not have more influence among politicians than an average construction worker, teacher, or chemist.

One thing to notice is that, just as people tend to like their own congressperson while disliking the rest, so do people tend to make distinctions among interest groups. If I do not like big corporations, then I will shake my head at what I view as the obvious corruption that comes with General Electric's lobbying expenditure of almost $14 million between January and June of 2005. But if I am an older person, I may not be bothered at all by the nearly $28 million spent in the same period on lobbying by the American Association of Retired Persons—in fact, I may cheer the AARP on as it fights for my interests! But regardless of its source, money tends to corrupt. How has Congress tried to police itself and address the concerns the public has about the corrupting influence of big money?

An early attempt to control the influence of lobbyists was the **Legislative Reorganization Act** (1946), also called the **Federal Regulation of Lobbying Act**. This act required lobbyists to state clearly who their clients were and what their policy positions were. This act was challenged on the grounds that it infringed on freedom of speech (among other things), but the Supreme Court rejected that claim in *United States v. Harriss* (1954). The Court did say that the law applied only to people who directly lobbied congresspersons; it did not apply to those who lobbied other branches of government or congressional staff assistants. Thus, in the years following this decision, the number of registered lobbyists stood at about seven thousand, while the actual number of people involved in trying to influence policy in Washington was closer to seventy thousand.

Another attempt to control lobbyists came in 1995, with the **Lobbying Disclosure Act**. Among other things, this act defined as a lobbyist anyone who spends at least 20 percent of his or her time lobbying government officials, and it required reports to be filed twice a year stating for what clients and on what legislative bills the lobbyists worked. The act did not require lobbyists to disclose whom they had specifically lobbied, and it did not apply to **grass-roots** lobbying efforts—that is, lobbying by nonprofessionals and concerned citizens—or to tax-exempt organizations such as churches. While debating this legislation, both houses placed restrictions on gifts that members of Congress could receive from lobbyists. The House banned gifts altogether, for example, and the Senate limited gifts to the value of $50. Both chambers banned all-expenses-paid outings.

A little more than a decade after the reforms of 1995, the Democrats won congressional elections promising "honest leadership and open government," and further restrictions were placed on lobbyists. Now, for example, lobbyists would have to report funds spent on parties and dinners at which attendees would make a contribution to a member of Congress.

But the problem persists. Political campaigns cost money, and sometimes it seems that politicians expect that their position should bring them the good things of life. The pervasive feeling is that big money and politics are inextricable. This has led to a widespread feeling of **cynicism** about politics. Aspiring political leaders often run on platforms of change and on "getting money out of politics," but in the American system as it exists today, the problem seems intractable, and many worry that it threatens democracy.

FORMS OF DISCIPLINE

Congress has the constitutional power to control and police itself; it has, in fact, made some efforts to do so. Whether Congress is really serious about policing itself is an open question, however. To be sure, congressional discipline of its own members is rare. The most severe form of discipline (and the rarest) is the **expulsion** of a member from Congress. It is rare, partly, because most members resign their seats before they can be expelled. During the Civil War, fourteen senators and three House members who supported the Confederacy were expelled from the Congress at Washington, D.C. (Some of them took up positions in the Confederate government; former U.S. senator Jefferson Davis became president of the Confederacy.) In 1980, the House expelled Michael Myers (D-Pennsylvania) for corruption.

Less serious than expulsion is **censure**—that is, formal reprimand. One would have thought that Representative Lovell Rousseau (R-Kentucky) might have been expelled for beating up a fellow congressman in 1866, but he was only censured. Ten years earlier, the leadership of the House attempted to expel Preston Brooks (D-South Carolina) for nearly killing Senator Charles Sumner in the Senate, but the expulsion vote fell short of the necessary two-thirds vote. Neither was Brooks censured, for he resigned and was then reelected. In 1990, to cite one more example, Senator David Durenberger was censured for unethical financial conduct.

Short of censure, congressional ethics committees can write letters criticizing the conduct of members and offering warnings against the kinds of activities that lead to investigations and that put Congress in a bad light and increase the amount of cynicism people feel about government. In February 2008, the Senate Ethics Committee unanimously and publicly "admonished" Larry Craig (R-Idaho) for trying to "evade legal consequences" related to allegedly improper behavior in a men's restroom in an airport. Craig was also criticized for not seeking proper permission to use leftover campaign money to pay for his legal case. The scolding was a rare public rebuke that carried no punishment beyond additional embarrassment for Craig. Months after the admonishment, political humorists continued to pile on.

OPERATIONS OF CONGRESS

One way we can keep track of congressional business is by reading the record kept of its transactions.

The *Congressional Record*

The Constitution requires that a record of congressional transactions be kept. Although Congress has maintained records of its proceedings from the beginning, publication of the *Congressional Record* began in 1873. It now fills hundreds of feet of shelf space in large research libraries. The *Congressional Record* was preceded by **Debates and Proceedings in the Congress of the**

The *Congressional Record* is the official record of the proceedings of the United States Congress. It is published daily when Congress is in session.

United States (1789–1824), the **Register of Debates in Congress** (1824–1837), and the **Congressional Globe** (1833–1873). Each volume of the *Congressional Record* is divided into four sections: (1) a daily digest, (2) a House section, (3) a Senate section, and (4) a section where Congress members' remarks can be extended. When listening to congressional debates on C-SPAN, one will often hear Congress members seeking permission to "revise and extend" their remarks. The revisions and extensions go into the *Congressional Record*.

Compensation

Section 6 of Article I of the Constitution requires that members of each congressional chamber are to be compensated for their labor from the U.S. Treasury. In 2008 the base pay for a member of the House and Senate was $169,300 per year. Majority and minority leaders in both chambers made $188,000. The Speaker of the House made $217,400. Benefits for health and other perquisites of office (such as a gym) are added.

Criminal Liability

Section 6 also says that, except for "Treason, Felony and Breach of Peace," members of Congress cannot be arrested while Congress is in session. Neither can members of Congress be prosecuted outside Congress for words spoken during congressional speeches and debates. The purpose of these protections is to prevent Congress members who hold unpopular views from being legally targeted on trumped-up charges. Obviously, its purpose is not to place Congress above the law. For example, in 2005 Representative Kevin Brady (R-Texas) was arrested for driving under the influence of alcohol. Vito Fossella (R-New York) was arrested for the same thing three years later. Neither representative lost his seat in Congress, however.

Finally, Section 6 stipulates that members of Congress cannot be appointed to civil offices created during their service in Congress or if compensation for an old office has increased during service.

TYPES OF TAXES

Article I, Section 7 of the Constitution says that all bills designed to raise revenue (income) for the federal government must originate in the House, though bills can be proposed by members of the Senate. In other words, legislation concerning **taxation** must be formally initiated in the House of Representatives. Because the government gets about 80 percent of its income via taxation, this is an important responsibility. Candidates for president may say that they want to lower taxes, but presidents do not have the power to do so. Presidents, like senators, can propose tax legislation, but only the House has the power to get the ball rolling. Remember that the United States was born partly as a result of a tax revolt. So the framers of the Constitution placed the power of formally initiating tax legislation in the political body that is closest and, theoretically, the most accountable to the people.

There are many varieties of taxes. The **income tax** is levied on sources of financial income. If you receive a regular paycheck, you probably also receive information about how much the government has taxed what you earned. Generally speaking, thanks to **loopholes** (legal ways to reduce your tax bill) in the tax laws, not much is simple when it comes to taxation. However, again speaking generally, the more you earn, the higher your tax rate. This is referred to as **progressive taxation**. In 2007, for example, married couples who made between $15,651 and $63,700 paid a 15 percent tax, while a married couple making more than $349,700 paid (or "contributed") 35 percent. The poor and **working poor** pay no income tax at all.

In addition to income taxes, people who earn paychecks face **payroll taxes**, which comprise the **Social Security tax** and the **Medicare tax**. (Employers are required to match what each of their employees pays in payroll taxes.) Unlike income taxes, these taxes come at a flat rate, and in 2007 wage earners who made more than $97,500 paid no such tax. Nor is this tax levied against investment earnings, and wealthier Americans invest more of their financial resources. Thus lower-wage earners pay most of the Social Security taxes. This is called **regressive taxation**.

Sales taxes, which are imposed by states and localities, not the federal government, are levied when you purchase books, CDs, and cars. Obviously, rich and poor pay the same sales tax rates. But because the wealthy tend to spend a smaller percentage of their incomes at the cash register, this tax is said to be regressive. On the other hand, the **estate tax** (sometimes called the **death tax** by critics) is progressive. This tax is levied against property left by people who have died.

Some of the arguing about taxes in American public life concerns the amount the wealthy pay. Democrats (and other left-leaning parties) tend to argue that the wealthy can afford to pay higher taxes and therefore should do so. Republicans and Libertarians (along with other fiscally conservative parties) argue that the wealthy use their resources to create jobs and that these jobs lead to greater tax income. Tax the wealthy more, they say, and there will be fewer jobs and, thus, less federal income. Those opposed to higher taxes on the wealthy also point out that Americans with high incomes already make a disproportionate tax contribution. In 2001, for example, wage earners in the top 10 percent earned 42 percent of American income but provided the federal government with 68 percent of its tax income.

Also contributing to the feeling of unease many people have over taxation is a general lack of awareness. By **April 15** of every year, when tax returns are due to the government, income earners know how much they have paid in income taxes. But because they do not file for payroll taxes, they are often unaware of how much the government has taken.

As we know, the United States was born in tax revolt, and one doesn't have to listen long to political campaigners to know that taxes are a constant concern of voters. It turns out, however, Americans are among the least taxed people in the industrialized world. In 2002 Swedes contributed (or lost) about 50 percent of their incomes to various forms of taxation, whereas Icelanders gave up about 38 percent, Australians about 32 percent, and Americans about 26 percent. (South Koreans paid about 24 percent.)

COLLECTION OF TAXES AND PAYMENT OF DEBT

Section 8 is the most detailed section of the Constitution's first article. Let's break it down. Among the key powers granted to Congress are (1) to require and collect taxes and import duties and (2) to borrow money for national purposes and to pay the nation's debts.

First, regarding taxation, the government body designed to collect taxes is the Internal Revenue Service (IRS), which follows the Internal Revenue Code—a "document" that is thousands of pages long and that keeps thousands of tax lawyers gainfully employed. The IRS is probably the only government institution of which law-abiding citizens have some fear. In the early 1990s, IRS offices were ranked according to how much unpaid tax money they brought in. This led to bureaucratic aggressiveness, to a hearing before the Senate Finance Committee in 1997, and to an apology from the IRS commissioner. Since then, the IRS has been kinder and gentler, but it will probably never be popular.

Next, let's discuss how the government borrows money. Then we'll take up the federal budget.

Ways the Government Borrows

If in a certain year the government spends more money (on, for example, public services and the military) than it takes in, the government is said to have acquired a **deficit**. The nation's debt—its **public debt**—is the sum of consecutive deficits. In 2006, the public debt stood at $4.8 trillion.

Like individuals and families, the government needs money to operate, for its operations are conducted by people, and people must be compensated for their labor. Where does the government get its money? As we have seen, the single greatest source of income is taxation—income taxes, payroll taxes, taxes on corporations, and taxes on particular items like beer, cigarettes, and gasoline. So why doesn't the government simply raise the amount of taxes it takes in to cover its costs? One answer is that it *does* do this, though not always openly. Sometimes taxes and fees that few people know about—called **hidden taxes**—pull more money from your pocket than you realize. Taxes are unpopular, and few aspiring politicians campaign on the promise to raise taxes, though Democrats do tend to campaign on raising taxes on the wealthy. There is a consensus that, at a point, taxes slow an economy because they make business growth more difficult and, thus, reduce the number of jobs employers create. Ultimately, the decline in jobs leads to a reduction in tax income, for the fewer jobs there are, the fewer incomes there are to tax.

Government also gains income from **tariffs**. Tariffs, also called **duties**, are taxes on goods imported into the United States. Well into the twentieth century, tariffs were the major source of government income. Partly as a result of increasing free trade agreements, such as the North American Free Trade Agreement (**NAFTA**), signed by Canada, the United States, and Mexico in 1993, tariff rates are falling or disappearing.

The sale of **bonds** helps the government manage its deficit. People purchase **savings bonds**, for example, with the expectation that they will get back what they paid, plus interest. Bonds sold today help to pay for bonds sold twenty years ago. During the two world wars of the twentieth century, the government sold "Liberty Bonds" to finance the hugely expensive war efforts. A worrying fact is that, in 2006, about 45 percent of the American government's debt was held by foreign organizations and individuals. If faith in the U.S. government's ability to pay its debt were seriously harmed and led foreign interests to stop lending money to the United States, the effects on the American economy would be dramatic.

The Budgeting Process

Before World War I, the Congress formulated numerous spending bills that amounted to a national **budget** and sought the president's approval for them. This was not an efficient process and, since the passage of the **Budget and Accounting Act** (1921), presidents have prepared budgets and sought congressional approval. The **Bureau of the Budget** was formed to assist the president with this process; in 1970, this bureau became the **Office of Management and Budget** (OMB).

At the start of each year, the president presents a budget for the next **fiscal year**, which runs from October 1 through September 30. The budget is thousands of pages long and explains in detail the president's reasons for the things he (or she) has called for. Obviously, the president does not personally write this document but relies on the OMB, which is part of the president's administration. The OMB seeks information from various government institutions on how much they will need to carry out their tasks. Of course, government departments will argue for the maximum amount of money they can get. The formulation of the budget is inevitably a very political process.

The budget the president sends to Congress includes information on (1) the amounts certain government agencies will be authorized to spend (**budget authority**), (2) how much government agencies are actually expected to spend (**budget outlays**), and (3) how much the government expects to take in via taxes and other sources (**receipts**). President Bush's plan for fiscal year 2007 (October 1, 2006–September 30, 2007) foresaw a deficit of $354 billion—a sum representing about $1,300 for each American citizen.

The budget sent to the Congress is not a finished product but a starting place for Congress. In the decades following World War II, the **Ways and Means Committee** in the House and the **Finance Committee** in the Senate considered the budget's information on tariffs, taxes, and other sources of income. Various **authorization committees** authorized spending on different projects (such as for upgraded dams in the Midwest), but unless the funds were actually approved by proper **appropriations committees,** the money was not spent. All along the way, presidents and legislators come under pressure from constituents, interest groups, and party demands. Inevitably, the desire to spend more money on more things—for the sake of completing worthwhile projects but also for the sake of pleasing constituents, donors, and party colleagues—grew. The process was very complicated. After 1974, with the passage of the **Budget and Impoundment Control Act**, congressional **budget committees** oversaw the still political and complicated budgeting process. The **Congressional Budget Office**, which assisted these committees, employed over two hundred people. And the national debt grew, particularly during the presidency of Ronald Reagan (1980–1988), while wrangling between the president and Congress and among Congress members and interests groups continued.

In an effort to get the problem of national debt under control, Congress passed the **Gramm-Rudman Act** (1985). This legislation required annual reductions in the annual deficit, with the final goal being an elimination of the national debt by 1991. This effort failed.

Congress and the president tried again in 1990, passing the **Budget Enforcement Act** (BEA). This act defined two types of federal spending. First, there is **mandatory spending** (required spending) for **entitlements** such as Social Security. (The government could not simply decide to reduce Social Security payments to the elderly.) On the other hand, there is **discretionary spending**—that is, spending that can change from year to year. In the first decade of the twenty-first century, for example, it became clear that more needed to be spent on upkeep of the nation's infrastructure—bridges, roads, and so on. The BEA called for **pay-as-you-go**, meaning that any increase in entitlement spending had to be offset by tax increases or by cuts in discretionary spending. The legislation also placed **caps** (upper limits) on discretionary spending. President George H.W. Bush agreed to a raise in taxes, thus breaking his famous promise of the 1988 presidential election: "**Read my lips: no new taxes**." The price he paid was the loss of the presidency in the 1992 election.

The BEA seemed to work, though the desire among political leaders to spend remained strong. The **Balanced Budget Act** of 1997, signed by President Bill

Clinton, led not only to a balanced budget but to a budget **surplus**—more income than spending—for the first time since the end of the 1960s. Republicans argued that the surplus should have led to tax reductions; Democrats argued that the surplus should be used to fund social programs, such as guaranteed healthcare for children.

In 2002 the requirements of the BEA expired; since then, the United States has seen annual deficits and a ballooning national debt driven mainly by conflicts in Iraq and Afghanistan related to the country's global war on terrorism. President George W. Bush signed tax reductions into law, and these helped to stimulate the economy. But the vast spending, combined with the tax cuts, led to a national debt, in October 2008, of over $10 trillion.

Relations with Other Nations

Section 8 of Article I also empowers Congress to regulate commerce between the states and between the Unites States and "Indian Tribes" and foreign nations. The **Interstate Commerce Commission** (ICC) was created in 1887. Its primary purpose was to regulate railroads that moved goods and services from one state to another. The ICC was abolished in 1995 and was replaced by the **Surface Transportation Board**, which has a regulatory interest in railroads, interstate trucking and moving vans, and pipelines.

The **Bureau of Indian Affairs** was established in 1824 and is under the jurisdiction of the Department of the Interior. In 2008 this bureau provided various services to some 1.7 million American Indians and Alaska Natives. At that time, the **Bureau of Indian Education** provided education services to about 44,000 students.

Citizenship

Section 8 empowers Congress to provide uniform rules regarding citizenship, or "naturalization."

In 2008 the **U.S. Citizenship and Immigration Services** (USCIS) declared the following as basic, general requirements for citizenship for immigrants to the United States (people born in the United States are granted citizenship immediately):

— a period of continuous residence (that is, physical presence) in the United States;

— the ability to read, write, and speak English;

— a knowledge of American history and government;

— commitment to the principles of the U.S. Constitution;

— a "favorable disposition" toward the U.S.

The USCIS became part of the Department of Homeland Security in 2003. (Many government bodies came into the Department of Homeland Security at the same time, including the U.S. Coast Guard, the Federal Emergency Management Administration, and the Transportation Security Administration, whose employees staff airport search points.) The USCIS employs about 15,000 people in 250 offices around the world.

Currency, Post Offices, and Inventions

Article I, Section 8 of the Constitution gives Congress the power to create currency, to create punishments for the counterfeiting of currency, and to establish post offices. The **U.S. Mint** (established in 1792) creates coins and maintains the nation's gold and silver reserves. The **Bureau of Engraving and Printing** produces the nation's paper currency. Both of these institutions are part of the Department of the Treasury. Money is distributed into the economy by the **Federal Reserve System**, which comprises twelve regional **Federal Reserve Banks**. These banks are located in Boston, New York, Philadelphia, Cleveland, Richmond (Virginia), Atlanta, Chicago, St. Louis, Minneapolis, Kansas City, Dallas, and San Francisco. The Federal Reserve, often simply called The Fed, is an independent government agency.

The Mint sells collectors' coins, among other things, and is self-funded. Income received beyond operating expenses is turned over to the Treasury. The national motto "In God We Trust" first appeared on paper currency, formally called **U.S. Federal Reserve Notes**, in 1963. The printed motto has been challenged in court as a breach of the separation of church and state many times but never successfully. During fiscal year 2007, the Bureau of Engraving and Printing produced about 38 million currency notes a day, with a value of about $750 million.

As of 2007, the **U.S. Postal Service** comprised some 37,000 post offices and other units of operation. In that year, the U.S.P.S. handled nearly 96 billion pieces of first-class mail and handled 45 million address changes.

The Constitution gives Congress the authority to "promote the Progress of Science and useful Arts, by securing for limited Times to Authors and Inventors the exclusive Right to their respective Writings and Discoveries"—in other words, to regulate copyright and patents.

If a person were to ask why the United States has been such a key source of invention in modern times, one answer would be the government protection that inventors can expect. (Of course, many other governments also protect **intellectual property rights**, but many others do not.) The U.S. government ensures that patented inventions are not copied and placed in the market for a certain number of years. Invention means risk, but the reduction of risk that government protection provides encourages inventors to move forward with their ideas. The **United States Patent and Trademark Office** (USPTO) is an agency of the Department of Commerce. Like the Mint, USPTO is fully self-funded as a result of the fees it requires. In 2008 the USPTO employed some 7,000 people.

The **U.S. Copyright Office** is associated with the **Library of Congress**. It became a distinct government entity in 1897. Copyright protects "original works of authorship" from being copied without permission for lengthy periods of time, after which they can be copied completely without permission. When a literary work has reached the point where it can be copied at will, it is said to have entered the **public domain**. Newspaper articles published in the 1920s and before, for example, are now considered public property, whereas articles published after the 1920s are not.

Federal Courts, War, State Militias

Article I, Section 8 of the Constitution calls on Congress to establish federal courts below the Supreme Court. Federal courts are discussed in detail in a later chapter. Suffice it here to note that, just as the framers of the Constitution could not have known the size of the bureaucracies the Congress would have to oversee, they could not have foreseen the sometimes seemingly godlike power the federal courts, especially the Supreme Court, would acquire. Nowhere does the Constitution explicitly grant to federal courts the power and influence they have acquired.

Congress also has the power to **declare war**, to raise and **regulate an army and a navy**, and to **finance military operations**, though no single appropriation may supply military operations for longer than two years. The last time Congress formally declared war was in December 1945, first against Japan and, soon after, against Hitler's Germany. But the United States has been in several wars since 1945. One could say that, technically, the wars in Korea, Vietnam, and Iraq were not wars because Congress never declared war. We might call them conflicts, though in reality they were no different from wars.

Rather than declare wars, since 1941 Congress has passed resolutions empowering the president to prosecute conflicts. The **Gulf of Tonkin Resolution** (1964), for instance, empowered President Lyndon Johnson to "take all necessary measures to repel any armed attack against the forces of the United States and to prevent further aggression." This opened wide the door to the long and agonizing conflict in Vietnam.

In the early 1970s, Congress saw that it had handed too much power to the president and passed the **War Powers Act** (1973), overriding President Nixon's veto, which limited a president's power in wartime. For example, this act required combat troops to return to the United States after sixty days unless explicit approval from Congress was gained.

In January 1991 and in October 2002, Congress authorized presidents to prosecute wars against Iraq. The first war saw the involvement of many nations who were united against Iraq's invasion and occupation of its neighbor Kuwait. The second conflict was much more controversial, in part because the United States had few allies, Britain being the strongest. Based on faulty intelligence, members of Congress widely believed that Iraq possessed weapons of mass destruction. Congress empowered the president to use "all means that he determines to be appropriate, including force." Iraq had possessed and used weapons of mass destruction and poison gases in the past, but as of 2008 (as the conflict in Iraq continued), no such weapons had been found. It appears that the weapons had been destroyed years before. The fact that Barack Obama had opposed the 2003 invasion of Iraq while he served in the Illinois state legislature partly accounts for his success as a Democratic nominee for U.S. president in 2008.

Related to Congress's position of authority in wartime is its constitutional responsibility to **provide for state militias** and to call up the "militia" for national purposes, such as to put down insurrections and to resist invasions. One rarely hears about this provision in the Constitution (found in Article I, Section 8). The militia that the Constitution's writers referred to has become formalized in the **National Guard**.

The chief of the National Guard Bureau is appointed by the president and reports to the secretary of defense and the military's chiefs of staff. Congress does provide general oversight in that these appointed positions must be approved by Congress, and these appointed officials are brought before congressional committees, which seek to hold them accountable.

Governance of Washington, D.C.

The Constitution empowers the Congress to **govern the District of Columbia** and military facilities in the states. The District of Columbia (better known as Washington, D.C.) is a unique entity in the United States. It is not a state and is not under the jurisdiction of any state. The Constitution gives Congress authority over the district "in all cases whatsoever." Both congressional chambers have standing committees devoted to the oversight of the district.

Residents of Washington, D.C., have no senators representing them, and since 1971 they have had a **congressional delegate**—that is, a member of the House of Representatives who can vote in committees but who may not vote for or against final passage of legislation. In this, the district's representation is similar to that of the American territories, Guam and Samoa. The Twenty-Third Amendment to the Constitution gave residents of the district the right to vote for president. The city's daily affairs are managed by local city leadership—under broad congressional oversight.

Some in the district argue for statehood or for joining the state of Maryland. In April 2007, the D.C. Fair and Equal Housing Act passed in the House. This would have given Washington, D.C., a representative with full voting powers, and it would have given an additional House member to Utah, which would have increased the number of seats in the House from 435 to 437. This bill was filibustered and defeated in the Senate.

POWERS CONGRESS DOES *NOT* HAVE

Article I, Section 9 of the Constitution has to do primarily with powers Congress does *not* have. One thing Congress may not do is **suspend habeas corpus,** except in cases of war or insurrection, or when "the public Safety may require it." *Habeas corpus* is Latin meaning "you have the body." The basic idea behind a writ of habeas corpus is that a prisoner (that is, the body) should be brought before a judge, and reasons for the prisoner's confinement should be explained to him and to the judge. Into the middle of the nineteenth century, this part of the Constitution was considered applicable only to federal prisoners. Among most Americans in the twenty-first century, the "right of habeas corpus" has been taken for granted throughout the United States. But there have always been problems. Into the mid-twentieth century, victims of lynching obviously were not afforded this right, often with the connivance of local police and officials.

In the early twenty-first century, some saw the detention of prisoners captured during the "war against terrorism" as a problem. Defining them as "enemy combatants," the Bush administration construed these captives as prisoners of war and thus not possessors of the constitutional rights afforded citizens and legal residents. A basic concern was whether all of the prisoners held at Guantánamo Bay in Cuba really had been enemy combatants. Some argued that these combatants needed the right of habeas corpus so they could hear the specific charges against them and defend themselves. No one questioned that some detainees at Guantánamo Bay were hardened terrorists. They did believe, though, that some of the imprisoned had committed no harm. In a series of cases decided in 2004 (*Hamdi v. Rumsfeld*), 2006 (*Hamdan v. Rumsfeld*), and a third case in 2008, the Supreme Court determined that the Bush administration's treatment of the prisoners was unconstitutional.

The Constitution prohibits Congress from passing **ex post facto laws** that make an act illegal after it has been done. If a person does something in January that is deemed illegal in the next October, in other words, he cannot be held liable because the act was not illegal at the time it was done.

In addition, Congress may *not* do the following:

- Impose taxes or duties on goods exported from any state, favor one state's ports over another, or tax goods shipped from one state to another

- Take money from the treasury unless expressly empowered to do so via legally passed appropriations

Finally, Congress may not give to anyone a **title of nobility**. At times presidents and their wives have been derided as acting like kings and queens, and some have said that John F. and Jacqueline Kennedy were American "royalty." This provision of the Constitution ensures that such talk remains only talk.

Chapter 6

The Presidency

It's strange that the Constitution has so little to say about the position held by the person Americans see as having more political power than anyone—the U.S. president. We have learned that the framers of the Constitution were reluctant to place a great deal of power in one person's, or one political body's, hands. And yet a major reason for the failure of the Articles of Confederation was their lack of a strong executive.

The job description set out for presidents in the Constitution is more detailed and much more substantial than what was in the Articles, yet the Constitution's language on the presidency is still general and vague. Perhaps one reason for this is the founders' knowledge that the first president, George Washington, would set admirable precedents. Washington refused, for example, to be called "your majesty," opting instead to be referred to as "Mr. President."

PRESIDENTIAL POWER AND RESPONSIBILITY

There's no question that the powers exercised by a president today go beyond the letter of the Constitution. For example, the Constitution does not empower a president to recognize the legitimacy of new foreign nations, as Harry Truman did in 1948 immediately after Israel declared itself a nation. The question is whether the recognition of other nations is an **inherent power** (an implied power, as discussed in Chapter 4), with a foundation in the constitutional authority presidents have to "receive Ambassadors." The consensus answer to the question is yes, the president does have this power.

Of all American elections, presidential elections are the most watched, precisely because presidents have accumulated so much power, especially since the Great Depression of the 1930s. Americans look to presidents to find solutions to national problems, whether in the aftermath of a natural disaster or following an economic crisis. Americans expect presidents to face up to, and respond to, the challenges presented by threats to national security. Americans also see that their presidents are the United States's most important diplomat, the commander-in-chief of the military and, in a sense, a symbol of the nation. If the nation is doing well, the nation feels that the president is doing well. At the same time, if the nation is not doing well, and even if the president has no direct control over what is wrong, the American people will turn their disfavor toward the president. Ronald Reagan, a generally popular president, made people feel good about America; Jimmy Carter, a generally unpopular president, did not.

A common American saying is that "anyone can grow up to be president." That is technically true of every natural-born citizen who is at least 35 years old and has resided in the country at least 14 years. In reality, though, the paths to the White House have been few. As of 2008, every president had previously served in the Senate, in the House of Representatives, or as a state governor. In 1992 Ross Perot wished to be the first to get into the **Oval Office** straight from the world of business, but his campaign was not successful. It is also possible for an atheist to be president, though every president has declared some Christian affiliation, John F. Kennedy being the only non-Protestant (he was Roman Catholic). It is also possible for a woman to be president, though as of the election of 2008, no woman had landed the job. In that year, New York Senator Hillary Clinton was a strong contender for the Democratic nomination, which went instead to Illinois Senator Barack Obama.

Until 1951, the year the **Twenty-Second Amendment** limiting a president's time in office to a maximum of ten years was ratified, it was possible to serve more than two full terms as president. Franklin Roosevelt was elected to the presidency four times. (If a vice president takes the presidency with less than two years to go in the recent president's term, the new president is eligible to run for office in his [or her] own right two times.) The precedent Washington set, though, was two terms, and the Twenty-Second Amendment set that precedent in constitutional stone.

What are a president's responsibilities? Next, portions of the Constitution are quoted and are followed with commentary. The portion of the Constitution that states the president's powers is Article II.

Power of the Executive: Article II, Section 1

"The **executive power** shall be vested in a President of the United States of America. He shall hold his office during the Term of **four years**. . . ." The section then goes on to discuss the electoral voting system discussed in Chapter 2, where presidential elections, held every four years, are also discussed.

The phrase "executive power" is not defined. In practice the phrase means that the president supervises the many governmental bodies created by Congress.

For example, the Transportation Security Administration (TSA), whose agents search our bags at airports, is ultimately under the president's supervision, as is the Central Intelligence Agency (CIA) and the Department of the Treasury. Of course, the president is not able to supervise the federal government's agencies personally. The president exercises his (or her) **power of appointment** by selecting **cabinet** members who preside over the various federal government agencies or who offer advice on vital issues. The director of the Office of Management and Budget (OMB) and the U.S. ambassador to the United Nations are also members of the cabinet. Most cabinet nominations must be approved by the Senate, and they usually are confirmed, though sometimes there is controversy. President Clinton was forced to withdraw his nomination of Zoë Baird for attorney general because it was discovered that she had hired an illegal worker and had not paid the worker's Social Security taxes.

Article II, Section 1 also states that to be eligible for president, a person must be a "natural born citizen"—that is, born on American soil. Early in the presidential election of 2008, there was some talk about John McCain being ineligible to run for president, since he had been born in the American-controlled Panama Canal Zone. This issue soon went away.

Military Command and Pardons: Article II, Section 2

The president is the **commander-in-chief** of all U.S. military forces. Day-to-day, the states' National Guards are under the state governor's control, but the president has the power to assume command, as President Dwight Eisenhower did in 1957, when the governor of Arkansas ordered the state's National Guard to prevent court-ordered desegregation from being carried out. Obviously, the U.S. military's daily operations are overseen by military commanders, the **Joint Chiefs of Staff**, and the secretary of defense. The ultimate authority, however, belongs to the president. When General Douglas MacArthur publicly differed with President Harry Truman during the Korean War, Truman removed MacArthur from command.

The president has the power to grant **pardons** and **reprieves** "for Offenses against the United States," though he does not have the power to pardon people who have been impeached. After the American Civil War, for example, President Andrew Johnson pardoned Southerners who had supported Southern secession, on the condition that they would take oaths of loyalty to the United States. For another example, in 1977 President Jimmy Carter pardoned all Americans who had fled to other countries or failed to register for the draft to avoid service in Vietnam. A presidential reprieve reduces the severity of a convicted person's punishment, though the person's guilt remains and some punishment is still delivered.

The White House is the official residence and principal workplace of the President of the United States. Built between 1792 and 1800, the White House has been the residence of every U.S. President since John Adams.

The president also has the power to make treaties with other nations, though they must be approved by two-thirds of the Senate. (The House of Representatives has no direct role in treaty making.) Although the Senate rarely defeats treaties—presidents are reluctant to make them without substantial Senate support—some Senate votes against treaties have been highly significant. The most significant treaty rejection followed World War I, when President Woodrow Wilson's plan for the United States to join the League of Nations failed. Less known is the Senate's rejection, in 1999, of the Comprehensive Nuclear Test Ban Treaty, agreed to by President Bill Clinton. This treaty would have, in effect, banned nuclear testing.

The president also has the power to nominate ambassadors, judges on the Supreme Court, and "other Officers of the United States," such as cabinet members and the director of the Federal Bureau of Investigation. The Constitution does empower a president to get around Senate confirmations, however. When Congress is not in session, the president may make a **recess appointment**, though upon the reconvening of Congress, the appointee must undergo a formal confirmation process.

A struggle between the Senate and president over an ambassadorial nomination moved center stage in late 2006, when President George W. Bush gave up his effort to install John R. Bolton as permanent ambassador to the United Nations. He had tried earlier to circumvent Senate opposition to Bolton's appointment by sending Bolton to the United Nations on a recess appointment.

Communication with Congress: Article II, Section 3

This last section on the presidency says that the president shall, "from time to time give the Congress Information of the State of the Union." Hence the name of an annual address to Congress delivered by the president: the State of the Union speech. Through the nineteenth century, presidents sent their annual "information" to Congress in written form. President Wilson delivered his State of the Union speeches in person, and through the twentieth century the speeches have been used less to provide information and more to set a policy agenda for the nation. Although both political parties are polite and deferential during State of the Union addresses, after a president gives his view of one or another policy, some members (usually in the opposing party) can be seen sitting and not clapping, while Congress members who agree with him often respond with standing ovations.

The presidential power, mentioned earlier, to "receive Ambassadors and other ministers" is also in Section 3, as is the statement that a president should "shall take care that the Laws be faithfully executed." Section 4 is concerned with impeachment (discussed in Chapter 4). At the heart of President Bill Clinton's impeachment trial in the late 1990s was a sex scandal, but a president cannot be impeached for adultery. The first three of the eleven charges brought against Clinton were as follows:

1. President Clinton lied under oath in his civil case when he denied a sexual affair, a sexual relationship, or sexual relations with Monica Lewinsky.

2. President Clinton lied under oath to the grand jury about his sexual relationship with Ms. Lewinsky.

3. In his civil deposition, to support his false statement about the sexual relationship, President Clinton also lied under oath about being alone with Ms. Lewinsky and about the many gifts exchanged between Ms. Lewinsky and him.

Some who favored Clinton's impeachment said that, his sex life aside, the president had lied under oath and had therefore not fulfilled his duty to "take care that the Laws be faithfully executed." This argument failed to persuade half the Senate, and thus the articles of impeachment fell short of the two-thirds majority vote required.

ADDITIONAL PRESIDENTIAL POWERS

One extension of presidential power sometimes linked to the concept of faithfully executing the laws is the **executive order**. Presidential executive orders, which themselves have the force of law, create or shape policies without congressional approval. President Eisenhower's taking over of the Arkansas National Guard (mentioned earlier) is an example of this. After World War II, President Truman desegregated the military by executive order and, also by executive order, President Clinton allowed homosexuals to serve in the military, though not openly.

Another way presidents can exercise their authority is by the use of **signing statements**. Usually, such statements, made when a president signs a piece of legislation into law, have given the president a chance to state how he intends to enforce the law. The first signing statements were made in the early 1800s, but President George W. Bush used them far more than any other president. Indeed, by 2008 he had issued some 800 signing statements—more than all his predecessors combined. President Bush's signing statements tended to express his opposition to parts of legislation because he deemed them unconstitutional or threats to national security. Some observers saw Bush's use of signing statements as another example of his alleged tendency to reach for more and more power. Others did not think the signing statements actually amounted to very much. As of late 2008, the issue had not been brought before any federal court.

Presidents also arrive at **executive agreements** with other nations. An executive agreement can be revoked by Congress, but a president doesn't need Congress's approval to make the agreement. In 1940 President Franklin Roosevelt agreed with Britain to trade access to British military bases for some old U.S. naval vessels.

The power of the presidency has been enhanced by Congress's **delegation of powers** to the president. During the early years of the Great Depression, President Franklin Roosevelt was given broad authority to respond to the economic crisis. If every measure had to go through the laborious legislative process, the government would not have been able to respond quickly to the crisis.

Another form of delegation of powers to the president came by way of **fast-track authority** for trade agreements with other nations. The purpose of fast-track authority, which expired in its most recent form in 2007, was to empower the president to make trade deals that Congress can either approve or disapprove but not amend, because the amendment process and a foreign country's response to the amendments significantly slows the process. Congress doesn't always grant fast-track authority. In the 1990s, a Democratic Congress, concerned about the effects of trade agreements on American workers and labor unions, refused to give the authority to President Clinton, a Democrat. Of course, Congress can hem in a president's power, such as happened when Congress passed the War Powers Act (1973), discussed in Chapter 5.

In turn, the president can hem in the power of Congress. As we have learned, a major tool a president has at his disposal is the **veto**. Some presidents have used the veto power extensively, others much less so. Franklin Roosevelt exercised the veto 635 times, Dwight Eisenhower 181 times, and Jimmy Carter 31 times. One thing presidents must be careful of is that their vetoes are not overridden often by two-thirds votes in the House and Senate. To have many vetoes overridden makes a president look weak—in fact, it is a signal of the president's weakness. Franklin Roosevelt's vetoes were overridden nine times—only .014 percent of the time. This is one measure of his power as president.

THE EXECUTIVE BRANCH OF GOVERNMENT

We sometimes hear the president referred to as "the executive." The president is, in fact, the central figure of the executive branch of government. Presidential elections seem to be about selecting one person to be president. In reality, presidential elections are about selecting a person who will preside over a vast bureaucracy and who will choose that bureaucracy's leaders, along with the aides and confidants who will assist him. Among the president's key personnel are a **chief of staff** (who, depending on the president, may or may not be empowered to closely manage White House operations), a **national security advisor** (who provides the president with regular briefings on military and intelligence matters), and a **Council of Economic Advisors**. The president will also hire different staff to handle different issues, such as event scheduling, meetings with interest groups, and media relations. Then there is the large **Office of Management and Budget** (OMB), the mission of which is to "assist the President in overseeing the preparation of the federal budget and to supervise its administration in Executive Branch agencies."

Each of these positions is included in the **Executive Office of the President**, which also includes the president's aides and their staffs (and White House operations). As of 2008, the Executive Office of the President comprised some 1,600 people and had a budget of nearly $375 million. New to White House operations (with the presidency of George W. Bush) is the Office of Faith-Based and Community Initiatives, which seeks to coordinate "efforts to empower community and faith-based organizations working to confront poverty and social needs."

We can get a sense of the vastness of the executive branch of government if we look at the order of presidential succession according to the **Presidential Succession Act** of 1947. We all know that the vice president follows the president in succession. Next in line is the speaker of the House of Representatives, followed by the president pro tempore of the Senate (the most senior member of the majority party in the Senate). Notice that here, as in so many places in the American government, powers are separated among different government bodies. Beginning with the fourth person in the line of succession, however, we turn to secretaries of federal departments included in the executive branch of government. Fourth in order of succession is the secretary of state, followed by the

> secretary of the treasury,
>
> secretary of defense,
>
> attorney general,
>
> secretary of the interior,
>
> secretary of agriculture,
>
> secretary of commerce,

. . . and the list continues.

Each of these titles represents a vast bureaucracy. For example, in 2003 the Department of Agriculture employed about 114,000 people. Obviously, the president can know very little detail about what is happening in this department. The president sets policies and relies on his secretaries to see to the implementation of the policies. Policy enforcement is left to the agencies.

Although individual department secretaries have substantial power, the power of the cabinet itself is fairly limited. For one thing, different cabinet members have different kinds of expertise—energy, agriculture, defense, and so on. It isn't possible for the cabinet to speak authoritatively in a single voice. Another challenge is that cabinet members are often chosen, in part, because of their ethnicity, gender, or geographical connections—not necessarily because the president knows them well. A third challenge is that full cabinets comprise at least 20 people. It is difficult for such a group to offer unified advice to the president.

RESPONSE TO CRISES

Perhaps another reason presidential cabinets do not behave well as advisory bodies is that a president's time is largely spent managing one problem or crisis after another. In moments of tension or political heat, it is natural for a president to turn to a few close advisors.

Successful **crisis management** also usually involves not acting impulsively or with undue haste. A president should have in place a system that makes review of problems and potential solutions possible. In other words, when a crisis strikes, a president should have a program in place that immediately gets the machinery of arriving at a solution going. Finally, a president should look for opinions from people who may disagree with him; this way, unstated assumptions may be exposed and analyzed, and decisions may be made with a greater sense of clarity. The president should resist **groupthink**—a situation in which people close to the president come to the same conclusion but without thorough analysis. People who are close to a president sometimes say that it is difficult not to tell him what he wants to hear.

Presidents want to handle problems and crises well for the simple reason that that's their job. But presidents also know that perceptions of them depend on how well they do in tough times. A president also knows that, more than any other American, he has the capacity to respond quickly to events. It's no surprise that the presidents who are regularly evaluated as being among America's best are those who responded well to great problems: Abraham Lincoln (the American Civil War), Franklin Delano Roosevelt (the Depression and World War II), and George Washington who, as president, took the nation through its first years under the Constitution. President Jimmy Carter, who is generally seen as not having handled crises well, is regularly ranked in the bottom half of presidential performers.

If presidents respond well to problems, this reflects well on their characters. For obvious reasons, Americans want their presidents to be honest and strong. Though Bill Clinton's presidency was saved by the Senate's refusal to vote for his removal from office, his image in the American mind was harmed. Even some of his defenders described him as a person you'd want to have as a political ally but not as a role model.

Of course, if a president is seen as weak or untrustworthy, the president's ability to persuade other politicians—members of Congress or foreign heads of state—is diminished. But a president also needs to be willing to compromise without seeming weak. Sometimes political compromise will put a president at odds with large elements in his own party, such as when George H.W. Bush raised taxes (thus going back on a campaign promise) and when Clinton agreed to put into place significant welfare reform, emphasizing work and getting off the welfare rolls.

PRESIDENTS AND PUBLIC APPROVAL

Presidents, like many people and organizations that want public approval, pay close attention to **approval ratings**—regular polls that show the extent to which the public approves of their performance. Typically, a president's ratings are fairly high during the first year in office, often seen as a "honeymoon period." Usually, first-term presidents who go into elections for a second term with approval ratings near 50 percent are not reelected. George W. Bush is an exception: his approval rating was 51 percent, and he still won the election of 2004.

Sometimes in moments of serious crisis, Americans will "rally around the flag," and this will manifest itself in high presidential ratings, for the American people want the president to respond well to crisis. Following the terrorist attacks of September 11, 2001, President George W. Bush's approval rating jumped to 90 percent. As the ensuing wars in Afghanistan and especially in Iraq dragged on, however, Bush's ratings fell. A national poll in late September of 2008 placed Bush's approval rating at a very low 26 percent. The only twentieth-century president to have a lower approval rating was Richard Nixon, whose approval was at 24 percent just before he resigned in 1974.

Initially, presidential candidates seek popularity on the campaign trail, and after they are elected they usually enjoy a honeymoon, during which the public gives them the benefit of the doubt and gives them some time to adjust to the presidency. After they've been in office a while, presidents will seek to get their message across, sometimes by delivering speeches from the **Oval Office** (their primary workspace in the White House) and sometimes in "town hall meetings"—informal question-and-answer sessions between citizens and the president. Very frequently, the president's views are conveyed by the **White House press secretary**, who "briefs" media representatives and takes questions from them. Some presidents, such as Bill Clinton, have been criticized for caring too much about poll numbers, while others, like Lyndon Johnson and George W. Bush, seem to have paid too little attention to the desires of most Americans.

As a result of their success and popularity, some presidents become icons of sorts to their parties. Republicans proudly refer to their party as "the party of Lincoln," and Republican aspirants to office have often associated themselves with Ronald Reagan. On the other hand, unsuccessful and unpopular presidents are left behind. No Republicans run for office drawing on the memory of Richard Nixon, and no Democrats seek to associate themselves with the political efforts of Jimmy Carter.

Presidents with strong approval ratings find it easier to push their agendas through Congress. This is all the easier if majorities from their party hold both houses of Congress. It's rare, however, for one party to hold the House, Senate, and presidency. This is because Americans tend to favor **divided government**: one party in charge of the White House and the other party in charge of at least one of the congressional bodies. It is common for the party that holds the presidency to lose congressional seats. Sometimes voters express their displeasure with the president by voting against his party. There also seems to be a sense, perhaps partly unconscious, that divided government is best. At first this seems counterintuitive because, in voting this way, Americans seem to ensure **gridlock**—a government that can't get important work done because it is divided. Overall, however, **bipartisanship** (that is, politicians of different parties working together) and compromise have helped government to function fairly well. Both parties complain about partisanship and regularly accuse the other party of partisan offenses, but, in reality, members from the parties regularly work together.

In Chapter 5 we discussed the work of lobbyists. It is important to know that the president is also a lobbyist. The president can seek to influence congresspersons with phone calls and meetings and public statements designed to spur public support. In addition, members of the president's **legislative liaison staff**, who work for the **White House Office of Legislative Affairs**, discuss legislative topics with members of Congress and simultaneously keep the president informed on a bill's status. If a bill hits a snag, the president or a presidential advisor can quickly talk with a congressperson to smooth out a problem. Of the many political voices seeking to be heard, the president's position gives him a clear advantage. Even if a president is deeply unpopular, his statements and speeches still receive media coverage.

The president is the leader of the nation and the **head of state**. The office of president combines political and symbolic functions that are kept separate in many other nations. For example, the president gets involved in the details of legislation, as the prime minister of Britain does. The president also participates in lofty state ceremonies the way British royalty does, though the pomp of such events is usually less heightened in the American context.

The president is the leader of a political party (and its main fundraiser), the commander-in-chief, and the lobbyist-in-chief. The president is also the nation's primary diplomat. Especially since the beginning of the twentieth century, American presidents have had a key spot on the international scene. Theodore Roosevelt, for example, helped Panama to become independent from Colombia, oversaw the beginning of work on the Panama Canal, brokered peace between Russia and Japan (and won the Nobel Peace Prize), and sent a U.S. Navy fleet on a global tour. President Nixon opened relations between the United States and China, and President Clinton reconstituted relations with Vietnam (which had been hampered since the Vietnam War ended in 1975). President Carter played an important role in brokering peace between Israel and Egypt. President Reagan helped push the Soviet Union into dissolution, partly by building a costly military that the Soviets would unsuccessfully try to keep up with. And President George W. Bush called for invasions of Afghanistan and Iraq in the aftermath of the terrorist attacks of 2001. Of course, Woodrow Wilson, Franklin Roosevelt, and Harry Truman led the country when it was engaged in world wars. A complete list of presidents' efforts, accomplishments, and failures in foreign policy would be very long.

THE VICE PRESIDENT'S DUTIES

What happens if a president dies in office? As we know, the vice president moves into the role of president. Traditionally, vice presidents have had little power and small roles as advisors. As far as the Constitution is concerned, their only explicit roles are to act as president of the Senate (and break tie votes in that body) and to be prepared to take over the presidency should that be necessary. Most vice presidents have been forgotten. The name Thomas R. Marshall—Woodrow Wilson's vice president—doesn't have much of a place in history. But, of course, some vice presidents have become well known because they themselves took presidential office, either in their own right or because the president they served under died in office or was assassinated. Andrew Johnson and Lyndon Johnson took over the presidency after the assassinations of, respectively, Abraham Lincoln and John F. Kennedy. George H.W. Bush won the presidency after two terms as Ronald Reagan's vice president.

The part of the Constitution that has the most to say about the vice president is the Twenty-Fifth Amendment, ratified in 1967, four years after the assassination of President Kennedy. This amendment states that upon the president's death, removal (via impeachment), or resignation, the vice president moves into the presidency. The new president is then required to choose a vice president, subject to approval by both houses of Congress. This amendment also sets out what a vice president may do if a president is incapacitated but hasn't resigned or been impeached:

> Whenever the Vice President and a majority of either the principal officers of the executive departments or of such other body as Congress may by law provide, transmit to the President pro tempore of the Senate and the Speaker of the House of Representatives their written declaration that the President is unable to discharge the powers and duties of his office, the Vice President shall immediately assume the powers and duties of the office as Acting President.

The amendment carries on with further instructions. As of 2008, this amendment has not been acted on, though it might have been after the assassination attempt on President Ronald Reagan in 1981. Reagan's vice president, George H.W. Bush, refused to invoke the Twenty-Fifth Amendment. (Later in Reagan's presidency, Bush was **acting president** for about eight hours, while Reagan underwent surgery.) In the amendment's background was the memory of Woodrow Wilson's illness following World War II, which prevented him from effectively carrying out his responsibilities.

THE FIRST LADY'S ROLE

In addition to a president's formal advisors and assistants, presidents sometimes rely on their spouses for advice. All but one president (James Buchanan) has been married. The **Office of the First Lady** has a staff of about 20. First Ladies are involved primarily with social ceremonies and events related to the White House, as well as with the promotion of worthy causes such as childhood literacy. Some, however, have been more actively political. Franklin Roosevelt's wife, Eleanor, even publicly challenged some of her husband's policies. More controversial was First Lady Hillary Clinton's 1994 effort to reform the nation's health-care system. Her plan was complicated and failed in Congress. In addition, many believed that she had been given too much power.

Chapter 7

Federal Bureaucracy and the Media

The federal government is the single largest employer in the United States. As of 2008, the U.S. government employed over 5 million people, including military personnel and postal workers. Many people find government work desirable, for job security is high, wages and benefits are good (relative to the private economy), and pension benefits are very good.

Still, the word *bureaucracy* has negative connotations. According to the popular image, a bureaucracy produces red tape, long lines, and overbearing regulations. We think of a bureaucrat as a person who favors procedures and paper pushing over people and career over common sense. Sentiments like these are reinforced when we undergo searches at airports that seem invasive, or when we try to start a new business and are overwhelmed by government forms to fill out, or when we stand in long, slow lines in a government office.

All of the presidents of the late twentieth and early twenty-first centuries promised to fundamentally change the way government did business. President Bill Clinton promised to "reinvent government," and the Republican vice-presidential nominee of 2008, Sarah Palin, vowed to reform government by "shaking up the 'good ol' boy network' in Washington." But the attempt to "rein in government" goes on.

Sometimes efforts to scale government back take the form of **privatization**—that is, handing over to private enterprise work that was formerly done by government employees. For example, much of the rebuilding of Iraq, following the U.S. invasion in 2003, was done by the large business Halliburton, and much of the security in Iraq was provided by the firm Blackwater USA. **Deregulation** has also been put into effect in sectors of the economy. The idea is that if government regulates less and allows private enterprise greater freedom, government growth will slow, because there is less regulation to enforce. (When the country experienced a financial crisis in the fall of 2008, many argued that deregulation of the financial industry had been a cause.) Finally, some argue for political **devolution**, or the turning over of functions carried out by the federal government to the states. This happened in the 1990s, when welfare programs funded by the federal government were largely given to the states to administer.

As a general rule, Republicans favor privatization, deregulation, and devolution more than Democrats do. In 1995, however, Democrats and Republicans agreed that the Interstate Commerce Commission (discussed briefly later in the chapter) had outlived its usefulness and had stemmed economic growth via excessive regulation; Congress abolished it.

Though we often don't think about the federal government's bureaucracy, it is the element of government that touches our lives, in one way or another, constantly. The federal bureaucracy brings us our mail (U.S. Postal Service), seeks to control profanity on the radio (Federal Communications Commission), promotes artistic expression (National Endowment for the Arts), keeps tabs on who's eligible for military service (Selective Service System), preserves the nation's records (National Archives and Records Administration), and many other services.

BUREAUCRACY DEFINED

But what exactly do we mean by *bureaucracy?* German sociologist Max Weber's suggestion that bureaucracies share five characteristics has been widely accepted. Weber says, first, that bureaucracies **specialize** and divide labor. For example, the U.S. Mint, Secret Service, and Bureau of Alcohol, Tobacco, and Firearms are all within the Department of the Treasury, while the Occupational Safety and Health Administration and the Bureau of Labor Statistics are within the Department of Labor. Second, bureaucracies follow a clear **chain of command**. One knows who is in charge of whom. Third, bureaucracies have clearly set out **rules and guidelines** for people within them to follow. Sometimes a situation seems to call for action beyond the rules or guidelines, but bureaucracies can be famously inflexible because of their commitment to rules. Fourth, bureaucracies maintain **written records**. One reason bureaucrats are often thought of as paper pushers is that they actually do move around a lot of paper that is filled with information—for instance, about how well procedures have been followed. Fifth, bureaucracies are staffed by **professionals**, that is, by people who plan to make their careers in the bureaucracy. As one succeeds in a certain position, he or she may move up the chain of command.

Of course, professionalization leads to **expertise** among career bureaucrats; not only do they become adept at navigating the world of the bureaucracy but they learn more about their areas of specialization (for example, military and foreign intelligence) than most members of Congress ever will. Expertise provides the bureaucracy with a kind of political power that can come in handy in times of budget cuts.

The professionalization of the federal bureaucracy has been assisted by the effort to depoliticize it. Into the late 1800s, most **civil service** jobs were political, meaning, for example, that a postmaster might lose his job if a president of a different political party was elected. Before reforms were set in place, a **spoils system** existed, meaning that with political victory went the "spoils"— the ability to give jobs to friends and supporters. The term for this kind of activity is *patronage*. The **Pendleton Act** of 1883 was the first law to make some government jobs off-limits to patronage. (President James Garfield had been assassinated by a disappointed government jobseeker.) By now, the vast majority of government jobs are not held by political appointees (just about eight thousand of 5 million government jobs are given by political appointment), and the Office of Personnel Management and the Merit Systems Protection Board (MSPB) serve to maintain the integrity of the civil service. In 2008 the MSPB's Web site put it this way:

> MSPB serves as an independent, bipartisan guardian of the merit systems under which Federal employees work. Merit-based civil service rules are essential to ensuring that Federal civil servants are well qualified to perform their jobs and are able to serve the public free from management abuse and partisan political pressure.

Although the growth of the federal bureaucracy has slowed and has even been turned back (very briefly) at times, the general trend since the founding of the United States has been growth. The "revolution" of Ronald Reagan's presidency was supposed to have included making government smaller, but Reagan's commitment to winning the Cold War against the Soviet Union led to the growth of the Department of Defense and thus to the overall growth of government.

New federal departments are created as new problems arise. As the United States began to settle the Midwest in earnest, the Department of Agriculture was founded (1862). When the country industrialized, large corporations began to take shape, and labor unions became increasingly influential, the government founded the Bureau of Labor (1884) and the Department of Commerce and Labor (1903). (The Department of Commerce and Labor was renamed the Department of Commerce in 1913.) An increased focus on social welfare programs in the 1960s led to the creation of the Department of Housing and Urban Development (1965) and, in response to the energy crisis of the 1970s, the Department of Energy was created (1977). And, for a final example, the unprecedented terrorist attacks on the United States in 2001 led to the creation of the Department of Homeland Security, a primary purpose of which was to help many organizations that already existed, such as the Coast Guard and the Secret Service, to communicate more effectively.

WHAT BUREAUCRACIES DO

With the exception of the Justice Department, which is led by the U.S. attorney general, the largest **executive departments** within the federal bureaucracy are headed up by **secretaries**. (In late 2008, for example, Robert Gates was secretary of the Department of Defense, and Michael Chertoff was secretary of the Department of Homeland Security.) The secretaries of the executive departments make up the majority of the president's cabinet (discussed in Chapter 6). Each secretary is appointed by the president and serves with the **advice and consent** of the Senate. The Senate may not approve a president's executive departmental appointment, but once the secretary is in place, the Senate cannot remove him or her. In 2006 many throughout the government called for the resignation of Secretary of Defense Donald Rumsfeld, but only the president could make the resignation happen.

Regulate

As we learned in Chapter 2, the primary purpose of agencies within the federal bureaucracy is to implement laws passed by Congress. Obviously, Congress is unable to closely supervise the implementation of the laws it passes, so this task falls to the bureaucracy, which must determine how to put the laws into effect. This involves devising rules and ways to enforce them. Thus bureaucracy plays the role of rule maker and rule enforcer.

Within the various executive departments are **independent regulatory commissions** (also called **regulatory agencies**) that write and enforce rules that regulate some element of industry. The Nuclear Regulatory Commission, for instance, oversees the nation's nuclear power plants. An early example of this kind of government body is the Interstate Commerce Commission (ICC), founded in 1887. The purpose of the ICC was to discover and end railroad practices that seemed predatory.

As the names of these commissions suggest, they are further removed from political concerns than the executive departments are. Whereas departmental secretaries are appointed by the president and lose their positions if the president leaves the White House, independent regulatory commissioners serve for fixed terms. They also are appointed by the president, but once their appointment is approved by the Senate, the president cannot remove them from office if he disagrees with what they do.

The next type of organization to note is the government corporation, which sells services and thus generates its own revenue. The U.S. Postal Service does this by selling stamps (and other goods), the U.S. Mint by selling coins, and the Federal Deposit Insurance Corporation by charging banks for the insurance it supplies to cover bank customers' savings accounts.

Next, there are independent agencies. These are not part of an executive department, though, of course, they still come under congressional and presidential oversight. Among the independent agencies are the National Aeronautics and Space Administration (NASA) and the Environmental Protection Agency (EPA), an organization with great regulatory power whose secretary holds a cabinet position.

Though the makeup and tasks of various organizations within the federal bureaucracy differ, they share basic functions. First, they engage in rule administration—that is, they ensure that congressional legislation, presidential policies, and court decisions are adhered to. When the president declares a state of emergency due to a natural disaster, for example, the Federal Emergency Management Agency (FEMA) makes federal aid available in the affected area.

Make Rules

Because legislation, policies, and court decisions are often broad, government organizations must also engage in **rule making**. To one extent or another, bureaucracies must decide how to act, given the mandates they face. In making decisions, bureaucracies make rules, and these rules have the force of **administrative law**. Each rule the bureaucracy devises goes into the *Federal Register*. By the year 2000, the *Federal Register* contained some ninety thousand pages. There is no way anyone could master the rules and regulations of the total federal bureaucracy.

What happens when there are disputes about the implementation of rules, or what happens when rules are broken? Just as bureaucratic bodies resemble the Congress when they make rules, they also resemble courts when they employ **rule adjudication** (which means to settle through a judicial process), also called **bureaucratic adjudicating**. By the year 2000, some 25 federal government organizations employed about 1,300 judges to determine whether rules had been broken and, if so, to determine a remedy. Judges employed by the National Labor Relations Board, for example, are empowered to enforce the National Labor Relations Act (also called the Wagner Act), which was passed in 1935. These judges hear allegations made by and against members of businesses and labor unions.

Redistribute Income

Another task of the federal bureaucracy—or parts of it—is income redistribution. This has been especially true since the Great Depression of the 1930s. The central job of the Social Security Administration, founded in 1935, has been to provide the elderly with income. A key job of the Aid to Families with Dependent Children (AFDC) program (1935–97) was to provide the poor with income. (In the 1990s, AFDC was replaced by the Temporary Assistance for Needy Families program.) The income the government has provided via these programs has been taken in by taxation. In other words, one person's income is taxed today to provide another person with income tomorrow.

THE POLITICIZED BUREAUCRACY

We have seen that the large majority of jobs within the federal bureaucracy are not liable to political appointment, and we would like to believe that the bureaucracy itself is not a political player. But the tasks that federal bureaucracies undertake inevitably politicize their operations. Although it is true that most employees with the Department of the Interior are not political appointees, the secretary of the department is appointed by the president, and he or she will set the department's agenda, based on the president's policies. Also consider that government departments and agencies often must interpret laws, policies, and court decisions. It is impossible that political biases will not shape interpretations. The **administrative discretion** that bureaucrats in leadership positions have helps make this possible, if not inevitable.

Also note that bureaucracies can get caught up in the complications of **divided government**. Suppose the White House is in the hands of a Democrat, but Congress (one or both houses) is in the hands of the Republicans. Government institutions must respond to both sides, if for no other reason than that both the president and the Congress have a say as to how much funding an agency will receive in the yearly budget. Congressional committees and subcommittees hold hearings that keep bureaucrats accountable for their actions and decisions, and at these meetings government departmental leaders can make pitches for more funding. Because certain bureaucracies and members of committees or subcommittees may have a common interest, such meetings can be mutually beneficial. House Armed Services Committee members usually have military facilities in their districts, for instance, so they have an interest in seeing the Defense Department well funded. The

Defense Department itself also has an interest in being well funded. Thus sometimes relationships between professional bureaucrats and Congress members can be characterized by the old phrase, "You scratch my back and I'll scratch yours." But congressional and bureaucratic agendas can also be at odds. In such a case, the bureaucracy will be pleased if it has a friend in the White House.

As bureaucratic leaders make their way through their careers, they must tend to **mission goals** and **survival goals**. Obviously, the job of the Department of Education is to promote good education in the country. As the department's Web site put it in 2008, one of its mission goals is to do the following:

> Supplement and complement the efforts of states, the local school systems and other instrumentalities of the states, the private sector, public and private nonprofit educational research institutions, community-based organizations, parents, and students to improve the quality of education.

But the Department of Education has critics and enemies, some of whom want it abolished. In 1994, Senator John McCain of Arizona said he favored doing away with the Department of Education, as well as the Department of Energy. Obviously, the 4,200 people the Department of Education employed in 2008 had a vested interest in seeing their department survive. The obvious way a department can prevent itself from being put out of business is by making itself seem indispensable or by making it clear that any effort to eliminate it, or to substantially reduce its budget and influence, would be politically costly. By forging ties with members of Congress, teachers, and teachers' unions, the Department of Education can ensure its future, for congresspersons would denounce efforts to diminish the department, and unions would target for political defeat the politicians who advocated budget cuts for the department. This is another way that a department can become involved in political action. The department assists its **clientele,** and the clientele assist the department. When President Reagan attempted to abolish the Small Business Administration (SBA) in the mid-1980s, he faced so much opposition from Congress members, interest groups, and (subtly) the SBA itself that he gave up.

Among a government bureaucracy's clientele, then, will be interest groups. Makers of weaponry, for example, will hire lobbyists to work for their interests in Congress and among government bodies, including the Department of Defense. At the same time, however, other interest groups will oppose high levels of military spending and will lobby for more funds to be spent on, say, urban renewal or the renovation of highways and bridges. Bureaucracies often find themselves stuck in these kinds of political battles and thus have an interest in making and keeping friends in Congress and the White House.

Sometimes federal organizations, congressional committees, and interest groups will form what are called **iron triangles**. Political interest groups lobby congresspersons to pass laws they want, and they encourage the bureaucracy to implement the laws in ways favorable to them (the lobbyists). Congress members gain from this because the lobbyists help them get reelected, and the lobbyists do research and provide other services that are useful to the Congress member. The lobbyists also make arguments in Congress that serve the interests of the bureaucracies. Everyone in the triangle wins: the lobbyists get what they want; the Congress members get election help and other services; and the bureaucracy's survival mission is strengthened. Whether the public benefits from iron triangles is a more complicated question. And with the dramatic proliferation of interest groups in the country in the past couple of decades, iron triangles have become less of a force. They have been largely displaced by **issue networks**, in which groups with a particular interest in a particular issue will band together to advocate that issue. Otherwise, the groups may differ on most things.

A final way the work of bureaucracies can be politicized is when their responsibilities overlap and they compete for turf. In the wake of the terrorist attacks of 2001, for example, the public learned that the Central Intelligence Agency (CIA) and the Federal Bureau of Investigation (FBI), along with other intelligence agencies, did not communicate well. Indeed, the lack of communication seemed deliberate, for it appeared that bureaucrats in these agencies were protecting the interests of their agencies and thus their own careers. This kind of thing has sometimes been called **bureaucratic imperialism**. After the terrorist attacks, reforms designed to improve cross-agency communication were put into place, and the Department of Homeland Security was formed.

Government had grown, but as of late 2008, there had been no further terrorist attacks on the United States. For that time period at least, the bureaucracy seemed to be working.

THE MEDIA

Though the work of government touches our lives every day—government regulates the water we drink, the medicine we take, and the speeds we are supposed to drive our cars—we don't often think about government's constant effect on our lives. Most of what we do know about government we learn through the media, which are sometimes referred to collectively as the **"fourth branch of government."** To be sure, the media have no constitutional standing as a part of government, but because media have such a powerful influence on politics and the operations of government, it is impossible to talk for long about government without bringing the work of the media into the discussion.

When political observers talk generally about the "media" or the **mass media**, they are referring to radio, television, and the Internet (**broadcast media**), as well as newspapers and magazines (**print media**). The media, then, are made up of many hundreds of information sources—town, city, and regional newspapers, blogs, local and national radio shows, and local and national TV news programs. The news media have several purposes, among which are to (1) hold politicians accountable, (2) inform the people about what government is up to, and (3) identify problems and present potential agenda items to the country. Most media are also for-profit organizations, however. So another key purpose of most media outlets is to make money.

Access But Not Information

There is no question that early twenty-first-century Americans have access to a greater volume of information about government and politics than their predecessors had. While newspaper readership has declined steadily for decades (until the early 1960s, most Americans learned about the news from newspapers), most Americans now learn about government and politics from TV and the Internet. But whether the typical early twenty-first-century American is well informed as a result is a different question.

The general picture is not very encouraging. Studies regularly show that Americans know more about celebrities than they do about the policy positions of political leaders, and TV comedy shows that spoof politicians make greater impressions on the public than the politicians' ideas. As one college student put it during the election of 2008, "When I see a picture of Sarah Palin, I just think of Tina Fey." Palin was a vice-presidential candidate; Fey was the *Saturday Night Live* comedian who spoofed Palin. This points us to what scholars refer to as the **television hypothesis**—that is, the idea that TV makes one feel informed when, in fact, that is not actually happening. Studies have shown repeatedly that those who rely on television for their news score lower on tests of knowledge about public affairs than those who get their news from other sources.

For-Profit News

As of 2000, about 70 percent of Americans claimed to get most of their news from TV. So why has mass TV viewership—the average American watches TV about three to four hours a day—not led to a well-informed citizenry? One answer is that TV stations are run by businesses that exist to make money, and it's just a sad fact that most people prefer entertainment to the serious exchange of ideas. Thus, a story's **newsworthiness** often depends on whether it can grab a viewership's attention, for the advertisers who provide TV stations with money require an audience. A detailed analysis of immigration policy won't hold many viewers; a **sensationalistic** or heart-touching **human interest story** related to immigration policies may. But in the process of delivering such **infotainment**, serious reflection on a serious policy matter gets pushed to the side. This is an example of **market-driven journalism** at work. Other news stories that focus on violence also serve this purpose. The news is regularly filled with stories of horrific murders that take place far away, while important but less riveting political matters go unnoticed. Thus the adage, "If it bleeds, it leads"—in other words, violence sells. It shouldn't surprise us that news and entertainment have melded in recent years. The major broadcasting companies are owned by big businesses: the Walt Disney Company owns ABC, for example, and General Electric owns NBC.

Because TV news shows, like all for-profit TV shows, rely on advertisers' dollars, they must get and hold an audience. Thus news programs often begin with a declaration about something shocking but often will not get around to that story for a while. Such techniques are called "hook and hold"—the news-caster hooks the audience with the interesting headline and holds them through other parts of the program, all the while promising to get to the juicy part of the show. The least interesting parts of a local news broadcast—those parts that have to do with run-of-the-mill national and international events—are placed in the middle of the show.

Even key political phenomena, such as presidential elections, cannot escape the "dumbing down" of for-profit TV. Significant elections become the subject of **horse race journalism**—a fixation on who's winning, who's losing, and the gamesmanship of campaigning. Sports analogies often come in handy. Candidates take "body blows" or try to deliver "knock-out punches" during debates; risky moves are likened to the "hail Mary passes" of a desperate football team; a well-delivered party convention speech is called a "home run." Once again, ideas and policy positions receive relatively little attention. Most of the focus is on image, personality, perception, and the effectiveness of snappy phrases, called **sound bites**, and easily digestible policy statements, called **talking points**. Politicians who want attention from the media, particularly the TV media, have to play along. They will need to devise sound bites, and they will want to create **media events**—events so big that the media will have to pay attention (and thus give the candidate some free advertising).

Leading politicians must also be willing to appear on popular late-night talk shows. Several politicians have launched their campaigns on the David Letterman and Jay Leno shows. In the early twenty-first century, three TV channels provided news coverage around the clock: Fox News, CNN, and MSNBC. This meant that a lot of time needed to be filled, which meant that a lot of time would be given to commentary on the news rather than to **hard news**. A typical hour of a 24-hour news channel will include more commentary on news than news proper. This has led to the growth of a large **pundit** class—pundits being professional commentators (also called talking heads).

Print Media

Of course, some Americans are better informed than others. A large majority of Americans 65 years and older—about 70 percent—follow the news daily. An equal percentage of young people (late teens through early twenties) can be called **news grazers**. They pick up a little news here and there. Not surprisingly, readers of serious news and opinion magazines, such as the *National Review* (right), *Weekly Standard* (conservative), *New Republic* (liberal), and *The Nation* (left) are better informed than most; however, the number of people who read such magazines is relatively small. Whereas consumers of NBC News, for example, are counted in the millions, readers of more intellectual news and opinion magazines are in the tens of thousands. Yet, in terms of political change and action, reaching a relatively small number of well-informed readers may amount to more than attracting larger and lesser informed viewers. **Attentive policy elites** (people who pay close attention to political matters) can disperse what they learn via a **two-step flow of communication**. This process can work the following way: a writer for the *National Review* writes a story that few will actually read, but among the readers is a national radio host (an attentive policy elite), who then discusses the article on the air.

Before the advent of radio, the daily newspaper (which became common in the late 1800s) was the primary source of news. The first president to use radio effectively was Franklin Roosevelt, who addressed the nation in **fireside chats**, in which he explained his anti-Depression policies. Once TV became widespread in the 1950s, it became a presence on the political scene. It is widely believed that Richard Nixon lost the 1960 presidential election to John Kennedy because Nixon did not look good on camera when the two debated. (A majority of Americans who listened on the radio felt that Nixon had won the debate.) The age of the image had arrived.

The Internet as News Source

TV remains a basic news source, but in recent years the Internet has become increasingly important. By making so much information so easily available, the Internet has made access to information about government and politics easy. All government agencies host Web sites. On the other hand, with the advent of Web logs, or **blogs**, anyone can act as a journalist, and plenty of misinformation can quickly pass from Web site to Web site and from e-mail to e-mail. During the presidential race of 2008, Internet rumors spread that Democrat Barack Obama was not a natural-born citizen of the United States (and thus not eligible for the presidency). On the other hand, bloggers have made genuine contributions to highly produced news. In 2004, for instance, bloggers revealed problems with a CBS story on George W. Bush's service with the Texas Air National Guard.

Bloggers also challenge various kinds of bias that exist in the mass media. At a basic level, a kind of bias *must* exist in the mass media, for limited time and resources force editors and producers—that is, media **gatekeepers**—to choose what will be seen or read. Bloggers can't comment on everything either, but there is no limit to the number of bloggers, so every imaginable issue has a blogging advocate. As we have seen, for-profit media also tend to be biased in favor of the sensationalistic. Bloggers can challenge this by writing about some topic in depth.

Bias in the Media

Usually, when we think of media bias, however, we are thinking of political bias. Are the media biased? The evidence for bias is strong. But whether the bias leans toward liberal ideas or conservative ones depends on what form of media we are talking about. As of 2008, talk radio is overwhelmingly conservative. There is a lot of variation, of course. Some talk show hosts are primarily fiscally conservative libertarians. Others focus on the concerns that arise from their social conservatism. Some, such as the radio talk kingpin Rush Limbaugh, are both fiscally and socially conservative. Others, such as the loud, smart, and shocking Michael Savage, spend almost as much time attacking the Republicans as they do the Democrats. Savage calls himself an independent conservative.

With the exception of Fox News, which had the highest ratings of all news channels in 2008, TV news programs tilt to the political left. Studies and surveys have consistently shown that Democrats and liberals receive more favorable treatment on TV news shows than conservatives and Republicans. A 2004 survey of the national press involving almost 550 journalists found that 34 percent of journalists considered themselves liberal, while just 7 percent accepted the label "conservative." Studies of the "tone" of news stories about the presidential campaigns from 1988 to 2004 showed that Democratic candidates received better press than their Republican counterparts, with the exception of the 1988 election, when George H.W. Bush defeated the Democrat, Michael Dukakis. In 2008 the Pew Research Center analyzed over 2,400 campaign stories from nearly 50 news sources. The study concluded that media coverage for the race for president has not so much cast Barack Obama in a favorable light as it has portrayed John McCain in a substantially negative one. Whereas 36 percent of stories on Obama were clearly positive (and 35 percent were neutral or mixed), just 17 percent of McCain stories were positive, while 57 percent were clearly negative. This had to do, in part, with Obama's very careful campaign, as compared to McCain's seemingly less-focused one.

The role of TV in American politics is difficult to feel good about. There are some good things to notice, however. TV played an important role in spurring acceptance of civil rights. Once Americans could see images of brutality against African Americans on their televisions, they favored civil rights reform. Another bright spot is **C-SPAN** (the Cable Satellite Public Affairs Network), supported by the cable-TV companies. C-SPAN broadcasts political events from all political parties (except for extreme fringe groups) without commentary. And when commentary is invited, the interviewers are meticulously neutral. Inevitably, the biases of guests on the program come through, but C-SPAN itself is famously nonpartisan.

GOVERNMENT AND THE MEDIA

Although the United States has the freest media in the world, the government does regulate the media, particularly radio and TV. The primary government agency responsible for this is the **Federal Communications Commission** (FCC). One of the FCC's primary goals is to prevent one corporation from gaining too much of the media market. Another is to maintain some level of decency on network TV. Pornography is not allowed on ABC, for example, though it is allowed on cable TV. And, obviously, much that is shown on the networks today would have been unthinkable 20 years ago.

Government relations with media have become tense in a time of war. During the Gulf War of 1991, the government prevented the media from getting much news and, as part of the war against terrorism (2001 to the present), the government has withheld much information from the media. The presidency of George W. Bush was called secretive and unfriendly to the media. Many Americans feel that the media are partly responsible for America's lost war in Vietnam. By reporting critical stories, the theory goes, the media undermined morale. Generally speaking, Americans favor both a free press and a press that makes national security a high priority.

The final point to make here is that an underlying theory about electronic media is that the airwaves are public and thus, theoretically, the government has the right to determine how the airwaves are used. Senator John McCain, the Republican candidate for president in 2008, maintained that the government should require networks to provide political candidates with free airtime. McCain thought that this would reduce a candidate's need for money and would thus help him or her avoid future obligations to big donors. As of 2008, McCain's proposed legislation on this matter had not found sufficient support.

Chapter 8

Federal Courts and Civil Liberties

Readers of earlier chapters in this book will not be surprised that the Constitution has little to say about what we call the federal court system. Perhaps most surprising of all, the Constitution does not explicitly grant to the Supreme Court the position it now has as the possessor of the final word about what is and isn't constitutional. The Constitution's comments on the federal courts are in Article III and can be read in less than a couple of minutes.

Let's walk through what the Constitution says about the courts. First of all, Section 1 of Article III says that the

> judicial Power of the United States, shall be vested in one Supreme Court, and in such inferior courts as the Congress may from time to time ordain and establish.

THE SUPREME COURT

Notice that the Constitution does not specify how many justices will sit on the Supreme Court. When the Court began its work in 1789, it included five justices. Since 1869 nine has been the number of justices sitting on the Supreme Court. In the 1930s President Franklin Roosevelt tried to "pack" more justices friendly to his policies on the Court, but he faced great resistance from Congress and backed off. It is unlikely that the number of Supreme Court justices will change soon; the current number seems to have become part of the informal Constitution that keeps government operating. Whatever the case, the number of justices will always be odd (7, 9, 11, and so on) to prevent tied decisions.

The Supreme Court's formal work begins each year in early October and carries into the summer. As the highest court in the land, many **plaintiffs** and **defendants** appeal to the Court for a hearing, and as long as the Supreme Court *might* hear one's case, hope is kept alive. But the Supreme Court decides on less than one percent of all cases decided each year in the United States. The Court decides which cases it will hear, and it declines to hear the large majority of cases that appeal to it. Cases the Court *does* hear tend to fall into the following categories:

- Lower courts hearing the case have made conflicting decisions.

- A lower court's decision is at odds, or potentially conflicts, with a previous Supreme Court decision.

- The case involves an issue with far-reaching national consequences.

- The **solicitor general**—a presidential appointee within the Justice Department who argues on the government's behalf—urges the Court to take the case.

For a case to be heard by the Supreme Court, the Court must issue a **writ of certiorari**, which calls for a lower court to send to the Supreme Court the records related to the case. At least four of the nine justices must agree to issue a writ of certiorari. (This is referred to as the **rule of four**.) Failing that, the case will not be heard. This is the fate of the some eight thousand petitions the Court receives each year. (Denial of a petition does not necessarily mean that the Supreme Court agrees with a lower court's decision.)

The number of cases the Court hears has decreased in recent decades. In the 1982-83 session, the Court heard and decided on 151 cases. The term ending in the summer of 2006 saw 69 cases decided by the Court. Some see this as an unhelpful trend, since the Court seems to be providing less guidance to lower courts. (No one would say, however, that Supreme Court justices are not very busy people.) Some observers maintain that the decline in the number of cases the Court hears is related to a general conservatism that has come into the federal court system as a result of Republican presidents appointing a majority of federal judges in recent decades.

Once the Supreme Court issues a writ of certiorari, the Court's justices and the four law clerks to which each is entitled begin doing research into the issues surrounding the case. During the hearings related to the case, the justices pose questions to lawyers for the opposing sides. These questions are often informed by the research the justices and their clerks have done. Usually, new evidence does not enter into the Court's hearings. Instead, arguments often are made about the merits and demerits of previous decisions. Attorneys make their cases in what are called **oral arguments**. The cases heard by the Supreme Court are recorded, but no cameras are allowed in the Court.

After the nine justices on the Court have heard a case, they meet to discuss and vote on it. No recording devices are allowed in these meetings, a central concern being the integrity of the justices' decision-making processes; when

The Supreme Court Building is the seat for the Supreme Court of the United States. The west façade of the building bears the motto "Equal Justice Under Law," while the east façade bears the motto "Justice, the Guardian of Liberty."

a recording device is on, it is difficult not to adjust what one says and, consequently, how one thinks.

The Court's decisions are issued in writing. Included in the Court's written **opinion** are its decision, the reasons for that decision, and a discussion of the legal matters involved. Sometimes a lower court's decision is **affirmed**, meaning that the Court accepts a previous court's decision. Sometimes a lower court's decision is **reversed**. In other instances, a case is **remanded**, meaning that the case is sent back to a lower court for retrial.

Sometimes an opinion is unsigned, in which case it's an opinion **per curiam** (by the court). Usually, all of the justices who agree with an opinion sign it. If the Court's chief justice sides with the majority, he (or she) writes the opinion. If the chief justice sides with the minority, the senior justice in the majority signs the decision.

A **unanimous decision**—that is, a Supreme Court decision on which all justices agree—is fairly rare. More commonly, cases are concluded with a

majority opinion (which states why most of the justices came to their decision) and a **dissenting opinion** (in which the justices who disagree with the majority state why they disagree). Justices often write a **concurring opinion**, meaning that they agree with a decision but for reasons different from those stated in the majority opinion. Each of these kinds of opinions can be important to future cases: a losing position today, argued in a dissenting opinion, can be part of an argument that eventually makes its way into a majority opinion.

Supreme Court decisions are quickly made public. The clerk of the Court makes the written opinions available to the public and posts the decisions on the Internet; the decisions are published in the *United States Report*.

LOWER FEDERAL COURTS

As we saw earlier, the Constitution calls for the creation of a Supreme Court and "inferior courts" to serve the needs of the federal government. Beneath the Supreme Court are **U.S. district courts** and special courts that have **jurisdiction** (authority) over certain matters. First, let's focus on the U.S. district courts.

U.S. district courts are said to have **general jurisdiction**. This means that they will hear cases on a wide range of topics. These courts are **trial courts**, concerned with matters related to the federal government or to federal law: evidence is shown and challenged; witnesses testify and are cross-examined; and so on. Most court cases begin in trial courts. Each state has at least one federal district court. As of 2008, there were 94 of these courts operating in the United States. If a plaintiff or defendant is dissatisfied with a district court's decision, an appeal can be made to a **U.S. court of appeals**, also called an **appellate court**.

There are 13 federal appellate courts in the United States. Also called U.S. circuit courts of appeals, one of these courts is in Washington, D.C., and 11 of the others cover broad areas in the country. The largest of the appellate courts is the Ninth Circuit Court, which has jurisdiction over the Pacific states, Alaska, Hawaii, Guam, and much of the West. The United States Court of Appeals for the Thirteenth Circuit has national jurisdiction over certain matters, such as when the defendant is the U.S. government. Unlike the district courts, appellate courts do not usually consider evidence. Their primary purpose is to determine whether the district court made a legal error or whether the lower court's judgment was unwarranted, based on the evidence presented at the earlier trial. If a plaintiff or defendant is displeased with an appellate court's decision, an appeal can be made to the U.S. Supreme Court.

Of course, federal court cases frequently bear on matters of political significance. Interest groups often submit **amicus curiae briefs**—that is, "friend of the court" briefs. The point of these briefs is to persuade the court that it should decide a case a certain way. Amicus curiae briefs make legal arguments. They also discuss the case at hand in light of **precedent**—that is, earlier federal court, especially Supreme Court, decisions.

Other federal courts have particular jurisdictions. For example, in 1978 the Congress passed the Foreign Intelligence Surveillance Act (FISA), which gave birth to the so-called **FISA Court**—a court that grants the federal government the power to place surveillance on suspected spies. This court operates in great secrecy (for reasons of national security): the court's seven judges meet in secret and do not publish their opinions. During the presidency of George W. Bush, the powers of the FISA Court were expanded, sparking controversy and leading some to say that the federal government wanted the power to spy on U.S. citizens.

SELECTION OF FEDERAL JUDGES

Article III, Section 1 of the Constitution says that federal judges "shall hold their Offices during good Behavior," which means that, so long as they are not found to have broken the law, they serve for as long as they wish. Article II, Section 2 says that the president must appoint Supreme Court justices, with the Senate's consent. This principle has been extended to all federal judges. So all federal judges are presidential appointments, and all serve for life unless circumstances (health, insanity, criminal behavior) warrant their removal.

In 2008 there were some 850 federal judgeships in the United States. Though a president needs to fill a court's seat only when it comes open (usually upon a judge's retirement), the president himself is rarely well versed on who the best candidates for a judgeship might be. So when a federal judgeship is open, the White House receives recommendations from many sources. The trouble a president can get into with a nomination was illustrated when George W. Bush nominated his White House counsel, Harriet Miers, for a seat on the Supreme Court. Politicians, activists, and commentators from Bush's own Republican Party responded strongly and negatively. Miers's nomination was withdrawn, and in her place Samuel Alito, much-approved by conservatives, was nominated and approved by the Senate.

Of course, a Supreme Court nominee's background, experience, and **judicial temperament**—the judge's fairness, even-handedness, and adherence to the Constitution—are very important. It isn't surprising that many go to the Supreme Court from lower federal courts; as of 2007, 30 Supreme Court justices had previously served as federal judges. Yet almost as many (25) have gone to the Court from private practice.

Ideally, once a person has been nominated for a federal judgeship, the Senate Judiciary Committee will hold hearings on the suitability of the nominee. In reality, some nominations are not acted on by the Senate. In the country's history, about 20 percent of the president's nominees have not been confirmed, usually for political reasons. (Between 1968 and 1987, the Senate rejected four nominees.) A nominee's candidacy can also be derailed if, as a result of **senatorial courtesy**, a senator from the nominee's state vetoes the nomination. Senators are not given this power by the Constitution, but the practice has acquired standing through practice. The party in control of the Senate does have the power to prevent the opposition party from applying senatorial courtesy.

THE COURTS AND CONTROVERSY

Although all nominations for federal judgeships can be controversial, the potential for controversy grows as the court in question is higher up on the judiciary chain. Nominations for appellate courts gain more attention than nominations for federal district courts, and nominations for Supreme Court seats are sure to attract the most attention. This may be especially the case when a person is nominated to be the Court's **chief justice**. This is because, in addition to managing the Court itself, the chief justice presides over the federal court system (with some 31,000 employees), as well as the Judicial Conference of the United States. This conference has an annual budget of about $6 million and, through the conference, the chief justice sets the federal court system's priorities.

Inevitably, nominations are politically controversial. Though we would like to believe that judges dispense justice without regard to political inclinations, it's just simply true that some judges are "liberal" and some are "conservative" and some are in-between. Presidential candidates often promote themselves or denounce opponents on the grounds of judicial nominations. During the presidential campaign of 2008, Republican John McCain said that "elections have consequences" and that if his opponent, Barack Obama, won the presidency, more liberal judges would be placed on the federal courts. Obama had previously voted in the Senate against the confirmation of President George W. Bush's two nominees, John Roberts and Samuel Alito, both of whom were confirmed with a majority vote in the Senate. As Obama feared and Republicans hoped, Roberts and Alito moved the Supreme Court in a conservative direction.

Many decisions from the Court presided over by Chief Justice Roberts were closely split, with 5-4 votes. It was easy to see that the liberal justices on the

Court would go one way and the conservatives another, with the centrist (Justice Anthony Kennedy) often deciding the issue. In 2007, for example, the Court upheld a federal ban on late-term (or "partial birth") abortion with a 5-4 vote, the deciding justice being Justice Kennedy.

The reason judgeships can be very controversial is that, once a judge is in place, his or her ideology is entrenched in the Court. Politicians come and go; federal judges stay for life. A judge's ideological leanings matter because of **judicial review**—the power to determine what is and what isn't constitutional. (The case that set this in place was ***Marbury v. Madison*** [1803].) In this capacity, federal judges possess enormous power. In 1973, as a result of the Supreme Court's *Roe v. Wade* decision, multiple state laws restricting abortion in the first trimester were annulled.

Partisans on both the political right and left worry about **judicial activism**—that is, judges acting as legislators and making policy as they see fit. Politicians complain about judges "legislating from the bench." (Formally, "judicial activism" refers to the idea that the Supreme Court should actively check the power of the executive and legislative branches of government.) Opponents of judicial activism call for **judicial restraint**, meaning that federal judges should decide narrow constitutional matters and not usurp the power of the other branches of government. Usually, liberal judges are thought to be more activist and conservative judges more "constraintist," but in the early twenty-first century, liberals denounced what they saw as the activism of a fairly conservative Supreme Court.

Generally speaking, when it comes to interpreting the Constitution, liberals tend to favor a **broad construction** approach. Judges who take this approach tend to interpret the Constitution in light of its underpinning principles and in light of evolving moral and cultural standards. Judges who favor **strict construction**, on the other hand, advocate an approach that reads the Constitution literally. They wish to be faithful to the letter of the words the Constitution's writers wrote; their counterparts want to be faithful to the spirit of a "**living Constitution**." Critics of this latter approach accuse judges of twisting the Constitution to say whatever they want it to.

Whether federal judges read the Constitution strictly or broadly, they wield enormous power and influence. Once the Supreme Court has spoken, it seems that nothing can check the Court's power. It's true that a court has no power to enforce its decisions, and when it comes to **judicial implementation** the president can ignore the Court, but this very rarely happens. The Congress can decline to make funding available to act on a Court's ruling but, again, this is rare. Congress can also pass legislation that puts limits on what judges can decide. The Religious Freedom Restoration Act (1993), for example, gave greater room to religious liberty. This law came in response to a feeling that the Supreme Court had gone too far in narrowing public religious liberty.

Federal courts can act as checks on each other. Lower courts can ignore Supreme Court decisions if they can argue that the higher Court's decision does not apply in a specific case. And the Supreme Court often overturns decisions from lower courts (the Ninth Circuit Court is, by far, the most overturned court in the appellate system). And the Supreme Court can check its own power by refusing to hear cases on hypothetical and political questions—those that are best dealt with by the Congress and the president). On the whole, however, we must say that the power of the federal courts, and especially the Supreme Court, is not checked to the extent that the powers of the other governmental branches are.

PROTECTION OF CIVIL LIBERTIES

One of the basic things we expect federal courts to do is protect our **civil liberties**—those freedoms guaranteed to us by the Constitution. The next chapter discusses **civil rights**—that is, privileges and powers granted to people as equals under the law. Sometimes scholars refer to civil liberties as "negative rights," meaning they limit the power of government. Civil rights, on the other hand, are "positive rights" in that they point to things government must do—for example, protect my right not to be discriminated against in a restaurant on account of my skin color.

When we speak of civil liberties that Americans enjoy, our primary text must be the Bill of Rights—the first ten amendments to the U.S. Constitution. Among the basic liberties given to Americans by the Bill of Rights are freedom of religion, freedom of speech, and freedom of the press. Let's walk through these one at a time.

Freedom of (and Freedom from) Religion

A large majority of Americans claim to have some kind of religious faith and, uniquely in the Western world, American presidents and politicians regularly bring speeches to an end with words like "God bless you, and God bless America." Americans' freedom to practice religion is found in the First Amendment, the relevant part of which says, "Congress shall make no law respecting an establishment of religion, or prohibiting the free exercise thereof."

First, notice the **establishment clause**: Congress may not found an official religion. At the time the Constitution was ratified, a few states did have official churches; it was understood at the time that the Constitution applied only to the federal government and not to the states. Since then, however, and especially since the mid-twentieth century, the establishment clause has been read to mean that no government in the country may seem to approve of any particular religion. This has led, among other things, to the removal of displays of the Ten Commandments from many public buildings and to the elimination of organized prayer in public school classrooms.

In obvious tension with the government's move away from doing anything that might seem like religious endorsement is the freedom of the individual, granted in the **free-exercise clause**, to engage in religious practices. How have the courts dealt with this tension and with the desire both to protect religious practice while not seeming to support any religion? The problem has often come up in questions related to education.

An important Supreme Court case is *Lemon v. Kurtzman* (1971), which provided courts and interest groups with a "Lemon test" to determine whether their activity was constitutional. In the decision, the Court disallowed a program that permitted a state to pay teachers at religious schools who taught non-religious topics. The Court said that the payment of the teachers entangled the state with a religious institution, since agents of the state would have to monitor the school's activities. The Court then provided the following test to help states know how to proceed:

1. When considering funding or any kind of involvement, the state should ensure that the program in question has no religious purpose.

2. The government involvement must not promote or inhibit religion.

3. The government action must not lead to its excessive entanglement with religion.

These general guidelines remained in place until 1997, when the Supreme Court took a different approach. In *Agostini v. Felton,* the Court said, in a 5-4 decision, that the First Amendment to the Constitution requires only government **neutrality** toward religion. This decision allowed public school teachers to teach remedial, nonreligious classes at religious schools at taxpayers' expense. The so-called **wall of separation between church and state**—a phrase borrowed from a letter Thomas Jefferson wrote to Baptist ministers—seemed to be lowered a bit. This seemed especially so when, in 2002, the Court allowed parents to use publicly funded school **vouchers** to pay tuition at religious schools (*Zelman v. Simmons-Harris*). (Vouchers are government funding that parents can use to pay for education at private or public schools. A purpose of vouchers is to spur competition for funding among schools and thereby enhance the schools' quality.) In 2002 the Court determined that public school rooms could be used by religious groups during after-school hours.

As noted earlier, religious displays have also caused dissension. In *Lynch v. Donnelly* (1984), the Court held that a Christmas manger display, along with a depiction of Santa, on public property was constitutional because (1) the display's primary purpose was to celebrate a national holiday, (2) it did not actively promote religion, and (3) the display involved no excessive entanglement of government with religion. The matter remains murky, however. In 2005 the Court allowed a display of the Ten Commandments at the Texas state capitol because it was one of several documents on display. However, the Court disallowed a display of the Ten Commandments at a Kentucky courthouse because its purpose seemed to be primarily religious.

What about school prayer? Since the early 1960s, the Court has regularly prohibited state involvement with prayers in school. *Engel v. Vitale* (1962) struck down a brief prayer said in New York public schools. The following year the Court prohibited Bible reading and the recitation of the Lord's Prayer in public schools. In 1992 the Court disallowed prayers at public school commencement ceremonies. Eight years later, the Court prohibited organized, student-led prayers at football games. Not surprisingly, many Americans felt that this relatively new interpretation of the establishment clause was trampling on the liberties called for in the free-exercise clause.

Although the federal courts have worked to prevent the government from entangling itself with religion, they have also tried to protect religious freedom. In the case *Sherbert v. Verner* (1963), the Supreme Court ruled that a state could not decline to give unemployment benefits on account of a Seventh-day Adventist's refusal to work on Saturday. According to the Court's standard of **strict scrutiny**, a law that discriminates against a religious practice must serve a "compelling government interest" and must be as unrestrictive as possible.

What about when religious groups use controlled substances? Rastafarians, for example, smoke marijuana as part of their religious practice. The Supreme Court's position has been that, for society to function well, one's religious beliefs cannot regularly go against societal norms (such as partaking of illegal drugs) or infringe on the general culture. In taking this position, the strict-scrutiny standard has been weakened. The place of religion in American public life remains unsettled.

Freedom of Expression

In addition to calling for freedom of religion, the First Amendment allows for freedom of expression: "Congress shall make no law . . . abridging the freedom of speech, or of the press; or the right of the people peaceably to assemble, and to petition the Government for a redress of grievances."

Although the language of the amendment seems clear, freedom of speech in the United States has never been absolute. No one has the right, for example, to openly discuss plans to assassinate the president. The scholarly consensus is that the Constitution's **free-expression clauses** have to do with the open discussion of public affairs. The Supreme Court has also determined that the clauses prohibit **prior restraint**, such as censorship. Yet citizens must also be willing to be held accountable for their views. People can be prosecuted who intentionally promote lawless action. Also, government may place limits on freedom of expression. Protestors may have to make their statements in a certain area, for example, but they may not block entrance to public buildings.

Something to bear in mind here is the **"clear and present danger" test**. This term stems from the Supreme Court case *Schenck v. United States* (1919). In this case the Court upheld the conviction of a defendant who had dispensed anticonscription literature during wartime. But soon the question arose as to whether suppressing unpopular or pernicious speech was more dangerous to the American republic than shutting speech down. Also in 1919, the Court upheld the conviction of a person who spoke against U.S. involvement in World War I but, in dissent, Oliver Wendell Holmes argued that the Court should favor a "free trade in ideas."

By the late 1960s, the Court was friendlier to the free expression of unpopular and radical ideas. In the case *Brandenburg v. Ohio* (1969), the Court struck down the conviction of a Ku Klux Klansman who had made threatening statements. The Court denied that the threat posed by Brandenburg's words was credible. Also in 1969, the Court sided with high school students who wore black armbands to protest the Vietnam conflict. The Court determined that the armbands did not create undue distractions or undermine school discipline (*Tinker v. Des Moines Independent Community School District*). The armbands were protected as a kind of **symbolic expression**.

Related to the "clear and present danger" test discussed earlier are **fighting words**—that is, words that incite a breach of the peace. In *Chaplinsky v. New Hampshire* (1942), the Supreme Court upheld the conviction of a Jehovah's Witness who had called a marshal a fascist. It was wartime, and the defendant's words seemed provocative. Less than a decade later, however, the Court protected the much more provocative speech of an anti-Semite. The country was no longer at war; fighting words seemed less dangerous. Later, in *Cohen v. California* (1971), the Court defended a person's right to wear a vulgar anti-Vietnam War slogan on his shirt. "One man's vulgarity is another man's lyric," the Court determined. In 1997 the Court determined that free speech rights applied to the Internet. The earlier efforts of Congress to restrict content on the Internet were struck down.

But just how far can free speech go? Blatant obscenity has not been protected as fighting words have been, but how does one define *obscenity?* In 1957 the Court offered a test to determine whether something is obscene: "Whether to the average person, applying contemporary community standards, the dominant theme of the material taken as a whole appeals to prurient [lustful] interest." It's easy to see that this test is difficult to put into effect. Another justice famously said that, even if he couldn't define obscenity, "I know it when I see it." In 1973 the Court again attempted to provide standards on how to know whether something is obscene:

1. The work appeals to prurient interests (that is, to the incitement of lust).

2. The work depicts sexual acts in an obviously offensive manner.

3. The work is void of any serious academic or artistic content.

But this, too, is inevitably problematic. What's offensive to some isn't offensive to others, and the concept of "art" is difficult to define.

Freedom of the Press

In addition to freedom of religion and speech, the First Amendment says that Congress "shall make no law . . . abridging the freedom . . . of the press." But, as with speech and religious practice, press freedom isn't absolute. Newspapers and magazines can be prosecuted for **libel**—the defamation of a person in writing. If, for example, a newspaper alleged, without evidence, that your neighbor is a Nazi and a court found that statement to be libelous, the publication could face legal punishment.

Libelous statements about public figures, however, are less likely to be prosecuted. In *New York Times v. Sullivan* (1964), the Supreme Court decided that false statements made about officials were protected unless one could prove malice—that is, the intention to do unwarranted harm. This also applies to celebrities and others who operate in the public sphere. Because it is very difficult to prove "malice" on the part of the person who wrote something untrue or defamatory, few slander cases are successful. In 1988 the Court decided against a plaintiff, a popular preacher, whom a magazine had satirized as having an incestuous affair with his own mother. Almost anything seems to go if the words are directed at public persons.

As mentioned earlier, the Supreme Court has not thought well of "prior restraint"—that is, the censorship of controversial material. In 1971 the U.S. Department of Justice sought to prevent the *New York Times* and *Washington*

Post from publishing documents that would be damaging to the government's public relations campaign concerning American involvement in Vietnam. In *New York Times v. United States*, the Supreme Court said that the government had not proven that the damage to national security outweighed the interest of the public in knowing what their government was up to. Several of the justices did suggest, however, that under unusual circumstances prior restraint could be put into effect in the future.

When pitted against public order, a free press's rights can be limited. In 1972 the Supreme Court determined that a news reporter did not have the right to withhold information about criminal activity, and in 1988 the Court decided that a school has a right to prevent a student newspaper from printing salacious or overtly provocative material if the school can show that its primary purpose of education will be damaged. And in the 2007 case *Morse v. Frederick*, the Court defended a public school official's confiscation of a student banner at a school-sponsored parade that said "Bong Hits 4 Jesus." Since the banner seemed to promote drug use, the Court majority said, it was contrary to a public school's purpose and not protected "school speech."

Sometimes the interests of a free press can conflict with the constitutional right of an accused person to a fair trial, granted in the Sixth Amendment. Since jurors can be influenced by news they read or hear, judges occasionally impose **gag orders** that prevent news about a trial from being published or disseminated. Most of the time, however, gag orders are deemed an infringement of the press's freedom.

As for speech that manifests itself in art and films, there are few restraints. The film industry regulates itself via its own film rating system. Radio and TV, on the other hand, are more highly regulated, but even here, few restrictions apply. Some "filthy" words may not be said on broadcast TV, but the rules do not apply to cable TV. Neither do the rules apply to satellite radio, which is outside the jurisdiction of the Federal Communications Commission.

Related to the right to express oneself is, in the words of the First Amendment, the "right of the people peaceably to assemble, and to petition the government for a redress of grievances." In practice, this right has merged with the right to freedom of speech. Protests of various kinds take place regularly across the country. Protests are often regulated, and public order has to be maintained, but citizens who wish to gather peacefully to make their grievances known face few barriers. Even the freedom of gang members to gather peaceably in public places has usually been protected. In 1999 the Supreme Court struck down a Chicago anti-loitering law directed at gang members, saying that the police had been given too much authority to determine what constituted loitering.

THE SECOND AMENDMENT: THE RIGHT TO BEAR ARMS

The Second Amendment to the U.S. Constitution reads as follows: "A well-regulated militia being necessary to the security of a free State, the right of the people to keep and bear arms shall not be infringed"—fewer than 30 words. But what do the words mean? Americans who advocate restrictions on gun ownership tend to say that the amendment applies to state militia which, in the eighteenth century (when the Constitution was written), would have been composed of armed citizens. Some of these observers say that the National Guard has taken the place of state militia and that the amendment is outdated.

Proponents of "gun rights," on the other hand, point out that the amendment is about an armed citizenry and, so long as the Constitution says what it says, the government cannot prevent the people from owning firearms. Hardly anyone argues that citizens should have the right to own operable bazookas. In 1934 the Supreme Court stated that citizens had a right to own guns associated with a citizen militia and thus required machine guns and sawed-off shotguns to be taxed and registered.

Although the registration and licensing of guns has regularly been deemed constitutional, bans on guns have run into trouble. In 2008, by a 5-4 vote, the Supreme Court deemed a ban on handguns in Washington, D.C., unconstitutional. One of the most conservative justices, Antonin Scalia, suggested that, as a practical matter, private gun ownership may be outmoded. But the Second Amendment says what it says and, Scalia argued, the Supreme Court's role is to abide by the words of the Constitution.

CRIMINAL RIGHTS AND SOCIAL ORDER

As we see in the next chapter, the federal government and federal courts claimed increasing jurisdiction in the United States during the twentieth century. It is difficult for Americans today to understand, for example, that for a long time the Sixth Amendment's guarantee of a trial by jury was not assumed to apply to state court cases, but this was not set in constitutional stone until the late 1960s, in the case *Duncan v. Louisiana*. (The Court did not require a certain number of jurors, though the minimum number is six, and that varies among the states.) As for the Sixth Amendment's guarantee to an accused person to "have the Assistance of Counsel for his defense," the Supreme Court has made this mandatory across the board. In the case *Gideon v. Wainright* (1963), the Court required legal counsel to be made available to all defendants.

In defense of alleged criminals' rights, the Supreme Court has also interpreted the Fifth Amendment's guarantee that no person "shall be compelled in any criminal case to be a witness against himself" to mean that a person who has been arrested should be advised of his rights. As viewers of TV police shows know, officers taking a man into custody tell him that (1) he has a right to remain silent, (2) if he says anything, it could be used against him in a court of law, (3) he has the right to talk to an attorney of his choice before questioning, and (4) a lawyer will be provided if he cannot afford one. These **Miranda warnings** (or "Miranda rights") stem from the case *Miranda v. Arizona* (1966). In 2000 the Supreme Court reasserted these rights and declared that Congress could not undo the rights via legislation. Some legislators, angry that criminal rights sometimes seem to trump victims' rights, had wanted to take action.

In the early 1960s the Supreme Court set in place the **exclusionary rule**, which says that evidence obtained illegally cannot be used against a defendant (*Mapp v. Ohio*). The Court drew this principle from the Fourth Amendment, which says the following: "The right of the people to be secure in their persons, houses, papers, and effects, against unreasonable searches and seizures, shall not be violated."

Sometimes in practice, however, the interests of law and order were sacrificed, as law enforcement agencies abided by the Court's doctrine. In 1984, then, the Court enunciated the **good faith exception** principle, meaning that if a warrant to gather evidence was based on faulty evidence but given in good faith, the evidence could still be used in trial. The Court stated that the point of the exclusionary rule was not to protect criminal behavior (as it sometimes seemed to do) but to prevent corrupt policing. In 2006 the Court sided again with law enforcement, deciding that, even if police fail to "knock and announce" before entering a home, evidence gathered afterwards may still be used against a defendant. Since the 1960s, there has been a clear turn away from an emphasis on criminal rights and toward societal protection.

THE WAR AGAINST TERRORISM

After the major terrorist attacks against the United States in 2001, the question of how to balance liberty against the need for social order came into sharp focus. Soon after the attacks, the Congress passed and the president signed the **USA Patriot Act**. The act expanded the government's ability to put Americans under surveillance and to monitor Internet and telephone communications within the country. The law was reapproved, with minor changes, in 2006.

The obvious purpose of the Patriot Act was to detect and capture terrorists before they could strike. Some worried, however, about a 300-page law that seemed to give the government vast power to pry into the lives of ordinary citizens. For example, the Patriot Act empowered government officials to look into a person's public library records or to track what videos a person rented from a store. Of course, the government could gather information on individuals before the Patriot Act was passed but only with a judge's consent after a case had been made to the judge. Now the government would only have to claim that it wanted to conduct a search to prevent a potential terrorist attack.

Many Americans weren't bothered by the Patriot Act. They felt that they had nothing to hide, and they favored the government having the power it needed to prevent terrorist attacks. And the number of Americans whose records were looked into was relatively small—some 3,500 in 2005—though that number was significantly higher than in years before. Others worried that the Patriot Act set a bad precedent: the legal expansion of the government's ability to pry into the private affairs of citizens and residents.

Chapter 9

The States:
Civil Rights and Federalism

The Tenth Amendment is among the lesser-known amendments listed in the Constitution's Bill of Rights. It states the following:

> The powers not delegated to the United States by the Constitution, nor prohibited by it to the States, are reserved to the States respectively, or to the people.

In other words, if the Constitution does not specifically empower the federal government to do something or specifically deny a state's ability to do something, then that power is in the hands of the state legislators or of the people, meaning that, through elections and by other legal means, the people can establish the kinds of laws and political forms that they desire.

One thing we know is that the latitude the states have to act has been increasingly restricted since the early twentieth century. If you had said the word *government* to a person in the year 1850, for example, he or she would likely have thought first of state or local government. The Civil War of the 1860s changed things. The war pitted Southern states, whose legislatures believed that state governments should be preeminent, against the states that remained loyal to the federal government in Washington, D.C. The victory of the federal forces established the preeminence of the federal government over the states, though for some decades states continued to have much more power and latitude to act than they do today. Following the exhausting periods of war and postwar construction, in other words, the federal government observed **states' rights**. In 1895, the Supreme Court declared a national income tax unconstitutional (the Sixteenth Amendment [1913] would entrench a federal income tax in the Constitution), and in 1916 the Court struck down a federal law outlawing child labor, deeming that issue to be a local problem for local authorities to respond to.

By the late twentieth century, however, the word *government* had come to be almost synonymous with the federal government. State and local governments now receive comparatively little notice in public affairs. The balance of power between the states and the national government has dramatically altered since the writing of the Constitution and the Tenth Amendment.

WHAT *FEDERALISM* MEANS

The United States practices **federalism**—that is, a political system that seeks to divide political power. Let's say that you live in Arkansas. The national, or federal, government has jurisdiction over some things in that state, and the state government at Little Rock has jurisdiction over different things. You pay federal taxes and state taxes (and also local taxes). In Arkansas you must use the currency of the United States when you buy a car, and the car was manufactured following federal government regulations. But if you get married in Arkansas, you will do so under Arkansas law. As of the summer of 2008, the states of Massachusetts and California allowed same-sex couples to marry, while other states had constitutional amendments prohibiting same-sex marriage. The underlying hope of the nation's founders was that the separation of state and federal government power would provide for another system of political checks and balances. States could offset (that is, check and balance) the national government, and the national government could offset the state governments.

Some of the terms we hear when discussing federalism are these:

> **Layer-cake federalism**: This metaphor implies that the powers of the central and state governments are separate but overlapping, distinguishable but overlapping—realistically speaking, a little messy.

> **Dual federalism**: This is the idea that the national and state governments are **sovereign** in their own distinct spheres—a view that seeks clear distinctions between the governments. The actual practice of evolving government seems to be more complicated.

> **Cooperative federalism**: This view emphasizes the point that the responsibilities of the state governments and the federal government overlap; it takes into account that the state and federal governments often share responsibilities—environmental protection, for example. The pastry metaphor to use here is **marble-cake federalism**—a system in which the powers of the governments are mixed and swirled, like the vanilla and chocolate of a marble cake. The oil industry in Alaska, for instance, faces regulations coming from both Washington, D.C., and Juneau (the state capital).

A basic and very important question that helped trigger the American Civil War is whether the states make the nation or whether the nation precedes the states. In other words: What comes first, the states or the nation? One can argue that the original thirteen states created the nation. Yet it is equally clear that the national government played a large role in the organization of the other thirty-seven states.

Balance of Government Power

Americans who believe that power should be closer to home advocate **states' rights**, and among their founding champions is Thomas Jefferson, primary author of the Declaration of Independence and third American president. Among the champions of those who argue for the preeminence of the federal government is Alexander Hamilton, coauthor of the Federalist Papers (*The Federalist*) and the nation's first secretary of the treasury. People who take a states' rights position read the Tenth Amendment and say that it means what it says. People who take the other position rely on the implied powers granted to Congress by the elastic clause (discussed in Chapter 4), which grants Congress the power to do what is "necessary and proper" to carry out its work.

A challenge the states' rights position has faced is that sometimes states seem to lack the ability to deal with vast problems. Take the Great Depression of the 1930s as an example: there is nothing in the Constitution that expressly grants the government the power to create jobs for people. Therefore, a strict reading of the Tenth Amendment would suggest that if a government is to create work for people, it should be done by the state governments. But the states lacked the capacity to deal with the magnitude of the economic depression (which affected the entire nation), while the Constitution's preamble says that the purpose of the federal government is to "promote the general welfare" of the country. Partly on the grounds provided by the elastic clause and partly for practical reasons, the federal government devised New Deal programs and oversaw their implementation. Increasingly, people looked more to Washington, D.C., for help and less to their state governments.

States' powers do come into play, however, in the process of amending the Constitution (see Chapter 2). Although Congress can propose a constitutional amendment (by two-thirds votes in both chambers), a super-majority of the states must consent if the amendment is to be ratified.

Role of the Supreme Court

It also seems clear that arguments between states and the federal government have helped to lift the Supreme Court to the position of near omnipotence that it seems to hold today. In any argument, someone has to decide, and for a society to function well, parties in dispute must agree to go along with what the decider decides. In disputes between the state and federal governments, the decider has often been the Supreme Court.

Through the mid-nineteenth and early twentieth centuries, the Court usually sided with states' rights positions. Since the mid-twentieth century, the Court has, on the whole, leaned in the other direction, though less so since the mid-1990s. In Chapter 4 we looked at the case *McCullough v. Maryland* (1819), which made an argument on behalf of a strong central government.

Since the nineteenth century, the federal courts have relied on the **commerce clause** of Article I, Section 2 of the Constitution to enhance the power of the national government. This clause says that Congress has the power to regulate commerce that takes place between the states. In the case *Gibbons v. Ogden* (1824), the Supreme Court began to interpret the word *commerce* quite broadly. Had the Court been of the same interpretive school in the 1850s, Congress would have been empowered to regulate the movement of slaves from state to state—a kind of commercial movement. But in *Dred Scott v. Sanford* (1857), the Court ruled that the federal government could not prevent Americans from bringing property (that is, slaves) from one state to another. This theoretically opened the entire United States to slavery, and the *Dred Scott* case was a major step on the road to civil war. The decision seemed like a victory for states' rights. (The issue of slavery was resolved by the Thirteenth Amendment, which eliminated slavery and forced labor, except for felons.)

The Court and Civil Rights

Certainly, the nation's slow-but-sure pursuit of **civil rights** has led the federal government to take precedence over state governments in a number of ways.

We know that the Constitution reserves to the states the duty to make rules about voting (so long as the rules do not counter other parts of the Constitution). Before the Civil War, as a result of these laws, very few African Americans could vote in either Northern or Southern states. Then the postwar Fifteenth Amendment made it unconstitutional to prevent blacks from voting simply on account of their skin color. But state laws requiring, for example, literacy tests and poll taxes continued to prevent blacks and poor whites from voting. Looking back, it seems inevitable that, if equal rights were to be protected, the federal government would *have* to step in.

The pursuit of civil rights involves the ideal of **equal opportunity**—the notion that all Americans should have an equal chance to succeed in life. Most Americans agree that equal opportunity is a good thing. But then agreement quickly breaks down. Some argue that institutions have actually aimed at **equal-**

Elizabeth Cady Stanton (seated) and Susan B. Anthony (standing) each played pivotal roles in the nineteenth-century century women's rights movement. In 1869, the women founded the National Women's Suffrage Association (NWSA), an organization dedicated to gaining women's suffrage.

ity of outcome—an approach that strives to *ensure* that everybody (all races and economic classes, for example) enjoys equality.

Ideally, equal opportunity allows individuals to have equal access to things that will help them succeed in life—for example, trustworthy law enforcement and good schools. Americans who favor equality of outcome, however, support plans that target specific groups for assistance. It's not difficult to see why there's controversy: inequalities inevitably exist in life. Some people are just better at math than others; some people are naturally more artistic than others; some neighborhoods are more peaceful than others. According to some political theorists, human life can be completely equalized; human experience suggests otherwise.

Some argue that because specific groups—usually racial minorities—have faced discrimination and therefore start the race of life at a disadvantage, the way to provide equal opportunity is to take **affirmative action** to "level the playing field." Most affirmative action programs seek to encourage minorities or under-represented groups to apply for employment positions. For example, a university that wishes to have more women faculty may send letters of encouragement specifically to women, in addition to advertising a position more generally. This strikes some as the promotion of inequality in the name of pursuing equality.

Affirmative action becomes more controversial when it moves beyond encouragement and toward *quotas* (a word with negative connotations) or *goals* (a word supporters prefer). Quotas, as they are usually called, set aside a certain number of positions for certain kinds of people—racial groups, ethnicities, males, or females. There is no question that this process is discriminatory against people who do not fit the need of the race- or gender-based quota or goal. The question is whether discrimination of this kind is justified to level a field made uneven by previous discrimination. The argument goes on.

To focus on the most enduring racial divide in the United States, let's look at the African American experience. As we know by now, the Fourteenth Amendment (1868) says that no state can "deny to any person within its jurisdiction an equal protection of the laws." And the Fifteenth Amendment (1870) says that the right of citizens to vote "shall not be denied . . . on account of race, color, or previous condition of servitude." Yet every American who knows just a little about history is aware that states, primarily in the South and parts of the Midwest, prevented most blacks from voting or did not provide blacks with equal legal protection. **Poll taxes**—a tax on voters—prevented many Southern blacks (and some poor whites) from voting. These taxes did not infringe on the letter of the Fifteenth Amendment, though they certainly flew in the face of the spirit of the Bill of Rights and post–Civil War amendments. **Black codes** (also called Jim Crow laws) entrenched segregationist practices in state laws; lynching, directed mostly at black men, was disturbingly common into the 1930s. Clearly, there were civil rights problems.

But enforced segregation did not infringe on the specific wording of the Fourteenth Amendment. If, according to one theory, it could be proved that equal access to justice and the promises of America could be gained in a segregationist system, then the Constitution was not damaged. Enter one of the most famous and among the most damaging of the Supreme Court's decisions: *Plessy v. Ferguson* (1896). This decision, involving passengers on railroads in Louisiana, put in place the doctrine "**separate but equal**." The letter of the Constitution was observed, while its spirit was challenged, and the obvious inequality of segregated facilities was ignored. The states acted (or, in case of lynching, often did not act) with few checks from federal authorities. At this time in American history, states' rights seemed to rule.

Desegregation

Change came about substantially as the result of the work of interest groups such as the National Association for the Advancement of Colored People, better known simply as the **NAACP**, which challenged the American conscience, lobbied government officials, and made court challenges. Strong moves against segregation also came from the federal government. In 1948, for example, President Harry Truman ordered the **desegregation of the military**. Around the same time, the U.S. Department of Justice was pursuing decisions for civil rights in federal courts. This, along with the work of the NAACP, led to one of the most influential Supreme Court cases of the twentieth century: *Brown v. Board of Education of Topeka* (1954). An enduring symbol of the Supreme Court's power to override state laws, *Brown* began the process of desegregation in the Southern and some mid-Western states. The Court relied on the **equal protection clause** of the Fourteenth Amendment to strike down segregationist state laws that had been built on the foundation of the doctrine "separate but equal." The Court instructed schools to desegregate with "all deliberate speed."

This order from the Court led to twentieth-century America's greatest struggle between state governments and the federal government. In Arkansas in 1957, Governor Orval Faubus called out the state's National Guard to prevent Little Rock High School from integrating. In turn, President Dwight Eisenhower (acting as commander in chief of the military) nationalized the Guard and sent in federal troops to ensure that black students could get into the school safely. Five years later, President John Kennedy sent some thirty thousand troops to Oxford, Mississippi, to put down riots that developed when a black student sought entrance into the University of Mississippi.

Brown began the work of dismantling **de jure segregation**—that is, segregation as a matter of law. Another challenge integration faced was **de facto segregation**—that is, segregation resulting from the fact that people of different colors lived in different areas and therefore went to different schools. One proposed solution was **busing**—the transportation of white students to schools attended mainly by black students, and vice versa. Though federal courts upheld the legality of busing through the 1980s, the practice was unpopular; busing for specifically racial reasons fell into disuse.

By the early 1990s, as a result of de facto segregation, racially divided schools became the norm again, especially in urban areas. The emphasis since the 1990s has been to raise educational standards at all schools. If the schools are going to be segregated by practice, not as a result of law, the government can still strive to ensure that they are equal. This idea led to the **No Child Left Behind Act of 2001**. By setting measurable goals, the program sought to

The Rev. Martin Luther King Jr., an African American clergyman, activist, and prominent leader in the civil rights movement, speaking to his congregation in Ebenezer Baptist Church in Atlanta, Georgia.

improve schools whose students were not doing well academically. Framed by the Tenth Amendment, the act allowed for state flexibility while also providing oversight and accountability at the federal level.

Of course, the pursuit of civil rights involved more than schools. It involved segregated public facilities like drinking fountains and private facilities like hotels; it also involved the right to vote. Partly in response to pressure from groups like the Southern Christian Leadership Conference, led by Martin Luther King Jr., and partly from a sense of disgust people felt as they saw the brutality often directed against Southern blacks on TV (a relatively new thing in the early 1960s), a general feeling grew that de jure segregation should end.

The Civil Rights Act of 1964 forbade discrimination on the basis of race, color, gender, religion, or national origin. Among other things, this act put into place the right of equality in employment and made discrimination illegal in restaurants and hotels because their business affected interstate commerce. The act banned discrimination in employment for any institution that received federal funds, and it established the **Equal Employment Opportunity Commission** (EEOC). The EEOC sets policy to carry out civil rights laws and has the power to investigate whether the laws have been broken. (Notice that, because some states seemed reluctant to provide "equal access" to the benefits of the Constitution's rights, the federal government empowered itself to do so.)

In the mid-1960s, the federal government also empowered itself to register citizens to vote if states or local jurisdictions failed to do so. The federal government disallowed the tests used, primarily in Southern states, to prevent African Americans from voting. These reforms came as a result of the **Voting Rights Act of 1965**. Within a week of the act's passage, nearly fifty federal voter registration examiners went to Southern counties where African American voter registration was low. Soon, the **Civil Rights Act of 1968** outlawed discrimination in most kinds of housing. These reforms point to a heightened national commitment to civil rights and also to the growing power of the federal government relative to state governments.

Where We Stand

The civil rights legislation of the 1960s seems to have achieved some of its purposes. In 1980, almost 56 percent of eligible black residents in the South were registered to vote, whereas in 1960 that figure stood at less than 30 percent. And as of 2008, more than nine thousand African Americans had been elected to office in localities, counties, and states, as well as in federal positions. By that time, about 94 percent of Americans said that they would be willing to vote for an African American running for president (compared to 38 percent in 1958).

On the other hand, wide disparities between blacks and whites persist in the early twenty-first century. For example, whereas just over 8 percent of whites lived in poverty in the early 2000s, almost 25 percent of blacks did. The reasons for this disparity level are debated. Liberals tend to call for persistent federal government action to eliminate the disparities. Conservatives also want to eliminate such differences but are less inclined to ask government to do most of the work; the government action they favor tends to be centered in localities and states.

THE WOMEN'S MOVEMENT

The major theme of this chapter is the often tricky and troubled relationship between the state and federal governments. In the past few pages, we saw that the federal government expanded its powers to provide for equal access to laws when it seemed that states and localities would not do so. If we look at the women's movement of the late twentieth century, we see something similar.

The Right to Vote

An early political objective of women's rights advocates was the right to vote. In 1848, at Seneca Falls, New York, early **feminists** such as Susan B. Anthony and Elizabeth Cady Stanton issued a Declaration of Sentiments, which drew on the language of the Declaration of Independence: "We hold these truths to be self-evident: that all men *and women* are created equal." Many women were actually opposed to women's **suffrage;** a prevailing idea was that men's proper sphere was public life and women's proper sphere was private life. But World War I, among other things, inevitably brought more women into the public square; they took up jobs that men who had gone off to war had left behind. And many women did not need the Nineteenth Amendment in order to vote; they had already been given the right to vote by their state legislatures.

However, the Nineteenth Amendment ensured that the vote for women could not be taken away by state legislatures and that they would have the vote in states where they had not had it before. The addition to the federal Constitution of the Nineteenth Amendment trumped the will of some state legislatures that opposed the amendment, but it was approved by the legislatures of thirty-six states, which comprised the three-fourths majority necessary to amend the Constitution. In this case, most states were willing to limit their own powers for the sake of a national good—the vote for women.

Between the ratification of the Nineteenth Amendment and the **women's movement**—sometimes called the **women's liberation movement**—of the 1960s, whatever political action that was devoted to the furtherance of feminist concerns accomplished little. The women's movement rode the wave of reform that led to civil rights legislation and to protests against the Vietnam War. Like those movements, the feminist movement sought action primarily from the federal government. In the 1960s and early 1970s, states saw many of their laws struck down by federal courts and overridden by the federal Congress.

The Right to Equality and Privacy

A key feminist organization, founded in 1966, was the National Organization for Women (1966), which aimed to make women the equals of men in all respects. They wanted **equal pay for equal work**; they wanted to break through the perceived **glass ceiling** that prevented women from advancing in the workplace; they wanted protections against **sexual harassment** and domestic violence; and most of them advocated greater reproductive freedom—that is, legal access to contraceptives and abortions. Opposition to abortion had been a feminist cause in the early twentieth century, and the organization Feminists for Life maintains this position. Other groups, such as **NARAL-Pro Choice** (formerly the National Abortion and Reproductive Rights Action League) and Planned Parenthood argue for abortion on demand.

State laws outlawing contraception and first-trimester abortion were struck down by the Supreme Court on the grounds that the Constitution guarantees a person a right to privacy and, the argument continued, decisions to procure contraception or abortions were private. The most significant case in this respect was **Griswold v. Connecticut** (1965), in which a barely enforced state law against contraception was declared unconstitutional. The Court acknowledged that the Constitution did not use the word *privacy* but, the majority of justices argued, a right to privacy could be discerned in several places—for example, in the right to association guaranteed by the First Amendment and in the right against self-incrimination guaranteed by the Fifth Amendment. The vague Ninth Amendment, which states that a person's rights are not limited to those expressly listed in the Constitution, also proved useful to the plaintiffs seeking to see the Connecticut law struck down.

Reproductive Rights

Griswold set the stage for one of most controversial Supreme Court cases in American history, **Roe v. Wade** (1973), which nullified state laws that made first-trimester abortion illegal. The Court did allow states to make laws regulating second-trimester abortions and, if states wished to make third-trimester abortions illegal, they could do so. This decision sparked a political war that continued into the twenty-first century, and what states could and could not do became murky and confused.

In the 1980s, the Court struck down state laws that required women to get counseling that aimed to discourage abortion, but in **Webster v. Reproductive Health Services** (1989), the Court upheld a Missouri law that prohibited abortions in publicly funded hospitals and clinics. In 1992, in **Planned Parenthood v. Casey** (1992), the Court upheld a Pennsylvania law requiring pre-abortion counseling, a twenty-four-hour waiting period, and parental or judicial permission for girls under eighteen. But then, in **Stenberg v. Carhart** (2000) the Court struck down a Nebraska law (and with it, thirty other state laws) that made late-term abortions illegal; these are often called **partial-birth abortions**. Underlying these cases, one sees not only the political struggle *Roe* sparked but also a struggle between state legislatures and federal courts.

To **pro-life** Americans (those opposed to abortion), *Roe* looks like one of the greatest federal government power grabs in history. Before that case, states made their own laws on abortion. They did so because the Tenth Amendment seemed to leave that issue to the state courts because the Constitution nowhere mentions it. But once a right to privacy was found in the Constitution, and once the decision to have an abortion was determined to be a completely private matter, the question of abortion's legality was taken away from the states.

Another key feminist goal was an **Equal Rights Amendment** (ERA), which had first been proposed in Congress in 1923. The first section of the proposed amendment reads: "Equality of rights under the law shall not be denied or abridged by the United States or by any state on account of sex." The ERA passed by two-thirds majorities in both chambers of Congress in 1972, but by the deadline for ratification ten years later, just thirty-five state legislatures had approved it—three short of the thirty-eight needed to meet the constitutional requirement of a three-quarters majority. Since 1982, the ERA has been introduced into every Congress, but it has never regained the momentum it had in the 1970s, partly because there is a growing sense that women have achieved a great deal without it.

Legislation and Significant Court Cases

Let's look at some other legislation and federal court decisions that have secured rights for women:

- The **Equal Pay Act** of 1963 required equal pay for work that was substantially the same. Since then, pay has moved toward equality though, for reasons that are debated, complete equality has not yet been achieved. In 1963, women were paid about 59 cents for each dollar a man was paid. By 2007 women received about 75 cents for every dollar a man received from an employer. One common argument is that women generally earn less than men because many of them take time away from work to give birth and raise children. This may also be a key reason why women hold less than 20 percent of American's highest corporate positions.

- **Title VII** of the Civil Rights Act of 1964 prohibited discrimination based on gender. In 1978, Congress expanded Title VII to prohibit discrimination on grounds of pregnancy or health problems related to giving birth. Thus it is illegal not to hire a woman because she is visibly pregnant.

- **Title IX** of the federal Congress's education legislation of 1972 stated that no "person in the U.S. shall, on the basis of sex be excluded from participation in, or denied the benefits of, or be subjected to discrimination under any educational program or activity receiving federal aid." When Title IX was passed, women earned about 9 percent of the medical degrees conferred in the country; by the mid-1990s, women earned almost 40 percent of medical degrees. Also by 1994, women were earn-

A group of feminists chained together to show support for the ratification of the Equal Rights Amendment (ERA), a proposed constitutional amendment that would guarantee equal rights under the law for Americans regardless of sex. The women held their hands in the shape of a womb to symbolize womanhood. The ERA never received enough support to become a constitutional amendment.

ing about 45 percent of Ph.D.s, as opposed to the 25 percent of 1972. Critics of Title IX say that it damaged many male-dominated sports programs when colleges were unable to provide comparable programs for women.

- Two Supreme Court cases, *Faragher v. City of Boca Raton* (1998) and *Burlington Industries v. Ellerth* (1998), ruled that employers are responsible for setting up safeguards against sexual harassment in the workplace. Employers often require employees to attend seminars where they are warned against sexual harassment.

Where We Stand

There is no question that the feminist movement has led to significant changes in American society. By the early twenty-first century, a majority of college students were women, and some cultural observers began to wonder if boys were being left behind. Some even wondered if boys needed affirmative action programs to help them catch up with their female peers.

In 2006, a woman, **Nancy Pelosi**, became speaker of the House of Representatives, and another woman, **Condoleezza Rice**, was secretary of state. Around the same time, the governor with the highest approval ratings was **Sarah Palin**, who gave birth to her fifth child while serving as governor, returning to work three days after the delivery. At the same time, **Sandra Day O'Connor** and **Ruth Bader Ginsburg** were justices of the Supreme Court.

In the congressional elections of 2006, 70 of the 139 women who ran for House seats won them. In the presidential party nominating campaigns of 2008, **Hillary Rodham Clinton** was a very strong Democratic candidate, though she lost the nomination to Barack Obama, and Palin was tapped to be Republican John McCain's vice-presidential running mate. Clearly, there was a widespread willingness among the electorate to vote for women. Although many remained discontented with what they saw as the persistent inequalities between the genders, no one could deny that early twenty-first-century America experienced more equality than it ever had before.

WHAT *COOPERATIVE FEDERALISM* MEANS

Though today the word *government* usually evokes images of goings-on in Washington, D.C., what Americans live with today is often called **cooperative federalism**—that is, the states and the national government seek to work together to solve problems. Practically, this makes sense; the federal government has greater resources to work with, and the states have greater knowledge about local affairs.

From the nation's beginning, the central government has given money to states, first, to help pay for schools; then in the early nineteenth century, the federal government assisted states with the building of canals and railroads. It isn't surprising that the amount of money going from the federal government to the states increased substantially during the Great Depression and then again in the 1960s, when President Lyndon Johnson's **"war on poverty"** and **Great Society** programs—for example, **Medicare** (medical assistance for the elderly), **Medicaid** (medical assistance for the poor), and **Project Head Start** (assistance to children from disadvantaged backgrounds)—went into effect.

The federal government makes funds available to states and therefore makes its presence felt in the states in several ways. By 1985, and across some four hundred different programs, the federal government gave to the states about $100 billion a year in **categorical grants**. These grants funded specific projects. In 2008 alone, some $230 billion flowed from Washington, D.C., to the states. These grants helped states pay for Medicaid, road improvements, education, and welfare programs. Whereas the federal government spent just 17 percent of the money spent by all government bodies in 1929 (when 60 percent was spent by localities), in 2008 federal government funds accounted for more than two-thirds of all government money spent.

Federal Grants to States

Why has federal government spending increased so much? One reason, as we've already noted, is that the federal government simply has greater resources to work with. Another reason is that federal agencies have been eager to provide money to the states to do work that the federal government can't do itself because the country is too large and complicated. A third reason is that with money comes power. States generally *like* receiving money from the federal government, but strings come with that money. Often a state will receive funds only if it complies with a national policy, such as making the legal drinking age twenty-one. The No Child Left Behind Act of 2001 did not require states to adhere to federal educational benchmarks, but states that wanted some of the billions of dollars made available by the act did need to adhere to national standards. Here, as on many other occasions, states have surrendered some of their autonomy in exchange for federal dollars—dollars that provide state and local politicians, bureaucrats, and officials opportunities to create programs and enhance their influence.

Block grants are federal grants that have fewer strings attached to them. Of course, state and local officials prefer these to categorical grants. In 2002, for example, the federal Department of Housing and Urban Development awarded almost $25 million in community-development block grants to the state of Arkansas.

Unfunded Mandates to States

Sometimes the federal government simply instructs states to meet certain requirements—related, for instance, to the environment or voter registration—without providing funding. These have come to be called **unfunded mandates**, and the Unfunded Mandates Reform Act (1995) obliges the Congressional Budget Office to determine when a mandate will cost a state more than $50 million to carry out. Yet unfunded mandates remain an issue between the state and federal governments, even though many of the state politicians who complain about them are also happy to take nearly "free" money from Washington, D.C., in the form of grants.

One unfunded mandate that led to much dissension was the **Real ID Act** of 2005. This act called for uniformity in state identity documents. From the standpoint of the Department of Homeland Security, Real ID is a nationwide effort intended to prevent terrorism, reduce fraud, and improve the reliability and accuracy of identification documents that state governments issue. Critics, however, said that the mandate amounted to a national identity card and heightened the possibility of identity theft and the invasion of citizens' privacy. The state of Maine was the first to pass a resolution opposing acting on the mandate. Many other states followed Maine's example.

Mistrust of Federal Power

Why do states sometimes resent the growing power of the national government? One reason is that federal policies that call for national uniformity can infringe on the sentiments of majorities within certain states. In the early twenty-first century, for example, laws concerning marriage were left to the states. But suppose the Supreme Court declared laws against homosexual marriage unconstitutional. Probably a majority of the electorate in Massachusetts would approve, while a majority in Utah would not. It's because federal action has largely driven rapid change that liberals have tended to favor national action. For the same reason, conservatives (who usually prefer slower change) have favored keeping power at the state level.

Another basic reason states sometimes resist the growth of the national government is that states, being smaller, have a better understanding of their own particular problems. This is related to a fairly widespread feeling that the national government isn't best equipped to solve every problem. In the early twenty-first century, this feeling was spurred by the national intelligence failures that made the terrorist attacks of September 11, 2001, possible and, soon after, by the failure of the **Federal Emergency Management Agency** (FEMA) in the immediate aftermath of Hurricane Katrina (2005), which devastated New Orleans and other parts of the Gulf Coast.

IMMIGRATION

The question of illegal immigration has also pitted states against the federal government. The **Immigration Reform Act** of 1986 aimed to penalize employers who hired illegal immigrants, and it gave amnesty to most of the undocumented aliens in the country. But the problem of illegal immigration continued to grow. Ten years later, the **Immigration and Naturalization Service** estimated that there were some 5 million people in the United States illegally. Another ten years later, in 2006, that number had doubled.

People of different political persuasions disagreed about how to respond to illegal immigration, but everyone seemed to agree that the federal government had failed in one of its most basic chores: to control the borders. Following the terrorist attacks of 2001, the federal government did move to gain greater control over the borders, and the number of apprehensions of illegal immigrants working in the country increased.

Sometimes concerns about immigration are dismissed as the stuff of simple bigotry, but there is no question that immigration has changed the United States since the mid-1960s, when President Lyndon Johnson signed the **Immigration and Nationality Act of 1965**. In addition to dramatically increasing the number of immigrants legally allowed into the nation each year (in the early 1920s, restrictions were placed on immigration), this legislation led to a great shift in the origins of most immigrants, with many fewer coming from Western Europe and many more coming from Latin America and Asia. Since 1965, the United States has experienced the most dramatic immigrant growth in its history, with about 1 million immigrants entering the country legally and perhaps as many entering illegally through the late 1990s and early 2000s.

In 2007, President George W. Bush, with allies in the two major parties, sought to pass comprehensive immigration reform. The reform proposal failed, mainly because many in Congress and in the conservative media argued that, like the law of 1986, this prospective legislation would give amnesty to the some 12 million people in the nation illegally. President Bush argued that he was not proposing amnesty; he said that workers who had "entered the country illegally and workers who have overstayed their visas must pay a substantial penalty for their illegal conduct" and must learn English, pay back taxes, pass a background check, and go to the "back of the line" when applying for citizenship. But because Bush's plan did not call for deportation of people in the country illegally, it could not escape the "amnesty" label, and it never came to fruition. The only immigration bill that did pass in 2006 provided for the construction of a fence, seven hundred miles long, on the U.S.-Mexico border.

Both of the major parties, like most Americans, know that immigration is good for the country. Well-educated immigrants have greatly contributed to American technology, and the labor of low-skilled immigrants has helped to keep food and other basic goods relatively inexpensive. Immigrants also offset the numerical decline, as a result of **baby boomers** aging and declining birthrates, of the native-born American population. Americans and politicians who are less concerned about immigration rates further point out that illegal immigrants do pay taxes—at the gas pump, at restaurants, at stores, and so on.

On the other hand, Americans and politicians who want greater controls over immigration argue that illegal immigrants take more out of the economy than they put in; they rely on tax-payer-supported health care, education, and other benefits. These observers also argue that inexpensive immigrant labor lowers pay rates generally. For example, a college student who might previously have charged $10 an hour for mowing lawns but who now faces immigrant competition may have to lower his fee to $7.00 an hour.

While the federal government has acted on the immigration issue, states and localities have also felt compelled to confront the problem. By 2008, some states required recipients of state welfare benefits to prove their American citizenship, and some states denied public university benefits to the children of illegal immigrants.

About ten years before, nearly 60 percent of California's voters had empowered their state to deny most public services to people in the country illegally by voting in favor of **Proposition 187**. Here, once again, the theme of power struggles between states and the federal government (primarily federal judges) appears: a federal court soon gutted the proposition approved by a large majority of California's voters. A federal judge also declared unconstitutional ordinances passed by the city council of Hazelton, Pennsylvania, which fined landlords for renting apartments to people in the country illegally.

THE NEW FEDERALISM

Although observers have noted a gradual trend of **devolution** of powers (a shifting of powers) from the federal government to the states since the 1980s, represented by an increase in numbers of block grants relative to categorical grants, federalism seems to have become less a partisan issue than in previous decades, thus the term political scientists sometimes use: the *new federalism*. Whereas, since the 1930s, Democrats had been seen as the party of "big government," it was a Democratic president, Bill Clinton, who devolved considerable power over welfare programs to the states (the **Personal Responsibility and Work Opportunity Reconciliation Act** of 1996), and it was a Republican president, George W. Bush, who greatly increased the presence of the federal government in education (the No Child Left Behind Act). Political rhetoric aside, both major parties now seem to favor a big federal government.

Chapter 10

Public Opinion
and Political Socialization:
The Case of the 2008 Election

No matter how one sliced it, the presidential election of 2008 was going to be historic. Either a woman, Sarah Palin (a Republican from Alaska), would be the first female vice president in history, or an American with an African father, Democrat Barack Obama, would be president. The earlier chapters were written during the campaign; this chapter was written in the days following Obama's victory. To illustrate relevant points, we will refer to the 2008 presidential campaign and election in this final chapter.

PUBLIC OPINION

The term *public opinion* is self-explanatory. It refers to the public's opinion about something. But after this, things get more complicated. On some matters, such as whether adult citizens should have the right to vote, there is **consensus opinion**, meaning that a large majority of Americans favor it. On other matters—whether, say, people in the country illegally should be given a path to citizenship or be deported—there is **divided opinion**, meaning simply that people disagree.

Sometimes public opinion changes. In the 1950s, the idea of homosexual marriage was not controversial. If the idea had been presented, almost everybody would have opposed it. There was a consensus of opinion. The election of 2008 showed that a majority of Americans still opposed gay marriage; every major presidential and vice-presidential candidate expressed opposition to it. But the minority of Americans that favored gay marriage had become substantial. This pointed to divided opinion. As of 2008, two states (Connecticut and

Massachusetts) allowed it, while voters in California passed an amendment to the state constitution making gay marriage illegal.

One thing to note about public opinion is that politicians who want to be elected must pay attention to it—in words if not always in action. By large majorities Americans favor the death penalty for murder, yet in 2005 the number of executions for murder was sixty while some sixteen thousand Americans were murdered. It is often easier for a politician to claim to support views held by constituents than it is to bring those views into political reality.

Sampling Public Opinion

Observers of American political life know that **polling** has become something of a cultural obsession since its inception in the 1930s, particularly because computers have made polling more sophisticated. Within a few days of the 2008 election, national polling organizations had begun taking polls related to the presidential election of 2012. One poll showed that 66 percent of Republican men and 61 percent of Republican women favored Sarah Palin—the defeated vice-presidential nominee—to be the GOP's presidential nominee in 2012. Democrats, on the other hand, had a low opinion of Palin, with 81 percent having an unfavorable view of her.

Theory of Polling

Pollsters do their work by randomly sampling residents of the country who represent different elements of the population—for example, Catholics, union members, Hispanics, and stay-at-home moms. According to the theory of **sampling**, the traits of individuals within representative groups generally reflect the views of the larger group.

The theory behind polling relies on three key factors. One, already mentioned, is **random selection**, meaning that the person who is selected had no better or worse chance than others of being chosen. Next, the **size** of the sample population must be sufficiently large to represent the large and diverse population of the United States. The third factor to consider is **variation**. For example, a man may be more conservative on a particular matter than the groups he's associated with. Because people and their views are complicated, pollsters do not present their work as being 100 percent accurate, but modern polling usually is accurate within a few percentage points. For example, an average of all national polls on the presidential election of 2008 showed Barack Obama leading his competitor, John McCain, by nearly 8 percentage points; Obama won by a little less than 7 percentage points. The polls, in other words, were very close to being accurate.

Statistics in Polling

Early on in this book, we discussed the **majoritarian** and **pluralist** models of democracy. Observers who take the majoritarian view tend to think that the public is fairly well informed and holds consistent views on public matters. However, polls lend more support to the pluralist position, which maintains that the public is not very well informed and can change its views on issues relatively quickly.

On some matters, polls reveal a **skewed distribution** of opinion, meaning that a large majority of Americans favor or oppose something. In 2005, for example, some 64 percent of Americans favored the death penalty for murder. On other issues, however, pollsters see **bimodal distribution**, which points to an almost evenly divided public. A **normal distribution**, when graphed, shows a bell curve—the fewest numbers of people being at the extremes and the highest number of respondents being in the middle. When Americans are asked about their political views, a normal distribution is usually the result: a few describe themselves as very liberal or very conservative, more define themselves as liberal or conservative, and the highest number call themselves moderate.

A **stable distribution** refers to opinion stability over time. For example, a large majority of American have long favored the death penalty for murder. On the other hand, some opinions change relatively quickly. In 1994 fewer than 50 percent of Americans approved of interracial marriage. Ten years later, that number had risen to about 75 percent. Clearly, Barack Obama's election to the presidency signaled that American feelings about race had changed dramatically in the space of a few decades.

One challenge pollsters have faced in recent years is the public's increasing unwillingness to answer the phone when pollsters call. Thanks to innovations such as caller-ID, people can identify callers and often do not answer calls from sources they do not know. This is largely a response to telemarketing, which many people consider a nuisance. As a result, by 2008 some 80 percent of telephone calls from pollsters went unanswered.

POLITICAL SOCIALIZATION

Where do people get their political ideas in the first place? Political scientists say that people pick up their views as a result of **political socialization**. Students of political socialization refer to **primary principles** (the idea that things learned earliest are learned best) and **structuring principles** (the idea that early learning shapes later learning). Obviously, many early memories are shaped by families. Many future adults who were young children during the election of 2008 will remember hearing adults discuss the election. They may remember (depending on the views of the people they heard speaking) that the Democratic vice-presidential nominee was a foreign policy expert or a talkative "gaffe machine." They may remember the disappointment of some who felt that an untested, unqualified person (Obama) had been elected instead of a true war hero (John McCain). Or, conversely, they may remember the joy their parents or other adults felt when the agent of much-needed change (Obama) beat the symbol of an outmoded way of conducting political business (McCain).

It isn't surprising that if both parents identify with one party, the child will also (usually) adopt that party's identity. And if the child leaves the party, he or she is more likely to become an Independent than to join the other major party. That said, it should be noted that party loyalty does not usually go as deep as loyalty to a family's religion. Religion answers the basic questions about human existence. Political parties are more time-bound and given to rapid change.

School **teachers**, particularly at the high school and college levels, can affect a person's political views. When students find their assumptions challenged, they may find themselves exchanging or altering their ideas. **Communities** and **peers** also can have a significant effect on a person's political outlook. If everyone seems to feel the same way about a political candidate, it's difficult not to adopt that view. But what if a peer group takes a view that is at odds with the view of the overall community? Oftentimes, the peer group will prevail. Most people would prefer the approval and recognition of their close peers to the approval of people who are further removed from them or who do not share their interests.

In the election of 2008, the "youth vote" went overwhelmingly for Barack Obama. "Young people feel a lot of ownership in the Barack Obama presidency," one young voter said. "There's a general sense that Obama is our generation's president; that he thinks and operates in a way we can understand." Certainly, some young people voted for Obama because they understood his political positions and approved of them. But just as certainly, many young people voted for Obama because it became the thing for their peer group to do. Obama symbolized the tolerance, cool-headedness, and diversity that many young Americans valued.

FACTORS RELATED TO POLITICAL OPINIONS

Although individuals have their own unique experiences and personalities, it's also true that people of similar backgrounds and subcultures tend to have similar views. It's true, for instance, that in recent elections Mormons have voted Republican, and residents of Massachusetts have generally voted Democratic. In the presidential election of 2008, Utah—the state with the highest Mormon population—voted for John McCain 63 percent to Barack Obama's 34 percent. The numbers from Massachusetts were the opposite: 62 percent for Barack Obama, 36 percent for John McCain (with the remainder of the votes going to candidates from third parties). In the former case, it's easy to make the connection: Mormon faith encourages respect for authority and promotes a pro-life (or anti-abortion) outlook. These kinds of views are generally more compatible with the Republican Party (and the minority Constitution Union Party) than with the Democratic Party (or the Green Party). As for why Massachusetts is among the the most liberal states in the union, perhaps one explanation is that it has a long history of being associated with influential institutions of higher learning such as Harvard University, the Massachusetts Institute of Technology, and Williams College.

Although there are many well-educated Republicans, it is generally true that higher **education** is generally associated with more liberal political views. A study of university professors' political views, published in October 2007, showed that about 62 percent of university professors identified themselves as very liberal, liberal, or somewhat liberal, whereas just 19 percent identified themselves as somewhat conservative, conservative, or very conservative. (The rest identified themselves as political moderates.) One explanation is that education is often associated with questioning norms, learning about different viewpoints, and reflecting on the value of civil liberties. These kinds of activities lend themselves to a greater openness to change, and cultural and political change is most associated with the Democratic Party. During the 2008 presidential election, one of Barack Obama's best-known slogans was "Change You Can Believe In."

What about **income**? Generally speaking, the higher a person's income, the less favorable the person is to a government that interferes with the economy, either through taxation, regulation, or welfare programs. This favors the Republicans (and Libertarian Party). But higher-income people also tend to favor abortion rights. Thus they sometimes find themselves at odds with the **social conservative** wing of the Republican Party. During the election of 2008, many of these socially moderate Republicans were put off by Sarah Palin's strong opposition to abortion, even in cases of rape and incest.

The **region** a person lives in can also shape his or her political views. This has been true from the country's beginning. The manufacturing Northeast tended to favor tariffs, for example, while the South tended to oppose them. (Obviously, the greatest regional split in the nation's history manifested itself during the American Civil War.) Although regional differences are not always easy to explain, they certainly do exist, and it seems safe to say that rural people tend to be more conservative on moral questions than urban residents. In the election of 2008, Barack

Obama won the Pacific Coast (except for Alaska, Sarah Palin's home state), the upper Midwest, and the Northeast. John McCain won most of the South and most of "middle America," for example, Kansas and the Dakotas.

A person's **race** or **ethnicity** can also affect how he or she views politics. In the decades following the Civil War, African Americans favored the Republican Party because of its associations with anti-slavery and because it was the party of Abraham Lincoln. During the Great Depression of the 1930s, the Democratic Party came to be more associated with civil rights and help for the poor, and black Americans generally shifted their allegiance to it. In the election of 2008, Barack Obama received over 95 percent of the African American vote.

In recent decades, Hispanics have been the fastest-growing minority in the United States. Partly because the Democratic Party has seemed to pay more attention to minorities' interests and to the problems associated with low **economic status** (that is, lower incomes and levels of educational attainment), Hispanics tend to vote Democratic. In late 2007, nearly 60 percent of American Hispanics claimed to identify with the Democratic Party, and in the presidential election of the following year, about the same percentage voted for the Democrat, Barack Obama.

Also significant is **religion**, which informs a person's views about the moral order. As a rule, evangelical Protestants and Orthodox Jews are much more likely to oppose abortion and gay marriage than Unitarians and Reform Jews. During the election of 2008, Sarah Palin's socially conservative views on such questions sparked controversy, and some disapproved of Palin's longtime attendance at evangelical churches. Palin's counterpart, the Democrat Joseph Biden, called himself a Catholic and declared himself personally opposed to abortion, though he also opposed government restrictions on abortion.

Political scientists have also noted some political differences between the genders. Whereas men and women hold basically similar views on abortion rights (they support and oppose them in the same numbers), women are more likely to believe that government should supply jobs to people than men are. Not surprisingly, then, women tend to vote for the Democratic Party more than men do. In the 2008 election, a majority of women voted for Barack Obama, while a majority of white men voted for John McCain. Four years earlier, George W. Bush came close to getting 50 percent of the women's vote. There was much talk at the time about "security moms"—mothers worried about threats to the nation such as terrorism—and Republicans have a political edge on questions of national security. In the end, Bush got just 48 percent of the women's vote.

Ideology plays an obvious role in shaping one's political outlook. If one has an ideological commitment to minimal government and identifies himself as a libertarian, then in principle he will likely be opposed to the creation of a new government department. On the other hand, if one is a socialist and has an ideological commitment to economic equality via taxation and the redistribution of wealth, then that idea will shape that person's response to government initiatives. Not many Americans have strong ideological commitments, however. Most hold "liberal" views on some things and "conservative" views on other things. Opposition to the death penalty is usually seen as a liberal value, while opposition to abortion is usually considered a conservative value. But some people are pro-life in a fuller sense: they are anti-death penalty and anti-abortion.

To what extent is basic knowledge about American politics possessed in the country? Researchers have found that, generally, Americans do have a basic sense of how their government works, yet this knowledge is not evenly distributed. Whites, the elderly, and the well-off tend to be better informed than African Americans, the young, and the poor. Men also tend to possess more political knowledge than women, though women consistently vote in higher numbers than men. The single greatest factor, however, is **education** level. A well-educated African American woman, for example, is much more likely to be knowledgeable about the country's political life than a poor white male. (Political ideology does not seem to have much bearing on political knowledge.)

Some people may not have strong political feelings and may know little about politics, but if they hear about a government policy (proposed or actual), they may have a feeling about it, based on how they think it will affect them. Political scientists refer to this phenomenon as the **self-interest principle**. An avid hunter will probably react negatively to a politician's desire to restrict gun rights, a person who eats at McDonald's every day will likely oppose a city council's plan to place additional taxes on fast food, and a smoker is more likely than a nonsmoker to oppose a local law that makes smoking in cars illegal when children are in them.

Sometimes opinions are shaped by perceptions of the **leaders** who offer them. A young man may possess very little political knowledge but have good feelings about Democrats because that was the party of his loving grandparents. So if a Republican suggests a policy, he may oppose it, whereas he might approve of the same idea if a Democrat offers it. For another example, researchers have shown that African Americans are more willing to accept statements about the need for greater self-direction if the statements are offered by African American spokespersons.

Political leaders understand this, which is why they pay attention to **issue framing**—that is, the manner in which a topic is presented to the public. If a political leader wants to encourage rock musicians to be less provocative, for instance, he might enlist the help of a person with standing among rock musicians; a statement from a Washington insider is unlikely to have much effect. For the same reason, government public service announcements directed at the elderly tend to use imagery that is attractive to older people.

Related to this is what some scholars call the **lifestyle effect**—the tendency for people at different stages of life to take certain viewpoints. Older voters, for example, tend to be more conservative. Of course, they may be convinced supporters of the Democratic Party, but they are less likely to favor the party's far left wing than are younger Democrats. We should also mention the **generational effect**—that is, the fact that certain events shape a particular generation's outlook. For example, baby boomers (Americans born between 1946 and 1964) tend to be cynical about government. This cynicism was partly shaped by the foreign disaster of the Vietnam War and the criminality of the Nixon administration at home.

AN ELECTION ABOUT TRUST

Although the amount of confidence, or **political trust**, Americans have in the country's political system and leadership changes from time to time, it seems safe to say that confidence in the nation's leaders has not been high in recent decades. A survey in 2007 showed that just 24 percent of the population thought that politicians "do the right thing" most or all of the time. The better news is that 75 percent believed that politicians acted correctly *part* of the time. Some observers worry about the future of a country in which a large majority of the population does not have a high view of the nation's leaders. Others say that democracy needs a skeptical public to work well because skeptical people will hold politicians accountable for their deeds and actions. The danger of widespread cynicism, of course, is the growth of political apathy.

In any case, there's no question that the presidential election of 2008 was, in many ways, about trust. John McCain told the American people that he could be trusted because he had experience and a long record of public service. Barack Obama inspired trust by presenting new ideas in eloquent terms, by effectively presenting himself as a steady personality, and by surrounding himself with accomplished advisors.

Following the election, as Obama began to assemble the people who would serve in his administration, he held frequent news conferences. At that time, the country was experiencing considerable economic turmoil. Among Obama's key goals was to inspire trust.

Practice Tests

CLEP American Government

Practice Test 1

CLEP American Government

This test is also on CD-ROM in our special interactive
CLEP American Government TestWare®

(Answer sheets appear in the back of this book.)

TIME: 90 Minutes
100 Questions

DIRECTIONS: Each of the questions or incomplete statements below
is followed by five possible answers or completions. Select the best
choice in each case and fill in the corresponding oval on the answer
sheet.

---

1. What type of voting system became well known immediately following
    the 2000 election?

    (A) Lever voting machines

    (B) Punch cards

    (C) Electronic

    (D) Optical scan

    (E) Internet voting

2. A person who votes based on what a candidate says he or she will do in
    the future is said to be

    (A) engaging in retrospective voting

    (B) responding to attack ads

    (C) responding to contrast ads

    (D) engaging in prospective voting

    (E) responding to name recognition

3. Should presidential candidates receive an equal number of electoral votes, the election is decided by

    (A) the legislatures of Maine and Nebraska

    (B) a constitutional convention

    (C) the House of Representatives

    (D) the Senate

    (E) the Supreme Court

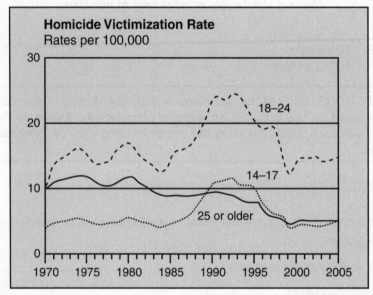

Source: Bureau of Justice Statistics (2008)

4. The graph above MOST suggests which of the following?

    (A) Murder rates rose notably in the first years of the twenty-first century.

    (B) Murder is a crime primarily associated with teenagers.

    (C) On the whole, the murder rate in the United States has remained steady since the late 1960s.

    (D) The murder rate remained fairly steady between 2000 and 2005.

    (E) High incarceration rates have led to a reduction in the murder rate.

5. "A form of government in which the people (defined broadly to include all adults or narrowly to exclude women and slaves, for example) are the ultimate political authority." These words best define what political arrangement?

    (A) Republicanism   (D) Constitutional monarchy

    (B) Democracy   (E) Mobocracy

    (C) One person, one vote

6. New England's town meetings are examples of

    (A) a parliamentary system   (D) democratic socialism

    (B) oligarchy   (E) concurrence

    (C) direct democracy

7. Under the pen name "Publius," Alexander Hamilton, James Madison, and John Jay wrote

    (A) *The Federalist Papers*

    (B) *The Anti-Federalist Papers*

    (C) *Common Sense*

    (D) *Leviathan*

    (E) *Second Treatise on Government*

8. In the seventeenth century, the signers of which of the following documents agreed to live under the colony's recognized authority and to wait for a royal charter, such as the Virginians had?

    (A) The Mayflower Compact

    (B) The Magna Carta

    (C) *The Federalist*

    (D) The English Bill of Rights

    (E) The Marshall Plan

9.   The last state to ratify the U.S. Constitution was

   (A) Delaware   (D) Vermont

   (B) New York   (E) Rhode Island

   (C) Pennsylvania

10. The purpose of the electoral college is to

   (A) decide in disputes between the executive and judiciary branches

   (B) choose the U.S. president

   (C) break tie votes in the Senate

   (D) promote higher education

   (E) regulate state election policies

11. In the debates over the Constitution, federalists and anti-federalists spoke
     of factions the way we today speak of

   (A) delegates   (D) interest groups

   (B) earmarks   (E) caucuses

   (C) executive orders

12. "All Bills for raising revenue shall originate in the House of Representa-
     tives." These words appear in which article of the U.S. Constitution?

   (A) Article 1   (D) Article 4

   (B) Article 2   (E) Article 5

   (C) Article 3

13. The English philosopher whose words are heavily drawn on in the Decla-
     ration of Independence was

   (A) Thomas Hobbes   (D) David Hume

   (B) John Locke   (E) Adam Smith

   (C) Edmund Burke

14. Insofar as the Constitution is concerned, members of Congress receive payment for their work from

    (A) their political parties   (D) political gifts

    (B) their state legislatures   (E) interest groups

    (C) the U.S. Treasury

15. The vice president of the United States is the president of what government body?

    (A) Federal judiciary

    (B) Senate

    (C) House of Representatives

    (D) Department of Homeland Security

    (E) Military

16. What is the minimum age specified in the Constitution for members of the House of Representatives?

    (A) 18   (D) 28

    (B) 20   (E) 30

    (C) 25

17. In recent decades, which of the following states has relied most heavily on mail-in voting?

    (A) Alabama   (D) Montana

    (B) Connecticut   (E) Oregon

    (C) Delaware

18. In which of the nation's founding documents could one point to an "elastic clause" to justify the existence of vast government agencies such as the Department of Health and Human Services?

    (A) The Articles of Confederation

    (B) Federalist Number 10

    (C) The Bill of Rights

    (D) The Constitution

    (E) *Marbury v. Madison*

19. The Tenth Amendment to the Constitution states that government powers "not delegated to the United States by the Constitution, nor prohibited by it to the States," are reserved for the

    (A) courts

    (B) political parties

    (C) state legislatures only

    (D) state legislatures and the people

    (E) state legislatures, the people, and the courts

20. The term *administrative discretion* refers to which of the following?

    (A) The president sets the nation's political agenda.

    (B) Congress sets guidelines for government agencies to follow.

    (C) One chamber of Congress fails to pass a bill that does pass in the other chamber.

    (D) Standing committees determine what bills will and will not receive attention.

    (E) Federal courts can declare unconstitutional laws passed by Congress and signed by presidents.

21. The Real ID Act of 2005 was an example of

    (A) a block grant   (D) cooperative federalism

    (B) an unfunded mandate   (E) Project Head Start

    (C) a categorical grant

22. Senators have the power to "talk a bill to death." What is the formal term for this procedure?

    (A) Filibuster   (D) Anarchism

    (B) Concurrence   (E) Gridlock

    (C) Cloture

23. A piece of legislation proposed to Congress is called

    (A) a docket   (D) casework

    (B) an earmark   (E) a lobby

    (C) a bill

24. What do unanimous consent agreements accomplish?

    (A) They move legislation quickly through the House committee system.

    (B) They provide for political party unanimity at nominating conventions.

    (C) They meld various concurrent opinions into a single document.

    (D) They provide for unanimous votes in the Senate.

    (E) They end debate in the Senate.

25. Article I is the longest section contained in the U.S. Constitution. What is the subject matter of this article?

    (A) Congress   (D) State governments

    (B) The Supreme Court   (E) The presidency

    (C) The military

26. An interest group perceives a problem and then works to encourage legislation that addresses the problem. Interest groups can legally promote their agendas by doing all of the following EXCEPT

    (A) paying a legislator in exchange for a vote in favor of the interest group

    (B) using the interest group's legislative power to swing the vote

    (C) writing letters to the president

    (D) using letters, e-mails, or phone calls to get the legislator's attention

    (E) organizing peaceful protests

27. When a bill has passed through a subcommittee, a full committee, and both Congressional houses, the president can still kill the bill via veto. What must happen for a presidential veto to be overturned?

    (A) A two-thirds vote must occur in both Congressional chambers.

    (B) A presidential veto cannot be overturned.

    (C) A two-thirds vote must occur in the Senate alone.

    (D) The president's cabinet may override his decision with a majority vote.

    (E) A two-thirds vote must occur in the House of Representatives.

28. If a president neither signs nor vetoes a piece of legislation within 10 days and Congress remains in session, what becomes of the bill?

    (A) It is pocket vetoed.

    (B) It becomes law.

    (C) It is referred to the states.

    (D) It is returned to the relevant Congressional standing committees.

    (E) It is referred to the courts.

29. *Gerrymandering* refers to the

    (A) political agreements made in Congressional committees to facilitate a bill's success

    (B) creation of a Congressional district to ensure the election of a person from a certain political party or ethnic or racial group

    (C) process of negotiation between the White House and Congress on proposed legislation

    (D) process that leads to a constitutional amendment

    (E) ways minorities were historically prevented from voting

30. Which of the following can most easily practice *home style*?

    (A) Presidents

    (B) Democratic senators

    (C) Republican senators

    (D) Members of the House of Representatives

    (E) Department secretaries, such as the secretary of the Department of Homeland Security

31. A Congressperson's franking privileges pertain to

    (A) international travel related to official business

    (B) official mail

    (C) the right to subpoena government officials

    (D) access to the Congressional gym

    (E) immunity from prosecution for things said in the course of a debate

32. Agreements between the United States and foreign nations can be made by a president's administration, but for the agreement to go into effect it must have the concurrence of

   (A) a majority of the Senate

   (B) a majority of the House and Senate

   (C) two-thirds of the Senate alone

   (D) two-thirds of both Congressional chambers

   (E) two-thirds of the president's cabinet members

33. The highest person in the military's chain of command is the

   (A) chairman of the Joint Chiefs of Staff

   (B) majority leader of the Senate

   (C) director of the Central Intelligence Agency

   (D) Speaker of the House of Representatives

   (E) U.S. president

34. A state's representation in the electoral college most directly reflects

   (A) its population

   (B) the combined number of the state's U.S. representatives and senators

   (C) a complicated formula taking into account population and economic output

   (D) success in selecting victorious political candidates in the past

   (E) political traditions that will likely be found unconstitutional when successfully challenged in court

35. Through the years, different presidents have held different levels of power vis-à-vis Congress, but the Constitution's framers wanted the U.S. president to

   (A) have power equivalent to the Speaker of the House

   (B) have power equivalent to the chief justice of the Supreme Court

   (C) have power equivalent to that of England's monarchs

   (D) have power that could check, but also could be checked by, other branches of government

   (E) have political power equivalent to the four largest state governors

36. Presidents can shape the nation's legislative agenda in all of the following ways EXCEPT

    (A) requiring the vice president, as president of the Senate, to participate in Senate votes

    (B) spelling out a legislative agenda in a State of the Union address

    (C) as leader of his (or her) political party, shaping the legislative direction of that party in Congress

    (D) using or threatening to use the veto

    (E) lobbying Congress members

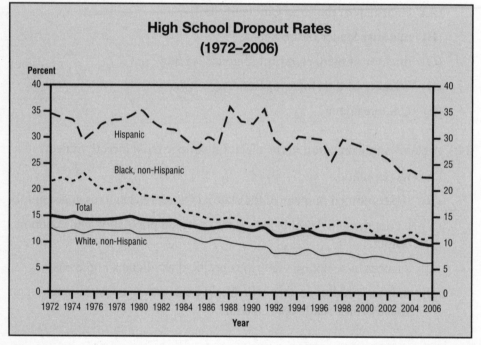

Source: National Center for Education Statistics

37. The above graph showing high school dropout rates suggests which of the following?

    (A) High school dropout rates have declined dramatically since the Civil Rights Movement.

    (B) Recent immigrants have a higher dropout rate than native-born Americans.

(C) The poor have substantially higher dropout rates than the middle class.

(D) Crime and dropout rates are correlated.

(E) The high school dropout rate is not a matter of national concern.

38. In times of national emergency, or when the government needs to act quickly and flexibly, Congress has done what with its federal powers?

(A) Delegated them to the president

(B) Delegated them to the courts

(C) Delegated them to the state legislatures

(D) Delegated them to local jurisdictions

(E) Delegated them to town mayors

39. According to the Constitution, the vice president gains the presidency if the president dies or is incapacitated. According to the Presidential Succession Act of 1947, if both the president and vice president are incapacitated, who rises to the presidency?

(A) The president pro tempore of the Senate

(B) The most senior member of the majority party in the Senate

(C) The speaker of the House of Representatives

(D) The mayor of Washington, D.C.

(E) The secretary of state

> **Which Bills?**
>
> - All Bills
> - Bills with Floor Action
> - Enrolled Bills
>
> **From Where?**
>
> - Both House and Senate
> - House Bills Only
> - Senate Bills Only

Source: Library of Congress (2008)

40. The item above is taken from a Library of Congress Web page (2008). To what general political process does the information refer?

    (A) Ratifying a constitutional amendment

    (B) Overriding a presidential veto

    (C) Passing legislation

    (D) Ending a filibuster

    (E) Regulating elections

41. According to a Supreme Court decision in 2008, the Second Amendment

    (A) should be understood to apply alone to state militias, that is, the National Guard

    (B) should be understood to apply to individuals and their right to possess firearms

    (C) allows for the right of the people to assemble peaceably and to make grievances known to the government

    (D) allows for the free exercise of religion

    (E) prohibits "excessive bail" to be imposed on an arrested person

42. The Bill of Rights' establishment clause

    (A) establishes the right against self-incrimination

    (B) gives the people the right to protest against government establishments

    (C) prohibits the federal government from promoting one religion as the religion of the state

    (D) establishes that people cannot be held after arrest without an indictment being brought against them

    (E) establishes that powers not expressly given to the federal government are left to the states or the people

43. The Supreme Court case *Engel v. Vitale* (1962)

    (A) made abortion legal across the country

    (B) made laws against contraception illegal

    (C) allowed the president to pursue anticommunist measures in Vietnam

    (D) eliminated prayer organized by public schools

    (E) required the desegregation of public schools

44. Charles Schenck was arrested and charged with the federal crime of trying to inhibit military recruitment in a time of war. What was the Supreme Court's decision in the resulting case, *Schenck v. United States* (1919)?

    (A) Schenck's right to speak and act against the war was protected by the First Amendment, though within vague limits.

    (B) Schenck's speech and action had presented a public danger in a time of war, and his conviction was upheld.

    (C) Schenck, not being a citizen, was deported before the case was decided.

    (D) A sharply divided court allowed Schenck's antiwar speech in the abstract but not when aimed at individuals who might be recruited.

    (E) The right to freedom of speech is absolute and the government was wrong to arrest him.

45. Which of the following acts, signed by President Bill Clinton, resulted in a balanced budget and a surplus for the first time since the end of the 1960s?

    (A) Budget and Impoundment Control Act

    (B) Gramm-Rudman Act

    (C) Balanced Budget Act

    (D) Patriot Act

    (E) Budgetary Restraint and Fiscal Responsibility Act

46. The effect of the Supreme Court case *McCulloch v. Maryland* was to

    (A) strengthen federal power at the expense of state power

    (B) strengthen state power at the expense of federal power

    (C) strengthen the Senate at the expense of the House

    (D) strengthen the House at the expense of the Senate

    (E) strengthen the presidency at the expense of Congress

47. The theory of sampling relies on which of the following key factors?

    (A) Random selection, sample size, and variation

    (B) Skewed, bimodal, and normal distributions

    (C) Mean, median, and mode

    (D) Traits, sentiment, and sample size

    (E) Demographics, geography, and political affiliation

48. Each of the following is a kind of third party EXCEPT

    (A) an economic protest party

    (B) an ideological party

    (C) an issue party

    (D) a verification party

    (E) a factional party

49. Which candidate is widely blamed by Democrats for being a spoiler in the 2000 presidential campaign?

   (A) Bernie Sanders

   (B) Al Gore

   (C) Joseph Lieberman

   (D) Howard Dean

   (E) Ralph Nader

50. The Grand Old Party (GOP) is a lesser-used name for what political party?

   (A) Democratic

   (B) Republican

   (C) Whig

   (D) Reform

   (E) Libertarian

51. Which of the following presidential candidates from the last two decades of the twentieth century is most closely associated with raising the issue of the federal government's budget deficit?

   (A) Ross Perot

   (B) George H. W. Bush

   (C) Bill Clinton

   (D) John Kerry

   (E) John Edwards

52. The States' Rights Democratic Party, also called the Dixiecrat Party, split from the Democratic Party in 1948 because it opposed

   (A) the New Deal

   (B) racial desegregation

   (C) war with China

   (D) war with Germany

   (E) the Democratic Party's reluctance to pursue civil rights legislation

53. All of the following are reasons two major parties dominate American politics EXCEPT

    (A) American voters tend to be centrist in their political outlook

    (B) Victory in electoral college votes pushes the political system toward two parties

    (C) Congressional seats are winner-take-all

    (D) Campaign financing is biased against third parties

    (E) Several state constitutions prohibit more than two political parties

54. What twentieth-century presidential candidate received fewer votes than his opponent but still won the election?

    (A) Harry Truman   (D) Gerald Ford

    (B) Woodrow Wilson   (E) George W. Bush

    (C) John F. Kennedy

55. *Marble-cake federalism* is a term political scientists use to describe

    (A) dual federalism   (D) sovereign federalism

    (B) unitary federalism   (E) layer-cake federalism

    (C) cooperative federalism

56. Which act forbade discrimination on the basis of race, color, gender, religion, or national origin?

    (A) Voting Rights Act of 1965

    (B) Civil Rights Act of 1964

    (C) Civil Rights Act of 1968

    (D) Fair Treatment Act

    (E) Equal Protection Act

57. What Supreme Court case nullified state laws that made first-trimester abortion illegal?

   (A) *Plessy v. Ferguson*

   (B) *Stenberg v. Carhart*

   (C) *Webster v. Reproductive Health Services*

   (D) *Roe v. Wade*

   (E) *Dred Scott v. Sanford*

58. Who was the first female speaker of the House of Representatives?

   (A) Condoleezza Rice

   (B) Sarah Palin

   (C) Hillary Rodham Clinton

   (D) Sandra Day O'Connor

   (E) Nancy Pelosi

59. The tendency of different races to live in separate communities and, therefore, to attend different schools is referred to as

   (A) de jure segregation   (D) de facto segregation

   (B) racial profiling   (E) busing

   (C) Jim Crow

60. The political system that divides political power between states and a federal government is referred to as

   (A) socialism   (D) democracy

   (B) right wing   (E) sovereignty

   (C) federalism

61. The Fifteenth Amendment made it unconstitutional to prevent citizens from voting based on race or skin color. Which of the following is an example of an initiative set up by some states to continue to prevent African Americans from voting?

   (A) Affirmative action   (D) Busing

   (B) Apartheid   (E) Poll taxes

   (C) Jim Crow laws

62. Which of the following acts penalized employers who hired illegal immigrants and gave amnesty to most of the undocumented aliens in the country?

    (A) Volstead Act

    (B) Immigration and Nationality Act

    (C) Homeland Labor Act

    (D) Immigration Reform and Control Act of 1986

    (E) Patriot's Initiative

63. How many votes are necessary for a unanimous consent agreement to be passed in the Senate?

    (A) Three-quarters majority   (D) 70 percent

    (B) Two-thirds majority   (E) 90 percent

    (C) 100 percent

64. All of the following programs were part of President Lyndon Johnson's Great Society and war on poverty programs EXCEPT

    (A) Medicare

    (B) Medicaid

    (C) Project Head Start

    (D) Social Security

    (E) Housing and Urban Development

65. Which of the following types of federal funding do states prefer?

    (A) Categorical grants   (D) Loans

    (B) Block grants   (E) Fiscal grants

    (C) Unfunded mandates

66. For a case to be heard in the Supreme Court, the Court must issue a call for a lower court to send to the Supreme Court the records related to the case. This call is referred to as a

    (A) amicus curiae brief   (D) writ of certiorari

    (B) court secondary appeal   (E) request of formal appeal

    (C) manifest subpoena

67. What Supreme Court case in 1966 guaranteed that no individual "shall be compelled in any criminal case to be a witness against himself"?

    (A) *Miranda v. Arizona*

    (B) *Duncan v. Louisiana*

    (C) *Gideon v. Wainwright*

    (D) *Roe v. Wade*

    (E) *Marbury v. Madison*

68. The Bill of Rights guarantees all of the following EXCEPT

    (A) the freedom of religion

    (B) the right to a fair trial

    (C) powers not delegated to the federal government by the Constitution are reserved to the states

    (D) the right to bear arms

    (E) the right of women to vote

69. Which of the following is NOT true of state militias?

    (A) They are established to enforce the will of the people.

    (B) They are used to put down insurrections.

    (C) They have been superseded by the National Guard.

    (D) They are supposed to resist invasions.

    (E) They are discussed in Article 1 of the Constitution.

70. To prevent jurors from hearing about a trial in the media, judges will sometimes impose what restriction on journalists?

    (A) Gag order

    (B) Writ of prevention

    (C) Discretion order

    (D) Order of cessation

    (E) Noncompliance order

71. The Supreme Court's power to determine what is and what is not constitutional is referred to as

    (A) judicial temperament

    (B) senatorial courtesy

    (C) judicial activism

    (D) judicial review

    (E) judicial implementation

72. All of the following are examples of legal symbolic expression EXCEPT

    (A) burning a draft card

    (B) burning a flag

    (C) libeling of a congressman in a newspaper editorial

    (D) wearing a black arm band in protest of war

    (E) wearing a T-shirt that reads, "The president is a fool"

73. Evidence obtained illegally cannot be used against a defendant. This principle is known as the

    (A) Miranda rule   (D) majority rule

    (B) exclusionary rule   (E) trial rule

    (C) solicitor's rule

74. In 1992 an independent ran for president. He advocated anti-incumbency and challenged the government to deal with the federal budget deficit. This candidate showed that third parties can provide a political outlet for dissident voters. His name was

    (A) Ralph Nader   (D) William Jennings Bryan

    (B) Ross Perot   (E) Eugene Debs

    (C) James Weaver

75. A theory of government that "emphasizes government-directed equalization of wealth and government control of industry" is referred to as

    (A) democracy   (D) monarchy

    (B) communism   (E) socialism

    (C) theocracy

76. Which of the following is NOT related to political activity on behalf of gender equality?

    (A) Equal Rights Amendment

    (B) Equal Pay Act

    (C) Title VII of the Civil Rights Act of 1964

    (D) *Gibbons v. Ogden*

    (E) *Faragher v. City of Boca Raton*

77. Which of the following courts is responsible for granting government agents the authority to post surveillance on suspected spies?

    (A) trial courts

    (B) FISC

    (C) appellate courts

    (D) circuit courts

    (E) common law courts

78. Which of the following terms refers to a potential check on federal judicial power?

    (A) Review

    (B) Implementation

    (C) Restraint

    (D) Temperament

    (E) Activism

79. In the Mayflower Compact, we see the emergence of two enduring principles important to the American political system: (1) a willingness to live under the rule of law and (2)

    (A) a bicameral legislature

    (B) separation of powers

    (C) checks and balances

    (D) separation of church and state

    (E) government by the consent of the governed

80. Civil liberties are freedoms guaranteed by the Constitution. Because civil liberties set limits on the extent to which the government can control citizens' affairs, they are sometimes referred to as

    (A) civil rights

    (B) inalienable rights

    (C) negative rights

    (D) positive rights

    (E) key rights

81. Which of the following cases stressed government neutrality toward religion?

    (A) *Agostini v. Felton*

    (B) *Zelmon v. Simmons-Harris*

    (C) *Engle v. Vitale*

    (D) *Lynch v. Donnelly*

    (E) *Lemon v. Kurtzman*

82. According to a Supreme Court decision, the clear-and-present-danger test prohibited what type of action?

    (A) Speaking against the government during wartime

    (B) Expressing a threatening, countercultural idea

    (C) Symbolically protesting a federal decision

    (D) Using provocative language that upsets the peace

    (E) Speaking publicly about how to prevent potential terrorist threats

83. Which of the following allowed President Lyndon Johnson to "take all necessary measures to repel any armed attack against the forces of the United States and to prevent further aggression"?

    (A) War Powers Act

    (B) Anticipatory Defense Act

    (C) Hanoi Resolution

    (D) Gulf of Tonkin Resolution

    (E) Truman Doctrine

84. Which of the following was called for in the Virginia Plan?

    (A) A bicameral legislature with representatives based on population

    (B) Equal state representation in a unicameral legislature

    (C) Political power sharing between the president and Supreme Court chief justice

    (D) A two-person presidency

    (E) A one-year presidency

85. What has been called "the most penetrating commentary ever written on the [U.S.] Constitution"?

    (A) Federalist Number 10

    (B) *The Federalist Papers*

    (C) *Common Sense*

    (D) Federalist Number 51

    (E) Three-fifths Compromise

86. Which of the following was created in 1887 to "regulate railroads that moved goods and services from one state to another"?

    (A) Bureau of Indian Affairs

    (B) Surface Transportation Board

    (C) Bureau of Indian Education

    (D) Interstate Commerce Commission

    (E) Article 1, Section 8 of the U.S. Constitution

87. According to the U.S. Citizenship and Immigration Service, all of the following are basic requirements for citizenship for immigrants in the United States EXCEPT

    (A) the ability to function in English

    (B) basic knowledge of American history and government

    (C) commitment to the principles of the U.S. Constitution

    (D) a period of continuous residence in the United States

    (E) memorization of the Pledge of Allegiance and the National Anthem

88. Which of the following institutions produces the paper currency for the United States?

    (A) Federal Reserve System

    (B) U.S. Mint

    (C) Bureau of Engraving and Printing

    (D) Federal Reserve banks

    (E) U.S. Patent and Trademark Office

89. Congress has the power to do all of the following EXCEPT

    (A) regulate an army and navy

    (B) declare war

    (C) finance military operations

    (D) supply military operations for up to five years

    (E) raise an army

90. According to pollsters who sample populations,

    (A) traits of individuals within majority groups reflect the views of minority groups

    (B) polling can significantly affect the outcome of national and state elections

    (C) traits of individuals within representative groups reflect the views of the group

    (D) U.S. polls generally reflect the views of most Western countries

    (E) sampling results can change drastically in the span of a few decades

91. The term *political socialization* refers primarily to which of the following?

    (A) The social structure within the Senate and House of Representatives

    (B) Cooperation, communication, and collaboration among the executive, legislative, and judicial branches of government

    (C) Political discussion among peers and colleagues

    (D) The tendency for children to share political views with parents

    (E) The tendency for individuals to undergo shifts in political affiliation during a university education

Mark Richard Abbott	
Position:	Member National Science Board (24) Nsf
Status:	Appointed
Date of Announcement:	June 15, 2006
Date Nomination Sent to the Senate:	June 16, 2006
Date of Confirmation by the Senate:	August 3, 2006

Source: The White House Web site

92. The process summarized in the chart above points to

    (A) the requirement in Article 2 of the Constitution that the president shall obtain the "advice and consent of the Senate" when appointing officers to serve in the federal government

    (B) the requirement in Article 2 of the Constitution that all matters concerning education be supervised by Congress

    (C) the development of the unwritten Constitution

    (D) the relatively great power the president holds relative to senators

    (E) the long-standing political gridlock that has prevented the government from working efficiently

93. Which of the following voters is LEAST likely to favor Republican candidates?

    (A) A voter who is a religious conservative

    (B) A voter who opposes taxation, regulation, and welfare programs

    (C) A voter who opposes abortion

    (D) A voter who lives in a small town

    (E) A voter who supports a small military

94. What polling term is used to describe a situation in which a large majority of Americans favor or oppose an issue?

(A) Normal distribution

(B) Skewed distribution

(C) Bimodal distribution

(D) Weighted distribution

(E) Stable distribution

95. Which of the following statements is NOT true?

(A) Members of Congress cannot be arrested while Congress is in session except for treason, felony, and breach of peace.

(B) Members of Congress cannot be prosecuted outside Congress for words spoken during congressional speeches and debates.

(C) Members of Congress cannot be appointed to civil offices created during a contemporaneous term in Congress.

(D) Members of Congress cannot hold office for more than 24 years.

(E) Members of Congress are compensated for their labor from the U.S. Treasury.

96. The Constitution gives the power of formally initiating tax legislation to which of the following?

(A) The people

(B) The president

(C) The Senate

(D) The Supreme Court

(E) The House of Representatives

97. Regarding U.S. taxes, all of the following statements are true EXCEPT

(A) Americans pay some of the highest taxes in the world

(B) U.S. income tax is progressive

(C) sales taxes are regressive

(D) estate taxes are progressive

(E) employers are required to match what each of their employees pays in Medicare and Social Security taxes

98. The main fiscal duties of Congress are

    (A) minting currency and regulating the stock market

    (B) regulating the stock market and collecting taxes

    (C) collecting taxes and import duties, borrowing money, and paying the nation's debts

    (D) borrowing money, paying the nation's debts, and regulating the stock market

    (E) regulating corporations and minting currency

99. All of the following provide the government with financial resources EXCEPT

    (A) tariffs and duties   (D) bonds

    (B) public debt   (E) hidden taxes

    (C) payroll taxes

100. The Budget and Accounting Act of 1921 had which of the following results?

    (A) It changed the fiscal year from January 1 through December 31, to October 1 through September 30.

    (B) It standardized the accounting procedures and rules for U.S. business and corporations.

    (C) It required Congress to formulate spending bills and seek presidential approval.

    (D) It required that all U.S. corporations submit to budgetary and fiscal regulation.

    (E) It required that the president prepare the budget and seek Congressional approval.

Practice Test 1

CLEP American Government

Answer Key

1.	(B)	26.	(A)	51.	(A)	76.	(D)
2.	(D)	27.	(A)	52.	(B)	77.	(B)
3.	(C)	28.	(B)	53.	(E)	78.	(B)
4.	(D)	29.	(B)	54.	(E)	79.	(E)
5.	(B)	30.	(D)	55.	(C)	80.	(C)
6.	(C)	31.	(B)	56.	(B)	81.	(A)
7.	(A)	32.	(C)	57.	(D)	82.	(A)
8.	(A)	33.	(E)	58.	(E)	83.	(D)
9.	(E)	34.	(B)	59.	(D)	84.	(A)
10.	(B)	35.	(D)	60.	(C)	85.	(B)
11.	(D)	36.	(A)	61.	(E)	86.	(D)
12.	(A)	37.	(B)	62.	(D)	87.	(E)
13.	(B)	38.	(A)	63.	(C)	88.	(C)
14.	(C)	39.	(C)	64.	(D)	89.	(D)
15.	(B)	40.	(C)	65.	(B)	90.	(C)
16.	(C)	41.	(B)	66.	(D)	91.	(D)
17.	(E)	42.	(C)	67.	(A)	92.	(A)
18.	(D)	43.	(D)	68.	(E)	93.	(E)
19.	(D)	44.	(B)	69.	(A)	94.	(B)
20.	(B)	45.	(C)	70.	(A)	95.	(D)
21.	(B)	46.	(A)	71.	(D)	96.	(E)
22.	(A)	47.	(A)	72.	(A)	97.	(A)
23.	(C)	48.	(D)	73.	(B)	98.	(C)
24.	(E)	49.	(E)	74.	(B)	99.	(B)
25.	(A)	50.	(B)	75.	(E)	100.	(E)

Detailed Explanations of Answers

Practice Test 1

1.   **(B)**   Punch-card ballots created a controversy following the 2000 presidential election; the "hanging" and "dimpled" chads that resulted when voters did not punch through the cards completely were difficult for vote counters to assess.

2.   **(D)**   Prospective voting is forward-looking voting: a voter supports the candidate based on what the candidate plans to do once in office. Retrospective voting (A) is voting based on an informed view of a candidate's or political party's past. Attack (B) and contrast (C) ads are designed, respectively, to create negative feelings toward a candidate's opponent and to draw distinctions between opponents. Sometimes voters simply vote for a name they recognize (E). This is one of the many advantages incumbents have.

3.   **(C)**   The Constitution dictates that the House of Representatives decides the outcome of the election, with each state's delegation getting one vote. In a presidential election, Maine and Nebraska (A) divide their electoral votes according to districts rather than via a winner-take-all system. In the event of an electoral college tie, neither the Senate (D) nor a constitutional convention (B) is involved in the presidential selection process.

4.   **(D)**   The graph's lines show little or no variation between 2000 and 2005, indicating that the murder rate remained relatively stable during this time period. It is probably true that high incarceration rates led to a reduction in the murder rate after the mid-1990s (E), but that cannot be inferred from this graph. And while the graph shows that teenagers (dotted line on the graph) are often linked to homicide (B), it also shows it to be linked to people, primarily males, in their early twenties (dashed line).

5.   **(B)**   Democracy is a form a government in which the citizens, via their power to elect government officials, are the ultimate political authority. Republicanism (A) advocates a political system without a monarch. Some republics, such as North Korea, are far from democratic. One person, one vote (C) expresses a democratic ideal, but not all democracies have given the vote to every

adult. For example, before the Nineteenth Amendment to the Constitution was adopted in 1920, women in many American states did not have the vote. A constitutional monarchy (D) can be a democracy, but it does not fit the definition given in the question. A "mobocracy"—that is, rule by the mob—is what most of the Constitution's framers feared. Thus, they established an indirect democracy.

6. **(C)** The town meetings common in New England are examples of direct democracy because citizens make direct decisions about local affairs. A parliamentary system of government (A) can be found, for example, in Britain and Canada. An oligarchy (B) is a government run by a few people. Democratic socialism (D) is distinguished from tyrannical forms of socialism in that it guarantees basic rights (e.g., free speech) and free elections. Unlike the regime in Cuba, for example, a democratic socialist government can be voted out of office. Concurrence (E) refers to a judge's agreement with the decision of a majority of judges on the court, though for different reasons.

7. **(A)** Hamilton, Madison, and Jay wrote *The Federalist Papers*; the most quoted of these, Number 10, was written by Madison. *The Anti-Federalist Papers* (B) were written in opposition to ratification of the Constitution. Among the anti-federalists' pseudonyms were "Brutus" and "Federal Farmer." *Common Sense* (C) was written by Thomas Paine in the early stage of the Revolution. Its purpose was to rouse the American public against the British. *Leviathan* (D) is an important work in political philosophy by the English theorist Thomas Hobbes. The *Second Treatise on Government* (E) by John Locke, another work in political philosophy, was highly influential on the American revolutionaries and Constitutional framers.

8. **(A)** The Mayflower Compact was agreed to by Pilgrim leaders who had landed at Plymouth Rock in Massachusetts. The Magna Carta (B) is a document from medieval England that established certain rights for British citizens. *The Federalist* (C), also known as *The Federalist Papers*, was a series of essays written to address the American controversy over ratification of the U.S. Constitution. The English Bill of Rights of 1689 (D) set an important precedent for the Americans who desired a federal Bill of Rights. The Marshall Plan (E) was a post–World War II development program for Europe.

9. **(E)** Rhode Island was the last state to ratify the Constitution; the vote was very close: 34 to 32. Delaware (A) was the first state to ratify, with a unanimous vote. New York (B) was the eleventh state to ratify; its vote was 30 to 27. Pennsylvania (C) was the second state to ratify, voting 46 to 23. Vermont (D) was not an original colony. It became the fourteenth state in 1791.

10. **(B)**   Each state contributes to the electoral college a number of electors equal to its representation in Congress (the federal House and Senate). These electors determine the outcome of the presidential election; their votes are *usually*—but not necessarily—based on the states' popular vote. Disputes between the executive and judiciary branches of government (A) can be decided only by higher federal courts. The Supreme Court is the place of last appeal, barring Constitutional amendment. The vice president, who is the president of the Senate, breaks tie votes in the Senate (C). Various government agencies promote higher education (D) through grant programs, student loans, and so on. States and localities regulate elections (E) within guidelines set by the Constitution and federal law.

11. **(D)**   What were called *factions* in the early days of the United States are comparable to today's interest groups. But the concerns of special interest groups today are much more varied than were those of the late-eighteenth century factions. Political delegates (A) represent the wishes of the majority on whose behalf they vote. Earmarks (B) are federal funds appropriated by Congress for local projects. Executive orders (C) are presidential directives that direct and create laws and policies within the federal bureaucracy. Caucuses (E) are closed meetings of members of a political party who meet to decide on political candidates and policy positions.

12. **(A)**   Article 1 focuses on both chambers of Congress. Article 2 (B) focuses on the presidency, Article 3 (C) on the courts, Article 4 (D) on the states, and Article 5 (E) on amending the Constitution.

13. **(B)**   John Locke was an English philosopher, some of whose words are used almost verbatim in the early part of the Declaration of Independence. The framers would have been aware, to one extent or another, of the writings of Hobbes (A), Burke (C), Hume (D), and Smith (E), but none of these had a greater direct influence on the Declaration than did Locke.

14. **(C)**   Article 1, Section 6 of the Constitution says that "Senators and Representatives shall receive Compensation for their Services."

15. **(B)**   Article 1, Section 3 of the Constitution says that the vice president is president of the Senate, though he has no vote, except in the case of a tie vote in the Senate—in which case the vice president can cast the deciding vote.

16. **(C)**   Article 1, Section 2 of the Constitution reads (in part): "No Person shall be a Representative who shall not have attained to the Age of twenty five Years." Senators must be at least 30 years old (E). As a result of the Twenty-Sixth

Amendment to the Constitution, 18-year-olds have the right to vote (A). In this context, the specific ages of 20 (B) and 28 (D) are irrelevant.

17. **(E)** All states have mail-in voting—for deployed military personnel, for example. But much more than any state, Oregon has emphasized mail-in voting for residents who could easily vote at local polls.

18. **(D)** The elastic clause, also called the necessary and proper clause, is in Article 1 of the Constitution. It empowers Congress to "make all Laws which shall be necessary and proper for carrying into Execution the foregoing Powers, and all other Powers vested by this Constitution in the Government of the United States, or in any Department or Officer thereof."

19. **(D)** In full, the Tenth Amendment reads as follows: "The powers not delegated to the United States by the Constitution, nor prohibited by it to the States, are reserved to the States respectively, or to the people."

20. **(B)** The term *administrative discretion* refers to Congress's authority to set guidelines that government agencies must follow. The other answers, while true, do not address the question. Presidents often do set the political agenda (A), but Congress and the states can do so as well. Chambers of Congress can check one another (C), such as when one chamber rejects a bill that has passed in the other chamber. Standing committees (D), like committees generally, are able to move some bills forward and squelch others. Federal courts (E) do strike down laws as unconstitutional.

21. **(B)** When the federal government simply instructs states to meet a certain requirement without providing funding, it is known as an unfunded mandate. The Real ID Act of 2005 called for uniformity in state identity documents.

22. **(A)** A filibuster is a tactic used by senators attempting to halt the progress of a bill; it usually takes the form of extended talking or speech-giving such that no vote can be taken. Often the mere threat of a filibuster can determine how a bill proceeds. A filibuster may be an example of gridlock (E), the term used when government is unable, or seems unable, to get anything done. Anarchism (D) is a philosophical opposition to any kind of formal government. Concurrence (B) refers to a judge's agreement with a court majority's opinions, though for reasons other than those expressed by the majority. Cloture (C) is the Senate action that brings filibusters to an end.

23. **(C)** A piece of proposed legislation is called a bill. A docket (A) is a court's agenda. Earmarks (B) are federal funds set aside by Congress members for local projects. A Congress member's casework (D) refers to the member's

solving of problems for constituents. A lobby (E) is also an interest group—a group with a particular interest that seeks to influence legislation.

24. **(E)** Debate in the Senate can go on and on, but for the purposes of moving legislation along, Senators can agree to limit debate. The other answers are not relevant.

25. **(A)** Article 1 of the Constitution delineates the structure, duties, and authority of both houses of Congress. The Supreme Court (B) is discussed in Article III. The presidency (E) is discussed in Article II. There are no Constitutional articles devoted solely to the military (C) or state governments (D).

26. **(A)** Though it seems that lobbyists working for interest groups may sometimes "pay off" legislators with gifts, dinners, and so on, such an exchange is illegal.

27. **(A)** To override a presidential veto, both houses of Congress must vote in favor of the override by a two-thirds majority. Though it is usually difficult to override a president's veto, the procedure for doing so is clearly established in the Constitution; thus (B) is incorrect. A president's cabinet (D) has no formal say concerning a presidential veto.

28. **(B)** If a president takes no action on a bill within 10 days of receiving it and Congress is still in session, the bill becomes law. The other answer that might be tempting is (A): if a president does not sign a bill and Congress adjourns, then the bill has undergone a pocket veto.

29. **(B)** Gerrymandering is the creation of a congressional district to ensure the election of someone from a certain political party or ethnic or racial group. It is unlawful but still happens as district organizers take advantage of legal ambiguities. The Supreme Court has allowed some rigging of districts in the interest of enhancing racial diversity in Congress.

30. **(D)** "Home style" refers to appeals to local interests. Since House members represent the smallest number of constituents, this is easier for them than for senators. Senators (B and C), representing entire states with different regions and subcultures, have a harder time appealing to all constituents. Presidents (A) have the broadest constituency of all. Department secretaries (E) want to serve the public well, but "home style" refers to things done by people who want to be elected or reelected.

31. **(B)** A congressperson's franking privileges allow him or her to send official mail at the government's expense. The other answers, while true, do not

address the question. Article 1, Section 6 of the Constitution grants Congress members immunity from prosecution for things said in the course of a debate (E), so long as their words do not amount to treason or assist in other crimes. Congress members do have travel allowances (A) and access to a congressional gym (D), and their government oversight role empowers them to subpoena officials (C).

32. **(C)** The framers of the Constitution were concerned about the United States entangling itself with other nations. Therefore, a rather high bar is set for approval in the Senate of foreign treaties. This supermajority requirement almost ensures that members of different political parties will have to consent to the treaty's passage.

33. **(E)** Article 2, Section 2 of the Constitution reads: "The President shall be Commander in Chief of the Army and Navy of the United States, and of the Militia of the several States."

34. **(B)** Article 2, Section 1 of the Constitution reads: "Each state shall appoint . . . a Number of Electors, equal to the whole Number of Senators and Representatives to which the State may be entitled in the Congress." Population (A) might be a tempting response because the number of representatives a state has in Congress is based on population. But all states have two senators regardless of population.

35. **(D)** The best way to arrive at the right answer to this question is to reflect on the historical context, the philosophy of separation of powers that pervades the Constitution, and the system of checks and balances that underpin the Constitution. The power of England's monarch was in decline by the writing of the Constitution (C), but the monarch still symbolized tyranny. The stated tasks of the president, the congressional leadership (A), and the Supreme Court (B) are fundamentally different. And the Constitution is devised in such a way that no power can go unchecked.

36. **(A)** Vice presidents vote in the Senate only in the case of a tie vote. The president can draw on all the other tools listed. Administration officials, for example, can lobby Congress members just as others can (E). Indeed, administration officials have easy access to congressional offices.

37. **(B)** Since the mid-1960s, Hispanics have comprised the largest immigrant group to the United States. In recent decades, the issue of immigration has largely centered on the numbers of Hispanic immigrants, particularly those in the nation illegally. It is true that the poor have higher dropout rates than the

middle class (C), and it is true that criminal activity and dropout rates are cor-related (D). The graph, however, does not point out these correlations.

38. **(A)**   In times of national emergency, or when government needs to act quickly and flexibly, Congress has delegated its federal powers to the president. For example, Congress gave President Franklin Roosevelt wide authority to act decisively to take action during the Great Depression. Congress may pass prob-lems and the power to act on them to courts (B), the states (C), and localities (D), including town mayors (E), but none of these moves would simplify things for a government that needs to act quickly.

39. **(C)**   The Speaker of the House becomes president in the event that both the president and vice president are incapacitated. The most senior member of the majority party in the Senate (B) is the president pro tempore of the Senate (A) and follows the House Speaker in the line of succession. The secretary of state (E) is fourth in the line of succession. The mayor of Washington, D.C., (D) is nowhere in the line of succession.

40. **(C)**   The give-away term in the graphic is *bill*. A piece of proposed legis-lation is referred to as a bill. Bills may be related to amending the Constitution (A), overriding a presidential veto (B), ending filibusters (D), and regulating elections (E), but none of these is specified in the graphic.

41. **(B)**   Answering this question correctly depends largely on knowing the content of the Bill of Rights, or the first ten amendments to the Constitution. The right of people to assemble peaceably and to make their grievances known to the government (C) and the right of freedom of religion (D) are established in the First Amendment. The Eighth Amendment prohibits excessive bail (E). It is the Second Amendment that deals with the right to "bear arms." In the 2008 case *District of Columbia v. Heller*, four of the nine Supreme Court justices expressed the view described in (A), but the majority decision was that the Second Amendment applied to individuals (B), not simply militias.

42. **(C)**   The establishment clause is the clause in the First Amendment that disallows the federal government from establishing a religion; it is followed by the clause protecting individuals' right to religious belief. The other an-swers describe additional provisions of the Constitution: the right to protest (B) is in the First Amendment as well; the right against self-incrimination (A) is found in the Fifth Amendment as is the prohibition against unlawful deten-tion (D); and the statement establishing that powers not expressly given to the federal government are reserved to the states or people (E) is found in the Tenth Amendment.

43. **(D)** *Engel v. Vitale* (1962) eliminated prayer organized by public schools. Abortion was legalized across the country (A) as a result of *Roe v. Wade* (1973). *Griswold v. Connecticut* struck down a law that made the use of contraception a crime (B). *Brown v. Board of Education* (1954) required the desegregation of public schools (E). Answer (C) is fictional.

44. **(B)** Though the meaning of the right to freedom of speech has steadily expanded, particularly since the early twentieth century, it has never been considered absolute. One cannot, as Justice Oliver Wendell Holmes said in the Court's unanimous decision, falsely yell, "Fire!" in a theatre since doing so would cause a panic. Similarly, the Court decided that in a time of war, when a nation is being threatened, limits on speech are justified.

45. **(C)** The Balanced Budget Act of 1997, signed by President Bill Clinton, led to a balanced budget and a budget surplus. The Budget and Impoundment Control Act (A) stipulated that a congressional budget committee would oversee the budgeting process. The Gramm-Rudman Act (B) required annual reductions in the annual deficit with the final goal being an elimination of the national debt by 1991, though it failed. The Patriot Act (D) was passed in the days following the terrorist attacks of September 2001 and was concerned with national security. The Budgetary Restraint and Fiscal Responsibility Act (E) is fictional, though a Fiscal Responsibility Act was passed in 2005.

46. **(A)** The Supreme Court ruled on *McCulloch v. Maryland* in 1819. Congress had passed a law establishing a national bank, an institution not mentioned in the Constitution. Federalists supported this idea; Democratic-Republicans and many state legislatures opposed it, seeing this expansion of federal power as an intrusion into affairs that should be reserved to the states. Maryland attempted to diminish the influence of the bank by taxing its operations. The Supreme Court ruled that Maryland's tax was unconstitutional, since state governments could not pass laws that were at cross-purposes with legitimate federal laws.

47. **(A)** The theory of sampling relies on random selection (the person who is selected had no better or worse chance of being chosen), sample size (must be sufficiently large to represent the large and diverse population of the United States), and variation (to account for differences within groups).

48. **(D)** A third party is a political party that achieves some prominence in a political system that normally has only two major parties. The Populist Party is an example of an economic protest party (A). The Socialist and Nazi parties are examples of ideological parties (B). The Prohibition Party was (and is) devoted to one primary issue—the elimination of alcohol for beverage purposes—and

therefore is an issue party (C). When Teddy Roosevelt led the Progressive "Bull Moose" Party out of the Republican Party, he was forming a factional party (E). The term "verification party" (D) is fictional.

49. **(E)** Ralph Nader ran as a Green Party candidate and won votes in Florida that otherwise would likely have gone to Democratic candidate Al Gore (B). This tipped Florida's popular vote in favor of Republican candidate George W. Bush, who ultimately received all of Florida's electoral votes and thus won the election. Joseph Lieberman (C) was Gore's vice presidential running mate. Howard Dean (D) ran for president in 2004. Bernie Sanders (A) is an independent, socialist senator from Vermont.

50. **(B)** The Republican Party is sometimes referred to as the Grand Old Party, or more commonly, the GOP. None of the other parties has a well-known second name.

51. **(A)** In the 1992 presidential election, Ross Perot ran as an independent and garnered 19 million votes but no electoral votes. Bill Clinton (C), who won that election, worked to bring the budget deficit under control.

52. **(B)** The Dixiecrats, led by Strom Thurmond, bolted from the Democratic Party over the issue of racial desegregation, which the Dixiecrats opposed. They resented the actions of some Democrats on behalf of civil rights, thus answer (E) is incorrect. Thurmond ran an independent campaign for president in the 1948 election, winning some southern states' electoral votes. The Democratic Party was responsible for the New Deal (A) during the Great Depression. Though relations with China were not good in 1948 (C), the United States did not go to war with that country. By 1948, the war with Germany (D) had been over for three years, and in any event, Thurmond favored the war against Germany.

53. **(E)** No state constitution forbids the formation of political parties. That would amount to an obvious breach of the First Amendment.

54. **(E)** George W. Bush lost the popular vote to Al Gore in the 2000 presidential election but won the electoral vote. Truman (A), Wilson (B), and Kennedy (C) won both the popular and the electoral votes in their respective elections. Gerald Ford (D), who gained the presidency after Richard Nixon resigned, lost the election of 1976 to Jimmy Carter.

55. **(C)** Cooperative federalism, sometimes called marble-cake federalism, refers to overlapping federal and state government jurisdiction. Dual federalism (A) is the term used when federal and state governments operate in separate

jurisdictions. Layer-cake federalism (E) refers to federal and state governments acting separately but often in overlapping ways. Sovereign federalism (D) and unitary federalism (B) do not exist.

56. **(B)** The Civil Rights Act of 1964 outlawed discrimination on the basis of race, color, gender, religion, or national origin. This act also made discrimination in restaurants and hotels illegal, since their business directly affected interstate commerce. The Voting Rights Act of 1965 (A) annulled tests used, primarily in Southern states, to prevent African Americans from voting. The Civil Rights Act of 1968 (C) outlawed discrimination in most kinds of housing. The Fair Treatment Act (D) and the Equal Protection Act (E) are fictional.

57. **(D)** *Roe v. Wade* nullified state laws outlawing first-trimester abortions, though states still had the authority to pass legislation regulating second and third trimesters. However, in 2000, *Stenberg v. Carhart* (B) struck down state laws that illegalized late-term abortions. *Webster v. Reproductive Health Services* (C) upheld a Missouri law that prohibited abortions in publicly funded hospitals and clinics. *Dred Scott v. Sanford* (E) and *Plessy v. Ferguson* (A) are not related to abortion rights.

58. **(E)** Nancy Pelosi's appointment to Speaker of the House is considered a major step in gender equality in America. Condoleezza Rice (A) was secretary of state in the administration of President George W. Bush. As of late 2008, Sarah Palin (B) was the governor of Alaska and had been the Republican vice presidential candidate in the election of 2008. By the same time, Hillary Rodham Clinton (C) had been a First Lady, a U.S. senator from New York, and U.S. secretary of state under President Barack Obama. Sandra Day O'Connor (D) was a Supreme Court justice.

59. **(D)** *De facto* is a Latin term meaning "in fact." De facto segregation is segregation that exists not through some specific intent, as in the passage of laws or state regulations, but as a result of social, economic, or other factors. One attempt to combat the negative effects of de facto segregation is the No Child Left Behind program, established in 2001, which strives to ensure that all schools are equal, regardless of the racial makeup. De jure segregation (A) is segregation that is codified in law; this is illegal in the United States. Racial profiling (B) is the act of using race or ethnicity as a basis for targeting individuals for criminal investigation. Jim Crow (C) was the label given to state and local laws that discriminated against African Americans. Busing (E), now out of political favor, attempted to make schools more racially mixed by busing children to schools outside their own neighborhoods.

60. **(C)** The United States government is a federal system: it divides political power between the federal, state, and local governments.

61. **(E)** Poll taxes, or a tax on voters, made it difficult for many blacks and poor whites in southern states to vote because they could not afford to pay.

62. **(D)** The purpose of the Immigration Reform and Control Act of 1986 was to curb illegal immigration in the United States. In 2007, President George W. Bush and Congressional members in both major parties tried to pass a comprehensive immigration bill, but the bill failed, primarily because some members of Congress felt that the bill would lead to more amnesty for illegal immigrants. The Volstead Act (A), passed in 1920, established prohibition. The other options are fictional.

63. **(C)** If a decision is unanimous, it means that there is 100 percent agreement.

64. **(D)** Social Security was set in place in the Great Depression, during the presidency of Franklin Roosevelt.

65. **(B)** Block grants have relatively few strings attached to them. Categorical grants (A) fund specific projects. Unfunded mandates (C) are federal requirements without funding. Fiscal grants (E) are fictional.

66. **(D)** A writ of certiorari is an official request by a higher court—in this case, the Supreme Court—to a lower court for all the records related to a case. Amicus curiae briefs (A) are legal opinions submitted to the Court by interested parties. The other answer options are fictional.

67. **(A)** *Miranda v. Arizona* outlined the fundamental rights of individuals when arrested—for example, that he or she has a right to remain silent. *Duncan v. Louisiana* (B) affirmed the right to trial by jury. *Gideon v. Wainwright* (C) requires the court to make legal counsel available to all defendants. *Roe v. Wade* (D) pertains to abortion rights. *Marbury v. Madison* (E) set in place the Supreme Court's power of judicial review.

68. **(E)** The Bill of Rights, or the first 10 amendments to the Constitution, placed limits on the power of the federal government, including freedom of religion, speech, press, and assembly, the right to keep and bear arms, limits on the quartering of troops, limits on the right of government to search, various rights for accused persons, and nonenumerated rights and powers reserved by the states and people. The Bill of Rights did not give women the right to vote.

69. **(A)**   Militias, established in Article 1, Section 8 of the Constitution (E), are called up for national purposes, such as to put down insurrections (B) and to resist invasions (D). They have been formalized as the National Guard (C). Under normal circumstances, militias are under the command of state governors.

70. **(A)**   A judge may issue a gag order to limit the amount of information immediately made public about a trial. Gag orders are, however, set in place relatively rarely as they can seem to conflict with a First Amendment right to a free press.

71. **(D)**   The Supreme Court explicitly gave itself the power of judicial review in the case *Marbury v. Madison* (1803). The power is not expressly granted in the Constitution.

72. **(A)**   Federal law declares burning a draft card illegal because it is federal property.

73. **(B)**   The Supreme Court drew the principle of the exclusionary rule from the Fourth Amendment, which protects the "right of the people to be secure in their persons, houses, papers, and effects, against unreasonable searches and seizures." In *Mapp v. Ohio*, the Court favored Mapp because agents of the state of Ohio entered her house without a warrant and arrested her after finding pornographic material in her basement.

74. **(B)**   Ross Perot gained more than 19 million votes in the 1992 presidential election. Ralph Nader (A) was a Green Party candidate who ran in the presidential election of 2000 and again in 2008. James Weaver (C) ran as a Greenback labor candidate in 1880 and as a Populist candidate in 1892. William Jennings Bryan (D) was a well-known Populist candidate who ran for the Democratic Party's nomination in 1896 and 1900. Eugene Debs (E) was a leader of the Socialist Party in the early 1900s.

75. **(E)**   Socialism is a system of government that advocates government regulation of wealth and industry. Democracy (A) is a system of government in which voters have the power to elect their leaders. Communism (B), though often confused with socialism, seeks to eliminate private property. Theocracy (C) is a government ruled by religious authority. A monarchy (D) is a system of government run by a king or a queen.

76. **(D)**   *Gibbons v. Ogden* (1824) involved Congressional oversight of interstate commerce. The Equal Rights Amendment (A) was first proposed in Congress in 1923 but has never been ratified. The Equal Pay Act of 1963 (B) required equal pay for work that was substantially the same. Title VII of the

Civil Rights Act of 1964 (C) prohibited discrimination based on gender. In 1978, Congress expanded Title VII to prohibit discrimination on grounds of pregnancy or health problems related to giving birth. The 1998 the Supreme Court decisions in *Faragher v. City of Boca Raton* (E), along with *Burlington Industries v. Ellerth,* ruled that employers are responsible for setting up safeguards against sexual harassment in the workplace.

77. **(B)** In 1978, Congress passed the Foreign Intelligence Surveillance Act (FISA), which authorized the Foreign Intelligence Surveillance Court (or FISC). The FISC oversees requests by the federal government to place surveillance on suspected spies. In federal trial courts (A) evidence is shown and challenged. Appellate courts (C) and circuit courts (D) do not usually consider evidence. Their primary purpose is to determine whether a lower court made a legal error, or whether the lower court's judgment was unwarranted based on the evidence presented at the earlier trial. A common law court (E) is fictitious. Common law (also called case law) refers to the body of law created through decisions of courts, rather than through legislative statute or executive action.

78. **(B)** While decisions made by the Supreme Court and other federal courts are important, they cannot be carried out unless implemented by the president and law-making bodies. Therefore, judicial implementation depends on the other branches of the government, which can potentially check the judiciary's power.

79. **(E)** None of the other options is referred to in the Mayflower Compact. The Compact was signed by settlers in Massachusetts in 1620. Their original plan was to settle under the jurisdiction of the Virginia Company, but the *Mayflower* was blown off course and the settlers landed in New England. Being outside the Virginia Company's jurisdiction, they needed to organize themselves politically until formal power from England could be established. The Compact represents the earliest American example of self-government.

80. **(C)** Negative rights limit the power of the government. The government must not, for example, forbid you from attending religious services on Saturday or Sunday. In contrast, positive rights (D) refer to things the government must actively do, such as protecting your right to attend religious services. Closely linked to the concept of positive rights is the better-known term civil rights (A). Your right to attend religious services is a positive right—a civil right—because you can count on the government to act to protect that right. Inalienable rights (B) are simply bottom-line political necessities and do not explicitly relate to the limit of government control. The Declaration of Independence lists three "inalienable rights": life, liberty, and the pursuit of happiness.

81. **(A)** *Agostini v. Felton* tempered *Lemon v. Kurtzman* (E), which set up a strong separation between church and state. The 1997 *Agostini* ruling stated that the government must act in a neutral manner on religious matters. *Zelmon v. Simmon-Harris* (B) followed *Agostini* and allowed courts to use publically funded school vouchers to pay tuition at religious schools. *Lynch v. Donnelly* (D) determined that certain public displays do not promote government entanglement with religion. *Engle v. Vitale* (C) outlawed prayers in public schools.

82. **(A)** The test was spelled out as a result of *Schenck v. United States* in the First World War era. The Supreme Court upheld the conviction of a defendant who had dispensed anti-conscription (i.e., anti-military draft) literature when the country needed men to fight overseas. By the latter twentieth century such an act would not be deemed criminal. Many young people protested the draft during the conflict in Vietnam.

83. **(D)** The Gulf of Tonkin Resolution of 1964 empowered Lyndon Johnson to "take all necessary measures to repel any armed attack against the forces of the United States and to prevent further aggression." In contrast, the War Powers Act of 1973 (A) limited the president's power during wartime.

84. **(A)** The Virginia Plan called for a bicameral legislature with representation based on population. In contrast, the New Jersey Plan called for a unicameral Congress and equal representation for all the states (B). The Connecticut Compromise melded the two plans to create the bicameral legislature of the U.S. government: the Senate has equal representation—two senators—from each state, whereas representation in the House of Representatives is based on state population.

85. **(B)** *The Federalist Papers* (sometimes called simply *The Federalist*), written by James Madison, Alexander Hamilton, and John Jay, argued in favor of the ratification of the U.S. Constitution.

86. **(D)** The regulation of the railroads that moved goods and services from one state to another was the reason that the Interstate Commerce Commission was created.

87. **(E)** As of 2008, the U.S. Citizenship and Immigration Service does not include the memorization of the Pledge of Allegiance to the American flag or the National Anthem in its list of general requirements for citizens. It does include each of the other answer choices.

88. **(C)** The Bureau of Engraving and Printing produces U.S. paper currency. The Federal Reserve System (A) distributes money through 12 Federal

Reserve banks (D), an independent government agency. The U.S. Mint (B) creates coins and maintains America's silver and gold reserves. The U.S. Patent and Trademark Office (E) is an agency of the Department of Congress that is self-funded. It ensures that patented inventions are not illegally copied and placed in the market.

89. **(D)** No single congressional appropriation may supply military operations for longer than two years.

90. **(C)** The theory of sampling states that traits of individuals within representative groups generally reflect the views of the larger group it represents.

91. **(D)** Political socialization refers in part to the tendency for children to share political views and affiliation with close family. Childhood memories have proven to be a strong influence on an individual's political affiliation.

92. **(A)** Article 2 of the Constitution states that the president must obtain the "advice and consent of the Senate" when appointing officers to serve in the federal government. The chart clearly states the dates the Senate received and confirmed Mark Abbott's appointment to the National Science Board. The president as an individual does hold greater power than individual senators (D), but the graph does not make this explicit. Given the relatively quick confirmation process (less than two months), this graph does not point to government gridlock (E).

93. **(E)** Of the given choices, a voter who supports a small military would be least likely to support Republicans, who have a political edge on questions of national security and tend to favor a strong and well-funded military.

94. **(B)** Polls reveal a skewed distribution when a large majority of Americans favor or oppose an issue. A normal distribution (A) shows a bell curve, a bimodal distribution (C) points to a nearly divided public, and a stable distribution (E) refers to opinion stability over time.

95. **(D)** Members of Congress can hold office for as long as they live and as long as they are legally reelected and as long as they maintain legal behavior and are not forced to leave office.

96. **(E)** The framers of the Constitution placed the power of formally initiating tax legislation in the political body that is closest and, theoretically, the most accountable to the people: the House of Representatives. Presidential and other political candidates may promise tax reductions but in reality have no direct, formal power to do so.

97. **(A)** Americans pay some of the lowest taxes in the world—about 26 percent on average. In Sweden, by contrast, citizens surrender some 50 percent of their incomes to the government.

98. **(C)** The main fiscal duties of Congress are collecting taxes and import duties, borrowing money to finance government operations, and paying the nation's debts. Congress is empowered to borrow money for national purposes.

99. **(B)** Public debt is not a source of government income. It is accumulated when the government spends more money than it takes in through other sources of income.

100. **(E)** The Budget and Accounting Act of 1921 required that the president prepare the budget and seek congressional approval. The Bureau of the Budget was formed to assist the president with this process. In 1970, this bureau became the Office of Management and Budget (OMB).

Practice Test 2

CLEP American Government

This test is also on CD-ROM in our special interactive CLEP American Government TestWare®

(Answer sheets appear in the back of this book)

TIME: 90 Minutes
90 Questions

DIRECTIONS: Each of the questions or incomplete statements below is followed by five possible answers or completions. Select the best choice in each case and fill in the corresponding oval on the answer sheet.

---

1. Where in the Constitution does Congress locate its authority to oversee governmental bodies not mentioned in the Constitution, such as the Department of Education?

   (A) Necessary and proper clause

   (B) Unwritten constitution

   (C) Bill of Rights

   (D) Execution clause

   (E) Admissions clause

2. Powers claimed by the president but NOT expressly called for in the Constitution are called

   (A) executive powers

   (B) inherent powers

   (C) delegated powers

   (D) inferential powers

   (E) trustee powers

3.   Which of the following stipulates that Congress may NOT put in place an official religion?

(A) Neutrality clause   (D) Second Amendment

(B) Establishment clause   (E) Exclusionary rule

(C) Free exercise clause

4.   Higher education is associated with more liberal political views because

(A) more than 95 percent of professors identify themselves as very liberal

(B) students have more exposure to liberal media

(C) higher education is associated with questioning norms, learning different viewpoints, and reflecting on the value of civil liberties

(D) higher education tends to depict conservatism as intellectually inferior

(E) young people rebel against the values of their parents

5.   Sometimes the federal government hands over to commercial enterprises work formerly done by government employees. This is known as

(A) privatization   (D) bureaucracy

(B) deregulation   (E) specialization

(C) devolution

6.   The Pendleton Act of 1883 was the first law to do what?

(A) Eliminate civil service jobs

(B) End a president's tenure in office (in this case, James Garfield's)

(C) Ban political bribes in the workplace

(D) Purposefully provide civil service jobs for the poor

(E) Make some government jobs off-limits to patronage

7.   With the exception of the Justice Department, the largest executive departments within the federal bureaucracy are headed by

(A) top military officials   (D) attorneys general

(B) U.S. senators   (E) secretaries

(C) elected judges

8. Which of the following, within various executive departments, write and enforce rules that regulate some element of industry?

   (A) Government corporations

   (B) Independent regulatory commissions

   (C) Independent agencies

   (D) Secretarial committees

   (E) Rule administrations

9. The U.S. Postal Service is a government corporation that sells services, thus generating

   (A) workers

   (B) federal government revenue

   (C) its own revenue

   (D) outside criticism

   (E) competing industry

10. Organizations within the federal bureaucracy ensure that congressional legislation, presidential policies, and court decisions are adhered to. This process is referred to as

    (A) rule administration   (D) administrative discretion

    (B) rule adjudication   (E) federal registration

    (C) rule making

11. The policy-making relationship between lobbyists, Congress, and the federal bureaucracy in which everyone involved wins is called

    (A) the brass ring   (D) the iron triangle

    (B) the federal lifeboat   (E) reciprocal bureaucracy

    (C) bureaucratic imperialism

12. In the 1990s, welfare programs funded by the federal government were largely given to the states to administer. This is an example of

(A) privatization

(D) bureaucracy

(B) deregulation

(E) specialization

(C) devolution

13. Which of the following are sometimes referred to collectively as the fourth branch of government?

(A) Voters

(D) Recent immigrants

(B) The president's advisors

(E) Nonprofit organizations

(C) The media

Congressional District 14

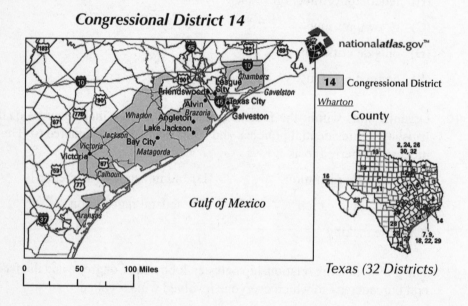

nationalatlas.gov™

14 Congressional District

Wharton County

Gulf of Mexico

0   50   100 Miles

Texas (32 Districts)

14. All of the following statements accurately describe what is shown by the map above EXCEPT

(A) members of Congress representing districts shown above are elected every two years

(B) Congressional districts as shown above are often constructed for political advantage

(C) Congressional districts as shown above are drawn every four years by federal judges

   (D) Congressional districts as shown above are drawn by state legislatures

   (E) federal Congressional districts are based on population and, therefore, rely on census data.

15. An easily digestible policy statement is often referred to as

   (A) infotainment

   (B) a sound bite

   (C) a talking point

   (D) hold and hold

   (E) condensed news

16. During elections, the media tend to focus on who is winning, who is losing, and the gamesmanship of campaigning. What is this journalistic style called?

   (A) Board-game journalism

   (B) Sensationalism

   (C) Horse-race journalism

   (D) Infotainment

   (E) Contest journalism

17. What is the substance of the television hypothesis?

   (A) Television makes one feel informed when he or she really isn't.

   (B) A story's newsworthiness depends on television viewership.

   (C) Human interest stories related to politics trump serious policy reflection.

   (D) "If it bleeds, it leads," that is, violence trumps intelligent news coverage.

   (E) Most television news is market-driven journalism.

18. The Real ID Act of 2005 was an example of

   (A) a block grant

   (B) an unfunded mandate

   (C) a categorical grant

   (D) cooperative federalism

   (E) Project Head Start

19. Within the Supreme Court, the "rule of four" describes the number of justices needed to

   (A) overturn previous case precedent

   (B) confirm a prospective chief justice

   (C) end the oral arguments of a given case

   (D) agree to a change in the numeric composition of the Supreme Court

   (E) accept a case for judicial review

20. The signing of the Immigration and Nationality Act of 1965 dramatically increased the number of

   (A) immigrants from Ireland and Britain

   (B) immigrants from Canada and Scandinavia

   (C) illegal immigrants

   (D) immigrants from Asia and Latin America

   (E) Republicans

21. In the Mayflower Compact, we see the emergence of enduring principles important to the American political system: (1) a willingness to live under the rule of law and (2)

   (A) a bicameral legislature

   (B) separation of powers

   (C) checks and balances

   (D) separation of church and state

   (E) government by the consent of the governed

22. The political philosophy that calls for the government to do what most people in the country want is

   (A) majoritarianism   (D) libertarianism

   (B) pluralism   (E) monetarism

   (C) liberalism

23. Under the Articles of Confederation, the central government was empowered to do all of the following EXCEPT

    (A) regulate coinage

    (B) create and operate a postal system

    (C) regulate Indian affairs

    (D) declare war

    (E) draft soldiers for national service

24. In an effort to define what is meant by *bureaucracy*, German sociologist Max Weber suggests that bureaucracies share five characteristics. Which of these is NOT among them?

    (A) They specialize and divide labor.

    (B) They follow a clear chain of command.

    (C) They are staffed by professionals.

    (D) They have fairly flexible rules.

    (E) They maintain written records.

25. In many ways, the American Bill of Rights is reminiscent of an earlier Bill of Rights put into effect in

    (A) France

    (D) England

    (B) Spain

    (E) Germany

    (C) Holland

26. The philosopher whose work most influenced the thinking of the Constitution's framers about political checks and balances and separation of political powers was

    (A) Machiavelli

    (D) Mill

    (B) Montesquieu

    (E) Montcalm

    (C) Montaigne

27. What important American document begins with the words, "We the people of the United States . . . "?

    (A) Bill of Rights

    (B) Declaration of Independence

    (C) Mayflower Compact

    (D) U.S. Constitution

    (E) Articles of Confederation

28. Each of the following is an example of direct democracy EXCEPT

    (A) a recall   (D) an initiative

    (B) a proposition   (E) a referendum

    (C) a class action

29. Which body of colonial leaders devised the Articles of Confederation?

    (A) The Association

    (B) House of Representatives

    (C) Senate

    (D) First Continental Congress

    (E) Second Continental Congress

30. When the media deliver infotainment in place of serious reflection on policy matters, they are indulging in what?

    (A) Horse-race journalism

    (B) Public inquiry

    (C) The television hypothesis

    (D) Market-driven journalism

    (E) Human interest priority

31. A typical hour of programming on a 24-hour news channel includes more opinion on news than actual news proper, which has led to a growing number of pundits. What are pundits?

    (A) Uninformed people

    (B) Cynics

(C) News grazers

(D) An attentive policy elite

(E) Professional commentators

32. Those in the media who choose what is ultimately published or broadcast are called

(A) filters

(B) gatekeepers

(C) bloggers

(D) news grazers

(E) colanders

Constituent Services

I want to serve my constituents in any way I can. Whether you need help with a federal agency, are trying to find out if federal grants are available for your project, or are considering applying to a service academy. I hope all the information in this section will be helpful.

Academy Nominations

Information on how to apply to one of the nation's military academies

Arranging a Trip to Washington, D.C.

If you are a planning to visit our nation's Capital, find out how my staff and I can help arrange tours and make your trip more memorable

Casework

If you are having trouble with a federal agency (i.e. Veterans Administration or Social Security Administration), my staff and I can help

---

Source: http://www.boozman.house.gov/ConstituentServices/

33. The excerpt above, from the website of a member of the U.S. House of Representatives, is a reflection of each of the following EXCEPT

(A) elected Congress members have resources that unelected aspirants to office usually do not have

(B) members of Congress must focus on both national and local issues

(C) Congress has oversight of the federal bureaucracy

(D) Congress persons determine who is admitted into military officer training schools

(E) members of Congress help to meet the needs of citizens living in their districts.

34. In the case of a tie vote in the Senate, to whom does the Constitution give the deciding vote?

    (A) President

    (B) Vice president

    (C) Speaker of the House of Representatives

    (D) Majority party whip

    (E) Chief justice of the Supreme Court

35. According to the Constitution, federal tax legislation must be formally initiated in

    (A) the White House

    (B) the state legislatures

    (C) the Office of Management and Budget

    (D) the Senate

    (E) the House of Representatives

36. The Constitution states that a person cannot serve in the Senate until he or she has been a U.S. citizen for at least how many years?

    (A) 5   (D) 10

    (B) 7   (E) 20

    (C) 9

37. Which twentieth-century U.S. president was impeached in the House of Representatives for lying in a court and obstruction of justice?

    (A) Calvin Coolidge   (D) Ronald Reagan

    (B) Lyndon Johnson   (E) Bill Clinton

    (C) Richard Nixon

38. When bureaucrats in certain agencies try to protect their agencies' interests, and thus their own careers, it is sometimes called

    (A) white-collar war   (D) interested bureaucracy

    (B) bureaucratic imperialism   (E) bureaucratic polarization

    (C) issue networking

39. The Voting Rights Act of 1982

    (A) gave the right to vote to 18-year-olds

    (B) disallowed poll taxes

    (C) disallowed literacy tests for prospective voters

    (D) encouraged the creation of congressional districts in which racial minorities would comprise majorities

    (E) allowed nonregistered voters to register and vote on the same day

40. Which of the following presidents regularly appears at the top of rankings for presidential greatness?

    (A) Abraham Lincoln   (D) Theodore Roosevelt

    (B) Franklin Roosevelt   (E) Harry Truman

    (C) George Washington

41. Each of the following gives incumbents an advantage over challengers for political office EXCEPT

    (A) unlimited time to speak in either chamber of Congress

    (B) press releases

    (C) name recognition

    (D) taxpayer-funded travel budgets

    (E) franking privileges

42. Insofar as the Constitution is concerned, the purpose of the census is to

    (A) determine the ethnic and linguistic makeup of the nation

    (B) reapportion the number of a state's U.S. senators

    (C) reapportion the number of a state's U.S. representatives

    (D) determine where Federal Reserve banks should be located

    (E) modify the number of judges sitting on the Supreme Court

43. The Constitution gives the power to declare war to the Congress. The last time Congress formally declared war was during the

   (A) Spanish-American War   (D) Vietnam War

   (B) First World War   (E) Gulf War

   (C) Second World War

44. Washington, D.C.'s delegate to Congress has what kind of power?

   (A) Full voting powers

   (B) The power to vote in committees but not in the full chamber

   (C) The power to vote in the full chamber but not in committees

   (D) Power limited to advising voting members

   (E) No voting power, except in the case of a tie among Congress members

45. The Constitution prohibits the House of Representatives from doing all of the following EXCEPT

   (A) passing ex post facto laws

   (B) imposing taxes on goods from southern states imported into northern states

   (C) spending money from the treasury that is not expressly accounted for in legislation

   (D) assigning to anyone a formal title of nobility

   (E) initiating tax legislation

46. What 1992 court case upheld a Pennsylvania law requiring pre-abortion counseling, a 24-hour waiting period, and parental or judicial permission for girls under 18?

   (A) *Roe v. Wade*

   (B) *Webster v. Reproductive Health Services*

   (C) *Planned Parenthood v. Casey*

   (D) *Griswold v. Connecticut*

   (E) *Stenberg v. Carhart*

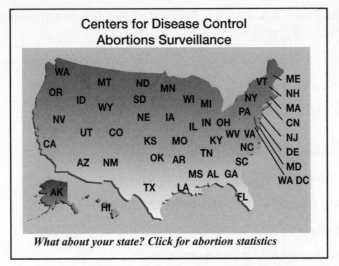

**Centers for Disease Control
Abortions Surveillance**

What about your state? Click for abortion statistics

Source: http://www.abortionfacts.com/statistics/statistics.asp

47. The map above reflects the fact that

    (A) abortion into the third trimester is legal in every state

    (B) the Supreme Court has required states to follow specific federal regulations on abortion

    (C) abortion is legal in some states and illegal in others

    (D) the proposed Constitutional amendment to make abortion illegal is likely to be ratified

    (E) abortion is legal across the country though dealt with differently in different states

48. What key feminist goal has been introduced into every Congress since 1982?

    (A) Equal Pay Act of 1963

    (B) Federal legislation requiring nationwide access to late-term abortions

    (C) Federal legislation requiring equal numbers of women and men in universities

    (D) Title VII

    (E) Equal Rights Amendment

49. Which of the following women served as secretary of state in the George W. Bush administration?

    (A) Condoleezza Rice
    (B) Nancy Pelosi
    (C) Sandra Day O'Connor
    (D) Ruth Bader Ginsburg
    (E) Hillary Clinton

50. Congressional standing committees

    (A) endure through congressional sessions
    (B) are formed to deal with temporary matters
    (C) pertain only to tax matters
    (D) pertain only to military matters
    (E) are formed to prepare parties for elections

51. In the United States, the state and national governments work together to solve problems. This form of government interaction is called

    (A) cooperative federalism
    (B) distributive federalism
    (C) power sharing
    (D) layer-cake federalism
    (E) unitive government

52. How often does the Constitution require the president to "give to the Congress Information of the State of the Union"?

    (A) Every year
    (B) Every six months
    (C) From time to time
    (D) At least twice during a presidential term
    (E) A minimum of six times during a presidential term

53. The U.S. president nominates ambassadors to foreign countries, but the ambassadorship must have the consent of

    (A) the Senate alone

    (B) the House alone

    (C) two-thirds of the state legislatures

    (D) a majority in the House and Senate

    (E) a majority of state governors

54. Beginning in the mid-1970s, fast-track authority was

    (A) granted by political parties to candidates to streamline the candidate nomination process

    (B) abused by Congressional members seeking financial contributions

    (C) put out of use due to chronic abuses

    (D) granted to the president by Congress to streamline the process of making trade deals with other nations

    (E) considered unconstitutional as a result of federal court decisions

55. When President George W. Bush ordered, without the consent of Congress, the establishing of military commissions to try captives captured in Iraq and Afghanistan, he was theoretically relying on what kind of powers derived from the war powers given to the president by the Constitution?

    (A) Executive powers   (D) Sovereign powers

    (B) Initiative powers   (E) Exclusionary powers

    (C) Inherent powers

56. Each of the following is an example of an executive order EXCEPT

    (A) President Bill Clinton's establishment of the military's "don't ask, don't tell" policy regarding homosexuals in the military

    (B) President Harry Truman's desegregation of the military

    (C) President Dwight Eisenhower's sending of troops into Arkansas to desegregate Little Rock High School

    (D) President Gerald Ford's pardon of ex-President Richard Nixon for any crimes that he may have committed

    (E) President George W. Bush's establishment of a White House office of faith-based initiatives

57. Which of the following is NOT included in the Executive Office of the President?

    (A) Office of Management and Budget

    (B) National security advisor

    (C) Presidential chief of staff

    (D) Federal Reserve System

    (E) Council of Economic Advisors

58. Which of the following statements about vice presidents is MOST accurate?

    (A) The framers of the Constitution envisioned vice presidents would hold more power and influence than they actually have had, especially since the Civil War.

    (B) The Constitution requires presidents to consult with vice presidents before vetoing legislation.

    (C) Until the election of 1896, House speakers moved to the position of vice president following a presidential election.

    (D) Vice presidents were more influential in the early twentieth century than they were in the late twentieth century.

    (E) Vice presidents were more influential in the late twentieth century than they were in the early twentieth century.

59. All of the following can prevent current presidential cabinets from being effective advisory bodies EXCEPT

    (A) congressional rules that limit a cabinet's advisory authority

    (B) the large sizes of modern cabinets

    (C) the fact that cabinet members tend to know a lot about their areas of expertise but not about all matters confronting a president

    (D) the fact that cabinet members are sometimes chosen to add racial or geographic diversity to the cabinet, not necessarily because they are close to the president

    (E) the reality that presidents have large personal staffs that they can turn to for advice

60. Which of the following does NOT appear in the First Amendment?

    (A) Free exercise of religion

    (B) Free exercise of speech

    (C) Freedom of the press

    (D) Freedom of trade

    (E) Freedom to petition the government

61. At what point was the Bill of Rights added to the U.S. Constitution?

    (A) Just before the Revolution began

    (B) At the same time as the Articles of Confederation

    (C) During the debates over the ratification of the Constitution

    (D) During the second term of George Washington's presidency

    (E) During Reconstruction, following the Civil War

62. A smoker who likes to light up while talking with friends at the table after a meal may know little about a candidate except that she supports laws banning smoking in public places. When the smoker votes against the candidate, he is acting on the

    (A) issue framing principle   (D) generational principle

    (B) self-interest principle   (E) political trust principle

    (C) lifestyle-effect principle

63. In *Lemon v. Kurtzman* (1971), the Supreme Court set out guidelines that, if followed, would theoretically keep government support of religious institutions—schools, for example—within the bounds of the First Amendment. All of the following are included in the Court's guidelines EXCEPT

    (A) a requirement that information about religions different from that of the institution being assisted be made available

    (B) a requirement that the basic purpose receiving the assistance be secular

    (C) the basic effect of the activity receiving support should not advance religion

    (D) the basic effect of the activity receiving support should not stand in the way of religious practice

    (E) the assistance must not entangle government in religion

64. In 2005, the Supreme Court decided cases involving the display of the Ten Commandments in public buildings in Texas and Kentucky, the results of which

    (A) allowed the display of the commandments in Texas and Kentucky because they reflect the religious heritage of most Americans

    (B) disallowed the displays since they suggested state support for religion

    (C) allowed the displays because they were accompanied by other, secular texts

    (D) determined that both displays successfully met the "Lemon test"

    (E) allowed one display and disallowed another display

65. How can Congress override a president's veto?

    (A) With a majority vote in both chambers

    (B) With a two-thirds majority vote in both chambers

    (C) With the support of two-thirds of the state legislatures

    (D) With a three-fifths vote in the Senate alone

    (E) With a national referendum

66. In the 1800s, before reforms were set in place, which of the following gave political victors the ability to give jobs to friends and supporters?

    (A) Civil service   (D) Personal benefits system

    (B) Spoils system   (E) Weighted system

    (C) Pendleton system

67. What is the most severe form of discipline that congressional members can receive from the Congress?

    (A) Censure

    (B) A critical letter from an ethics committee

    (C) Expulsion from Congress

    (D) A prison sentence

    (E) Revocation of franking privileges

68. Which of the following is NOT included in the *Congressional Record*?

    (A) A daily digest

    (B) A section summarizing, though not quoting, expunged remarks

    (C) A House section

    (D) A Senate section

    (E) A record of debate

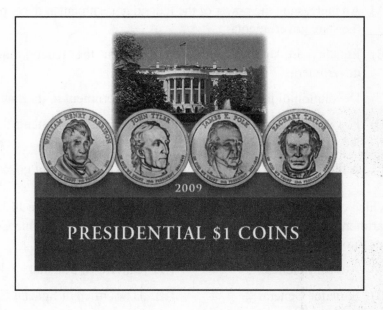

69. The image above was produced to support the services of which of the following?

    (A) U.S. Mint

    (B) Bureau of Engraving and Printing

    (C) Federal Reserve

    (D) Federal Deposit Insurance Corporation

    (E) U.S. Postal Service

70. Which of the following was NOT an independent or third-party candidate for president?

    (A) Ralph Nader

    (B) John Anderson

    (C) Theodore Roosevelt

    (D) Strom Thurmond

    (E) Jimmy Carter

71. Which of the following statements BEST summarizes the power relationship between the federal and state governments since the 1980s?

    (A) An increase in the power of the federal government at the expense of the state governments

    (B) Equality in sharing of powers between the federal and state governments

    (C) Devolution of power from the federal government to the states

    (D) Power struggles between the federal and state governments that have led to national gridlock

    (E) A dramatic shift of power from the states to the federal government

72. Which of the following is a presidential appointee within the Justice Department who regularly makes legal arguments to the Supreme Court on behalf of the U.S. government?

    (A) Attorney General

    (B) Solicitor General

    (C) Inspector General

    (D) Chief U.S. Marshal

    (E) U.S. Office of Special Counsel

73. Which of the following documents that helped to make the U.S. Constitution possible came first?

    (A) English Bill of Rights

    (B) American Bill of Rights

    (C) Magna Carta

    (D) *Second Treatise on Government*

    (E) *Spirit of the Laws*

74. The United States splits political power between the state and federal governments. This form of power sharing is called

    (A) nationalism

    (B) appropriate jurisdiction

    (C) federalism

    (D) shared jurisdiction

    (E) demonstrative government

75. Americans who believe that political power should be held close to home advocate

    (A) federal rights   (D) assumed powers

    (B) states' rights   (E) provisional rights

    (C) implied powers

76. What clause in the Constitution grants Congress the power to regulate interstate trade?

    (A) Enhancement clause   (D) Commerce clause

    (B) Regulation clause   (E) Gibbons clause

    (C) Common market clause

77. Which of the following led the federal government to take precedence over state governments in the twentieth century?

    (A) Civil rights   (D) Representative rights

    (B) Severance rights   (E) Procedural rights

    (C) Affirmative rights

78. The political notion that all Americans should have a chance in life to succeed is encapsulated in the term

    (A) *civil rights*   (D) *equal opportunity*

    (B) *freedom of choice*   (E) *affirmative action*

    (C) *equality of outcome*

79. The Supreme Court case *Plessy v. Ferguson* (1896) put in place the doctrine of

    (A) separate but equal

    (B) federal action against lynching

    (C) equal voting rights

    (D) affirmative action

    (E) de jure integration

80. Which of the following spurred the process of desegregation in the southern and some midwestern states?

    (A) *Plessy v. Ferguson*

    (B) Desegregation of the military

    (C) No Child Left Behind

    (D) Busing

    (E) *Brown v. Board of Education of Topeka*

81. A writer for the *Partisan Review* writes a story few will read, but one reader is a national radio host who discusses the article on the air. Thus, the original writer actually does reach many people. What term below BEST applies to this process?

    (A) Gatekeeping

    (B) Two-step flow of communication

    (C) News grazing

    (D) Fireside politics

    (E) Step-ladder communication

82. The first president to use radio effectively was

    (A) Franklin Roosevelt   (D) Lyndon Johnson

    (B) Richard Nixon   (E) Harry Truman

    (C) John Kennedy

83. Which of the following outlawed discrimination in most kinds of housing?

    (A) Fair Housing Act of 1965

    (B) Voting Rights Act of 1965

    (C) Civil Rights Act of 1968

    (D) Civil Rights Act of 1964

    (E) Equal Opportunity Act of 1968

84. Which of the following seeks to encourage underrepresented or minority groups to apply for employment positions?

    (A) The House Equal Action Committee

    (B) Jim Crow legislation

    (C) The Twenty-Sixth Amendment

    (D) Tariffs

    (E) Affirmative action

85. Which of the following established the Equal Employment Opportunity Commission (EEOC)?

    (A) Voting Rights Act of 1965

    (B) Civil Rights Act of 1964

    (C) Equal Access Act of 1965

    (D) Women's Rights Act of 1974

    (E) Civil Rights Act of 1968

86. Which of the following terms refers to the perceived barrier preventing women from advancing in the workplace?

    (A) Glass ceiling   (D) Picket fence

    (B) Back door   (E) High wall of separation

    (C) Good boys' wall

87. *Griswold v. Connecticut* set the stage for which 1973 controversial Supreme Court case?

    (A) *Webster v. Reproductive Health Services*

    (B) *Planned Parenthood v. Casey*

    (C) *Stenberg v. Carhart*

    (D) *Roe v. Wade*

    (E) *Faragher v. City of Boca Raton*

88. Why can't one hope to master the rules and regulations of the federal bureaucracy?

    (A) Few are legally able to know what they are.

    (B) Many of them are outdated and irrelevant.

    (C) They change often.

    (D) They are usually written in code.

    (E) They would fill hundreds of volumes.

89. If the Republicans have control of the White House and the Democrats have control of Congress (one or both houses), the government is said to be

    (A) split

    (B) divided

    (C) under administrative discretion

    (D) under bureaucratic adjudication

    (E) provisional

90. Which president launched a "war on poverty"?

    (A) Harry Truman   (D) Gerald Ford

    (B) Lyndon Johnson   (E) Richard Nixon

    (C) John Kennedy

91. The primary purpose of the Interstate Commerce Commission was to

    (A) regulate railroads that moved goods and services from one state to another

    (B) build infrastructures such as railroads and highways that linked one state to another

    (C) collect tariffs and duties on interstate commerce

    (D) regulate interstate oil pipelines

    (E) dig canals connecting major rivers and lakes to enhance trade

92. The first Supreme Court case to apply the First Amendment's language on freedom of speech to a state law was

    (A) *Abrams v. United States* (1919)

    (B) *Gitlow v. New York* (1925)

    (C) *Cohen v. California* (1971)

    (D) *Brandenburg v. Ohio* (1969)

    (E) *Chaplinsky v. New Hampshire* (1942)

93. Which of the following presidents is most associated with the substantial reform of federal government welfare programs?

    (A) Calvin Coolidge

    (B) Harry Truman

    (C) Lyndon Johnson

    (D) George H.W. Bush

    (E) Bill Clinton

94. Each of the following is a reason that working for the federal government is attractive EXCEPT

    (A) high job security

    (B) good wages relative to the private workplace

    (C) good health insurance benefits

    (D) annual food allowances

    (E) good pension benefits

95. The Joint Chiefs of Staff comprise

    (A) the nation's economic leaders

    (B) the appointed heads of the federal departments such as the Department of the Interior

    (C) the committee that brings Senate and House bills into agreement

    (D) leading military officials

    (E) the federal judiciary

96. What is the *hopper*?

    (A) The box into which members of the House of Representatives drop proposed legislation

    (B) The person who reports to the House when a bill has passed in the Senate

    (C) The file into which the president places legislation he has vetoed

    (D) A political indictment brought against a federal judge

    (E) The date given for a congressional election

97. The purpose of congressional special elections is to

    (A) determine whether a majority or supermajority of votes is needed to pass a bill

    (B) break a tied presidential election

    (C) appoint a replacement for the president pro tempore

    (D) fill a seat vacated when an election is not under way

    (E) override a president's veto

98. Members of which of the following parties would be least likely to support a federal government program that taxed middle-class Americans in order to give the poor free access to a college education?

(A) Libertarian Party

(B) Green Party

(C) Democratic Party

(D) Republican Party

(E) Prohibition Party

99. When a president sends a budget to the Congress, all of the following are included EXCEPT

(A) tariff legislation

(B) budget outlays

(C) receipts

(D) general economic statements

(E) budget authority

100. Which Republican president altered the nation's political landscape by attracting many Democratic voters?

(A) Franklin Roosevelt

(B) John Kennedy

(C) Ronald Reagan

(D) Dwight Eisenhower

(E) Gerald Ford

Practice Test 2

CLEP American Government

Answer Key

1.	(A)	26.	(B)	51.	(A)	76.	(D)
2.	(B)	27.	(D)	52.	(C)	77.	(A)
3.	(B)	28.	(C)	53.	(A)	78.	(D)
4.	(C)	29.	(E)	54.	(D)	79.	(A)
5.	(A)	30.	(D)	55.	(C)	80.	(E)
6.	(E)	31.	(E)	56.	(D)	81.	(B)
7.	(E)	32.	(B)	57.	(D)	82.	(A)
8.	(B)	33.	(D)	58.	(E)	83.	(C)
9.	(C)	34.	(B)	59.	(A)	84.	(E)
10.	(A)	35.	(E)	60.	(D)	85.	(B)
11.	(D)	36.	(C)	61.	(C)	86.	(A)
12.	(C)	37.	(E)	62.	(B)	87.	(D)
13.	(C)	38.	(B)	63.	(A)	88.	(E)
14.	(C)	39.	(D)	64.	(E)	89.	(B)
15.	(C)	40.	(A)	65.	(B)	90.	(B)
16.	(C)	41.	(A)	66.	(B)	91.	(A)
17.	(A)	42.	(C)	67.	(C)	92.	(B)
18.	(B)	43.	(C)	68.	(B)	93.	(E)
19.	(E)	44.	(B)	69.	(A)	94.	(D)
20.	(D)	45.	(E)	70.	(E)	95.	(D)
21.	(E)	46.	(C)	71.	(C)	96.	(A)
22.	(A)	47.	(E)	72.	(B)	97.	(D)
23.	(E)	48.	(E)	73.	(C)	98.	(A)
24.	(D)	49.	(A)	74.	(C)	99.	(A)
25.	(D)	50.	(A)	75.	(B)	100.	(C)

Detailed Explanations of Answers

Practice Test 2

1.   **(A)**   The necessary and proper clause, also known as the elastic clause, grants Congress the authority to pass "all laws necessary and proper" for enforcing the congressional powers enumerated in the Constitution. The unwritten constitution (B) refers to departments of government not specifically called for by the Constitution but generally accepted in American political life. The Bill of Rights (C) refers to Amendments 1 through 10 of the Constitution, and the admissions clause (E) is Article 4, Section 3, which concerns the admission of new states into the Union. The execution clause (D) is fictional.

2.   **(B)**   Powers claimed by the president but not expressly called for in the Constitution are called inherent powers. For example, during the Civil War, President Abraham Lincoln placed a blockade on the Southern states without congressional approval. His argument was that the war powers given to the commander-in-chief empowered him to do this, and he did not have time to get Congress's permission. Later, Congress and the Supreme Court agreed with Lincoln. This expanded for future presidents the area of powers inherent in the Constitution's language on the president as commander-in-chief.

3.   **(B)**   The First Amendment's establishment clause states that the federal government may not establish a state religion. The free exercise clause (C) is also in the First Amendment and guarantees an individual's freedom to practice religion. The Second Amendment (D) concerns the right to bear arms. There is no neutrality clause (A) in the Constitution concerning religion, though the language of the First Amendment does suggest that the government should not favor any religion, but rather maintain a position of neutrality. The exclusionary rule (E) is related to the Fifth Amendment and says that evidence obtained illegally cannot be used in court against a defendant.

4.   **(C)**   A large majority of the professoriate claims to be liberal to one extent or another, but not 95% (A). A 2007 survey showed that about 62% of university professors identified themselves as very liberal, liberal, or somewhat liberal, and 19% identified themselves as somewhat conservative, conservative, or very conservative. (The rest identified themselves as political moderates.)

Because of this, political conservatives may be depicted as intellectually infe-rior (D), but if this is so, it is because of the professoriate's political leanings. It is true that higher education is associated with questioning norms, learning different viewpoints, and reflecting on the value of civil liberties (C), but this doesn't necessarily have to lead to an embrace of political liberalism.

5. **(A)** Privatization is one way the government seeks to control costs and reduce bureaucratic red tape.

6. **(E)** The Pendleton Act made some government jobs off-limits to pa-tronage, a first step in reforming the political "spoils system" that led to wide-spread political corruption. Currently, as a result of the reforms begun with the Pendleton Act, most government jobs are not held by political appointment.

7. **(E)** Secretaries of the executive departments—for example, the Depart-ment of the Interior, Department of Defense, and so forth—comprise the ma-jority of the president's cabinet. They serve with the advice and consent of the Senate, and though the Senate must approve the president's secretary nomina-tions before they can be appointed, once they are in place, the Senate is unable to remove them from office.

8. **(B)** Also known as regulatory agencies, independent regulatory com-missions are further removed from political concerns than are the executive de-partments, making them better able to achieve their objectives without political interference.

9. **(C)** The U.S. Postal Service generates its own revenue. The U.S. Mint is another example of a government corporation because it sells coins, also generating its own revenue.

10. **(A)** Rule administration is one of the functions that all the various orga-nizations within the federal bureaucracy share. Congress passes legislation that the bureaucracy must determine how to implement.

11. **(D)** The term *iron triangle* is used to describe the three-sided, mutually beneficial cooperation that often occurs between lobbyists, Congress, and the federal bureaucracy. Lobbyists influence Congress to pass favored laws and the bureaucracy to implement these laws in ways that favor the lobbyists. Congress members garner votes by supporting legislation that pleases special interest groups. And bureaucrats ensure their own survival since they are charged with implementing the new legislation touted by the lobbyists. In recent years, iron triangles have been largely displaced by issue networks.

12. **(C)**   *Devolution* is defined as the turning over of functions done by the federal government to the states and local jurisdictions.

13. **(C)**   Most of what we know about government is learned through the media. The media have a powerful influence on politics and the operations of government. The media comprise hundreds of information sources that are typically for-profit organizations.

14. **(C)**   Federal judges have disallowed some districts that have obviously been gerrymandered to overwhelmingly favor a political party. However, judges do not routinely draw federal Congressional districts.

15. **(C)**   In the media, complicated ideas and policy positions receive relatively little attention. The media wish to simplify information. Thus, politicians often condense their basic ideas into talking points. Infotainment (A) mixes political or other hard news with entertainment news. Sound bites (B) are catchy phrases politicians use to make points and to get media attention. The term "hold and hold" (D) is fictional. Condensed news (E) is something many busy Americans want, but this term does not answer the question.

16. **(C)**   Horse-race journalism often takes on the language of sports and puts most of its focus on image, personality, and popular perceptions of candidates.

17. **(A)**   Studies and surveys regularly show that Americans know more about celebrities than they do about the policy positions of government leaders. Studies also show that those who rely on television for their information know less about public affairs. Thus, though most Americans watch three to four hours of television per day, they are not well-informed. Television executives know that entertainment sells.

18. **(B)**   When the federal government simply instructs states to meet a certain requirement without providing funding, it is known as an unfunded mandate. The Real ID Act of 2005 called for uniformity in state identity documents. Federal block grants (A) are given to states to use at their own discretion, though to achieve a certain general end. Categorical grants (C) are given to the states to achieve a specific purpose. Cooperative federalism (D) is a system of government in which the federal and state jurisdictions overlap. Project Head Start (E) is a federally funded child development program for low-income children.

19. **(E)**   Four of the nine justices must agree to accept a case, or issue a writ of certiorari. Case precedent is only overturned via court rulings, which would call for a vote of five justices generally (A). The Supreme Court does not confirm or deny chief justice appointees, the Senate does (B). Oral arguments are

set at 30 minutes per side in any given case by informal amendment (C). Only Congress could change the numerical size of the Court from its current nine, which is highly unlikely to happen.

20. **(D)** When President Lyndon Johnson signed the Immigration and Nationality Act of 1965, it greatly increased the number of immigrants legally allowed into the nation each year. Most of these immigrants came from developing countries, chiefly Asian and Latin American.

21. **(E)** The Mayflower Compact was the written document signed by the Puritan settlers (Pilgrims) of Plymouth Colony establishing the rule of law within the colony and the principle of government by consent of the governed. The compact is silent on the makeup of a legislature (A), separation of political powers (B), and political checks and balances (C). The Pilgrims had no interest in the separation of church and state (D).

22. **(A)** Majoritarianism calls for majority rule: decisions are based on the preferences of the numerical majority of voters. The pluralist model of democracy (B) argues that government operates as people with different political ideas compete in public life. Liberalism (C) is difficult to define, though it has always emphasized the importance of human freedom. In its modern form, it argues for government action to promote greater equality. Libertarianism (D) argues for minimal government. Monetarism (E) is an economic school of thought that focuses on inflation and the amount of money available in an economy.

23. **(E)** The Articles of Confederation did not allow for the federal government to draft soldiers. Thus, states could refuse to send troops to meet a national need. This was one of the many reasons the central government under the Articles was deemed too weak.

24. **(D)** Bureaucracies can be famously inflexible because of their commitment to rules.

25. **(D)** A key element of England's Glorious Revolution was the written Bill of Rights, which placed limits on the monarch's power. None of the other countries listed—France (A), Spain (B), Holland (C), or Germany (E)—had written bills of rights before the United States.

26. **(B)** Montesquieu's *Spirit of the Laws* was very influential with respect to the U.S. Constitution. Machiavelli (A) was an important Renaissance political philosopher, and Mill (D) was an important nineteenth-century proponent of liberalism. Montaigne (C) was a French official and essayist; Montcalm (E) was a French general.

27. **(D)** The words appear in the Constitution's preamble. The Bill of Rights (A) has no preamble or introductory sentence. The Declaration of Independence (B) begins with the words, "When in the course of human events. . . ." The Mayflower Compact (C) begins with the phrase, "In the name of God, amen." The first sentence of the Articles of Confederation (E) is functional and uninspiring.

28. **(C)** A class action lawsuit is brought to court by one person on behalf of many in a similar situation. Recalls (A), propositions (B), initiatives (D), and referenda (E) are all examples of direct democracy.

29. **(E)** The Second Continental Congress devised the Articles of Confederation. The Association (A) was organized by the First Continental Congress (D) and called for a complete colonial boycott on British goods. The creation of the Congress, comprising the House of Representatives (B) and the Senate (C), came with the writing of the Constitution, following the effective failure of the Articles of Confederation.

30. **(D)** The media realize that in order to keep a general audience's attention, they must often provide news that is horrific or sensationalistic. According to the well-known saying, "If it bleeds, it leads," meaning that a grizzly crime is likely to receive more news attention than a tedious but important trade bill. Horse-race journalism (A) treats politics like a sport, focusing on who's up and down, who's winning and losing. Human interest stories (E) forgo serious news for discussions of, for example, politicians' hairstyles, personal lives, and clothing choices.

31. **(E)** In the early twenty-first century, three TV stations began providing around-the-clock news coverage, which created time to fill. Rather than filling it with hard news (the collection of which costs money), they gave much time to "talking heads," otherwise known as pundits.

32. **(B)** Limited time and resources force editors and producers, the media gatekeepers, to choose what will be seen or read. News grazers (D) pick up news here and there; they have no commitment to being well-informed. Gatekeepers certainly act as filters (A) but are not referred to as such. Bloggers (C) are contributors to Web logs, or blogs. The term *colanders* (E) is fictional in this context.

33. **(D)** Congress has general oversight of the publicly funded military academies, but it does not specifically determine who is and is not accepted into the academies.

34. **(B)** Article 1, section 3 of the Constitution reads: "The Vice President of the United States shall be President of the Senate, but shall have no vote, unless they be equally divided."

35. **(E)** Article 1, section 7 of the Constitution reads: "All Bills for raising Revenue shall originate in the House of Representatives."

36. **(C)** Article 1, Section 3 of the Constitution reads (in part): "No person shall be a Senator who shall not have attained to the Age of thirty years, and been nine Years a Citizen of the United States." To serve in the House of Representatives, a person must have been a citizen for at least seven years. In this context, the other numbers are not relevant.

37. **(E)** Bill Clinton was impeached in the House but was ultimately acquitted and served out his full second term in office. The allegations stemmed from an investigation into a sexual scandal. Coolidge (A) was among the twentieth century's upstanding (and rather dull) presidents. Johnson (B) was widely disliked by the end of his first full term in office, and he chose not to run for reelection, but he was not impeached. Nixon (C) would have been impeached for a political cover-up had he not resigned—the only president to do so. Reagan (D) came under substantial congressional criticism for funneling money to anticommunists in Nicaragua (contravening a law against doing so), but he was not impeached.

38. **(B)** One way bureaucracies can be politicized is when their responsibilities overlap and they compete for "turf" so as to protect their own interests; this tendency is sometimes called bureaucratic imperialism.

39. **(D)** Responding to concerns that racial equality was not being sufficiently realized in the county, the Voting Rights Act of 1982 encouraged the creation of congressional districts in which racial minorities would comprise majorities. Eighteen-year-olds (A) gained the right to vote from the Twenty-Sixth Amendment (1971). Poll taxes (B) and literacy tests (C) were abolished by civil rights legislation of the 1960s.

40. **(A)** It isn't surprising that the president who led the nation through its greatest crisis, the Civil War, would achieve such status. The other four presidents are regularly listed highly in surveys. Notice that each of the highly ranked presidents is linked to the crisis of war. Franklin Roosevelt (B) led the nation through most of World War II. George Washington (C) presided over the Continental Army during the American Revolution. Theodore Roosevelt (D) became well known during his time of leadership in the Spanish-American

War. Harry Truman (E) led the nation through the end of World War II and led the country during most of the conflict in Korea.

41. **(A)** Debate in the House of Representatives is consistently limited and, by unanimous consent, is often limited in the Senate. Press releases (B), name recognition (C), taxpayer-funded travel budgets (D), and franking privileges are all advantages held by incumbents.

42. **(C)** Representation in the House of Representatives is based on population. States that gain population, gain representatives; states that lose population relative to growing states, lose representatives. The government has long used the census to determine the national and ethnic origin of residents (A), but the Constitution does not require this. States have the same number of senators regardless of population (B). The Congress has the power to create more, or reduce the number of, Supreme Court seats if it wishes to (E), but this is not directly related to information gained from the census. The census has no bearing on the location of Federal Reserve banks (D).

43. **(C)** Congress last declared war during World War II. Decades earlier, it had declared war in the Spanish-American War (A) and the First World War (B). Congress empowered the president to enact authorized military action before the Vietnam War (D) and the Gulf War (E).

44. **(B)** The District of Columbia's delegate can have whatever voting power Congress determines since oversight of the district is constitutionally given to Congress. At present, that power extends to voting only in committee, not in the full chamber. Washington, D.C., not being a state, is not eligible for the federal representation states have, such as Senators and voting House Representatives.

45. **(E)** Both chambers of Congress are prohibited from passing ex post facto laws (A), taxing goods that are shipped from state to state (B), spending treasury money not accounted for in legislation (C), and giving titles of nobility (D). Only the House of Representatives may formally initiate tax legislation.

46. **(C)** *Planned Parenthood v. Casey* was part of a series of cases in the aftermath of *Roe v. Wade* that illustrates the political struggle *Roe* sparked as well as the tensions between federal courts and state legislatures.

47. **(E)** As a result of the Supreme Court case *Roe v. Wade* (1973), state laws that outlawed abortion were deemed unconstitutional. However, the practice of abortion throughout the country remains complicated. Restrictions exist in some states that do not exist in others. No Constitutional amendment to outlaw abortion has been put into the ratification process.

48. **(E)**   The first section of the Equal Rights Amendment (ERA) reads: "Equality of rights under the law shall not be denied or abridged by the United States or by any state on account of sex." The amendment was first proposed in Congress in 1923 and was passed by a two-thirds majority in Congress in 1972, but failed to be ratified 10 years later. The ERA has never regained the momentum it had in the 1970s. By the early twenty-first century, women outnumbered men in colleges and universities (C).

49. **(A)**   Condoleezza Rice was both the second woman and the second African American to serve as secretary of state. Nancy Pelosi (B) became the first woman Speaker of the House in 2006. Sandra Day O'Connor (C) and Ruth Bader Ginsburg (D) were the first women justices appointed to the Supreme Court. Hillary Clinton (E) has been a First Lady, a U.S. senator, a presidential candidate, and in 2009 became President Barack Obama's secretary of state.

50. **(A)**   Congressional standing committees carry over from one congressional session to the next, hence the term *standing*. Committees that are formed to deal with temporary or special issues (B) are called select committees. Standing committees are concerned with several issues, not just taxation and military matters (C and D). Congressional committees are not formed for the purpose of preparing political parties for elections (E).

51. **(A)**   Cooperative federalism, also known as marble-cake federalism, makes sense theoretically, though not always in practice, because the federal government has greater resources to work with while the states possess a greater knowledge of local affairs. The idea is that the powers of the two governments are mixed and swirled like the chocolate and vanilla in a marble cake. Layer-cake federalism (D) refers to a system in which federal and state responsibilities are clearly defined and distinct.

52. **(C)**   By tradition, the president gives a state of the union address annually, but the Constitution does not explicitly require this, relying instead on the vaguer requirement from "time to time."

53. **(A)**   House members and state legislators (C) and governors (E) are free to make known their views about ambassadors, and the president may even seek their advice—for example, a president might ask a governor of a southwestern state for advice on prospective ambassadors to Mexico. But, formally, advice and consent comes through the Senate.

54. **(D)**   Fast-track legislation allows Congress to agree or disagree with trade deals, not amend them. One reason is that amendments change agree-

ments and these changes affect the other nation or nations that are party to the trade deal. Thus, the process can be indefinite and terminal.

55. **(C)** President Bush exercised his inherent powers in establishing military tribunals to try alleged terror suspects captured in Iraq and Afghanistan. The argument in support of this action is that the Constitution's language about the president as commander-in-chief, along with practical concerns about the complications taking the matter to Congress would incur, gave the president the inherent power to act swiftly for the good of the nation.

56. **(D)** Executive orders are based on the Constitution's language regarding the president's obligation to see that laws are "faithfully executed" and the executive branch of the government well managed. The power of the pardon for crimes committed against the United States is explicitly given to the president in the Constitution and does not rely on executive order.

57. **(D)** The Federal Reserve System is essentially the central bank of the United States. It can be influenced by Congress and the executive branch, but it is an independent government body.

58. **(E)** Vice presidents were more influential in the late twentieth century than they were in the early twentieth century. Vice President Al Gore (in the Clinton administration), for example, was a very active and public vice president. The trend continues in the early twenty-first century: Vice President Dick Cheney (in the George W. Bush administration) was the most powerful vice president in American history to that point.

59. **(A)** Congress can limit a cabinet member's influence via oversight, but it has set no limits on what cabinet members can say to presidents. Contemporary cabinets comprise about 20 people with different areas of expertise (B and C), and thus, meetings of the cabinet tend not to be very productive. While presidents want to ensure that all cabinet members are highly competent, they are also under pressure to ensure that their cabinets are diverse (D). The president also may turn to personal friends, aides, and allies (E), thus making the need for advice from cabinet secretaries to whom he may not be close less necessary.

60. **(D)** The freedom to engage in legal trade is certainly implied in the nation's founding documents—in, for example, the stated right to "life, liberty, and the pursuit of happiness." But this freedom is not expressly acknowledged in the First Amendment.

61. **(C)** The key framers of the Constitution did not think a bill of rights was necessary, but as the debates over the Constitution continued, it became

clear that such a document was necessary to gain the support of some anti-federalists. Following the Civil War (E), three important amendments were passed in quick succession (Amendments 13, 14, and 15).

62. **(B)** The candidate's position runs counter to the sociable smoker's self-interest. Issue framing (A) has to do with how a political idea is pitched to the public. For example, one politician might pitch an anti-smoking law as an infringement on personal liberty while another will speak about it in terms of public health. The lifestyle effect (C) refers to the tendency for people at different stages of life to take certain viewpoints and to vote differently. The generational effect (D) points to the fact that generations tend to differ in general terms—for example, the generation that grew up during the Second World War participated in civic clubs more than baby boomers did. Political trust (E) simply refers to the amount of trust people have in public officials.

63. **(A)** A basic component of the "Lemon test" was that assistance to a religious institution could not lead to the government's supporting religion (C) or inhibiting religion (D). To require that other religions be taught, as (A) suggests, would be to force exclusivist religions to give other religions attention. Such a requirement would contradict the requirements in (C), (D), and (E).

64. **(E)** These decisions underscore the ongoing confusion that surrounds the paradoxical desires to protect religious belief and practice while limiting religion in the public sphere. The display was allowed in Texas because the commandments were accompanied by other secular documents and were deemed to reflect the broad heritage of the country. The Kentucky displays were deemed to be purely religious and were therefore disallowed. This shows that the "Lemon test" (D) of *Lemon v. Kurtzman* (1971) did not last long.

65. **(B)** A supermajority of two-thirds in both chambers of Congress is required to override a presidential veto. For a bill to get to a president's desk, it must have received a majority of votes in both chambers (A). State legislatures (C) cannot directly override a presidential veto. The United States does not use formal national referenda (E), though elections are often said to be referenda on political aspirants.

66. **(B)** The spoils system led to pervasive patronage—for example, the giving of political jobs in exchange for help with elections. This led to widespread corruption. The Pendleton Civil Service Act (1883) began the process of significantly reducing patronage in the federal government.

67. **(C)** The Congress can vote for the expulsion of one of its members. It is rare; a congressperson accused of wrongdoing usually resigns before this

becomes necessary. Censure (A) and critical letters from ethics committees (B) are also forms of punishment that the Congress can impose on a fellow congressional member. A congressperson may spend time in prison (D), but Congress cannot impose this sanction.

68. **(B)** No such section exists. The four sections of the *Congressional Record* are a daily digest (A), a House section (C), a Senate section (D), and a section where Congress members' remarks can be extended.

69. **(A)** The U.S. Mint produces coins and sells collectors' coins as a way of financing its own operations. The Bureau of Engraving and Printing (B) produces the country's paper currency. The Federal Deposit Insurance Corporation (D) insures bank deposits. The U.S. Postal Service (E) is not directly related to the production of currency though, like the Mint, it pays for its own services by selling stamps and other services.

70. **(E)** Jimmy Carter, a Democrat, won the presidency in the election of 1976. Both Carter and John Anderson (B), an Independent, lost to Ronald Reagan in 1980. Theodore Roosevelt (C) ran for president on the Progressive ticket in 1912. Strom Thurmond (D) ran as a States' Rights Democrat (or Dixiecrat) in 1948. Ralph Nader (A) ran for president as a Green Party candidate in 1996 and 2000, and as an Independent in 2004 and 2008.

71. **(C)** There has been a gradual trend toward devolution, or a shift, of powers from the federal government to the states since the 1980s, represented by an increase of block grants relative to categorical grants. Of course, power struggles between the federal and state governments (D) persist, but choice (C) best answers the question.

72. **(B)** All of the options are positions within the Department of Justice. The Attorney General (A) is the top law enforcement officer in the federal government. In matters of exceptional importance, the U.S. Attorney General may represent the president's position in the Supreme Court. The Inspector General (C) fights against waste, fraud, and abuse within the Department of Justice. The Chief U.S. Marshal (D) oversees the nation's federal police force. The primary purpose of the Office of Special Counsel (E) is to protect the federal employment merit system from fraud, bribery, corruption, and so on.

73. **(C)** The Magna Carta, issued in 1215, set some limits on the English monarch's powers. The English Bill of Rights (A) followed the English Glorious Revolution of 1688. John Locke's *Second Treatise on Government* of 1690 (D), relates some of the basic ideas expressed in the U.S. Declaration of Independence. The emphasis on separation of powers and political checks and

balances in Montesquieu's *Spirit of the Laws* (E), published in 1748, influenced the writers of the Constitution. The American Bill of Rights (B) was written shortly after the Constitution, partly to win over anti-federalists who wanted a written list of rights added to the Constitution.

74. **(C)** The United States practices federalism. The federal, or national, government has jurisdiction over some state affairs, and the state government has jurisdiction over other areas. A more nationalist government (A) would likely maintain more centralized control. The other options provided are fictional terms.

75. **(B)** Among the founding champions of states' rights is Thomas Jefferson, primary author of the Declaration of Independence and third American president. People who hold this position emphasize the language of the Tenth Amendment: "The powers not delegated to the United States by the Constitution, nor prohibited by it to the States, are reserved to the States respectively, or to the people."

76. **(D)** The federal courts have relied on the commerce clause of Article 1, Section 2 of the Constitution to enhance the power of the national government. The other options are fictional.

77. **(A)** By the mid-twentieth century, it was clear that many southern states would not provide African Americans equal protection under the law as required by the Fourteenth Amendment. States also used texts and taxes to prevent African Americans from voting. To remedy this situation, the federal government enhanced its power at the expense of the states. A symbol of this is President Dwight Eisenhower's order to federal troops to see to it that Little Rock High School in Arkansas was desegregated.

78. **(D)** The term *equal opportunity* refers to the political notion that all Americans should have a chance in life to succeed. Of course, for there to be equal opportunity, civil rights (A) must be protected and free choices (B) made available. Some argue that affirmative action (E) is necessary to ensure equal opportunity for certain groups who have been historically disadvantaged.

79. **(A)** The Court determined that so long as facilities were of equal quality, racial segregation was constitutional. The practical problem was that facilities for whites and blacks were rarely of equal quality. The separate-but-equal view was overturned by *Brown v. Board of Education of Topeka* (1954).

80. **(E)** *Brown v. Board of Education of Topeka* was one of the most influential Supreme Court cases of the twentieth century. Relying heavily on the

equal protection clause of the Fourteenth Amendment, the Court overturned the separate-but-equal doctrine of *Plessy v. Ferguson* (A). *Brown* symbolized the Supreme Court's willingness to override state laws for the sake of constitutional principle. Busing (D) to eliminate de facto segregation came as a result of the civil rights work that followed *Brown*. President Harry Truman's desegregation of the military (B) was an important step on the road to the dismantling of legal segregation. No Child Left Behind (C) was an education reform act passed during the first term of the George W. Bush administration.

81. **(B)**   The given scenario illustrates the two-step flow of communication, whereby an informed reader (an opinion leader) pays close attention to information and then disperses what he or she has learned to the masses. In terms of political change and action, reaching a small number of well-informed readers (i.e., "attentive policy elites") may amount to more than addressing many lesser informed individuals because the lesser informed many are influenced by the opinions of the well-informed few.

82. **(A)**   Before radio, the newspaper was the primary source of daily news. Franklin Roosevelt first used the radio effectively in his "fireside chats." His addresses to the nation explained his economic policies during the Great Depression.

83. **(C)**   The Civil Rights Act of 1968 outlawed discrimination in most kinds of housing. This act, along with the Civil Rights Act of 1964 (D) and the Voting Rights Act of 1965 (B), point to a heightened national commitment to civil rights and to the growing power of the federal government relative to state governments.

84. **(E)**   Affirmative action is an effort to ensure equal opportunity for historically disadvantaged groups by factoring race, gender, and ethnicity into decisions of employment and education. Some argue that because specific groups start life at a disadvantage due to discrimination, affirmative action—such as specifically encouraging members of that group to apply for a position—is necessary. Others believe that this amounts to the promotion of a new kind of inequality. Affirmative action is a response to the legacy of segregationist Jim Crow laws (B). The Twenty-Sixth Amendment (C) gave the vote to Americans who have reached their eighteenth birthday.

85. **(B)**   The Civil Rights Act of 1964 forbade discrimination on the basis of race, color, gender, religion, or national origin. It banned discrimination in employment for any institution that received federal funds, and established the Equal Employment Opportunity Commission (EEOC), which sets policy to carry out civil rights laws and has power to investigate whether the laws have been broken.

86. **(A)** The perceived glass ceiling prevented women from being equal to men in the workplace. In the 2008 presidential election, the Republican vice presidential nominee, Sarah Palin, spoke many times about the need to break the glass ceiling "once and for all." All of the other answers are irrelevant.

87. **(D)** *Roe v. Wade*, citing the constitutional right to privacy established in *Griswold v. Connecticut*, struck down as unconstitutional most state laws outlawing first-trimester abortions. *Roe* did allow states to make laws regulating the second-trimester abortions and gave states power to make third-trimester abortions illegal. This sparked a political war concerning what states could and could not do. Before this case, states made their own laws on abortion.

88. **(E)** Each rule the bureaucracy devises goes into the *Federal Register*. By the year 2000, the *Federal Register* comprised a breathtaking 90,000 pages.

89. **(B)** A divided government occurs when the White House is in the hands of one party and Congress is in the hands of the other. In the national elections of 2008, sensing that they would lose seats in the House and the Senate and that the Democrat Barack Obama would win the White House, Republicans asked for votes by pointing to the importance of divided government—one of the many ways that political power can be checked and balanced.

90. **(B)** President Lyndon Johnson's "war on poverty" began in the 1960s. At the time, the amount of money going from the federal government to the states increased. Among the war's tools were Medicare, Medicaid, food stamps, and housing assistance.

91. **(A)** The primary purpose of the Interstate Commerce Commission (created in 1887) was to regulate railroads that moved goods and services from one state to another. It was abolished in 1995 and replaced by the Surface Transportation Board.

92. **(B)** The case of *Gitlow v. New York* concerned Benjamin Gitlow's arrest under a New York law for handing out socialist literature. The majority of the Court agreed with Gitlow's conviction, but the decision established the principle that the First Amendment applied to state laws. In *Abrams v. United States* (A), Oliver Wendell Holmes dissented from the Court's decision to uphold Abram's conviction for publicly opposing America's position on the Russian Revolution with the claim that "the ultimate good desired [in a free society] is better reached by free trade in ideas." In *Cohen v. California* (C), the Court overturned a conviction of an anti-Vietnam protestor. *Brandenburg v. Ohio* (D) allowed hateful but not genuinely threatening speech from a Ku Klux

Klansman. In *Chaplinsky v. New Hampshire*, the conviction of a Jehovah's Witness for calling a marshal a "fascist" was upheld because Chaplinsky's "fighting words" in a time of war presented a present danger.

93. **(E)** The Personal Responsibility and Work Opportunity Reconciliation Act of 1996 required work and job training in exchange for benefits, among other things. Calvin Coolidge (A) was president before the advent of a large federal welfare system. Lyndon Johnson (C) is most associated with the rapid growth of welfare programs. Neither Harry Truman (B) nor George H. W. Bush (D) is associated with significant welfare reform.

94. **(D)** Some federal employees, such as military personnel in certain circumstances, do get food allowances. As a general rule, however, federal employees do not get such a benefit. Federal employment is secure (A) relative to many occupations in the general economy. Before a person can be fired from a federal position, a specific and sometimes lengthy process has to be followed. Federal job wages (B) keep up with inflation, and while some government jobs (such as low-ranking military personnel) do not make a lot of money, they do receive other benefits such as housing. (Another notable exception is that federal judges do not earn as much as they might working privately. Supreme Court justices have regularly told Congress that this prevents many excellent prospective judges from entering the federal system.) Health insurance (C) and pension benefits (E) are very good. A retired military veteran, for example, receives lifelong healthcare and a monthly pension.

95. **(D)** The Joint Chiefs of Staff comprise leading military officials who advise the president.

96. **(A)** The hopper is the box into which members of the House of Representatives drop proposed legislation.

97. **(D)** A special session of Congress may be needed to break a tied presidential election (B). None of the other answers is relevant.

98. **(A)** Libertarians advocate minimal government control and argue for the elimination of many government agencies, such as the Department of Education. The Green Party (B) is socialistic and many of its members would advocate such a program, as would some Democrats (C) on the party's left wing. Under some conditions, moderate Republicans (D)—sometimes called RINO's (Republicans in Name Only)—might support such a scheme. The Prohibition Party (E), once powerful though now without any formal influence, is dedicated to the abolition of alcohol for beverage purposes.

99. **(A)**   The president cannot create legislation. He can only approve or veto legislation. Budget authority (E) refers to the amounts government agencies will be able to spend. Budget outlays (B) state how much government agencies are actually expected to spend. The term *receipts* (C) refers to the amount the government expects to take in via taxes and other sources. The document the president sends are prefaced with general statements on the economy (D).

100. **(C)**   The so-called Reagan Democrats helped the Republican gain two smashing presidential victories in 1980 and 1984. Roosevelt (A) and Kennedy (B) were Democrats. Ford (E) lost the election of 1976. Dwight Eisenhower (D) was a popular wartime general who won both of the elections he contested handily (1952 and 1956), but his presidency isn't associated with the capture of a substantial Democratic voting bloc. Twenty years after Reagan's presidency ended, Republicans wondered how to win back the "Reagan Democrats" who were lost to Barack Obama in 2008.

Practice Test 1

CLEP American Government

Answer Sheet

1. Ⓐ Ⓑ Ⓒ Ⓓ Ⓔ	35. Ⓐ Ⓑ Ⓒ Ⓓ Ⓔ	68. Ⓐ Ⓑ Ⓒ Ⓓ Ⓔ
2. Ⓐ Ⓑ Ⓒ Ⓓ Ⓔ	36. Ⓐ Ⓑ Ⓒ Ⓓ Ⓔ	69. Ⓐ Ⓑ Ⓒ Ⓓ Ⓔ
3. Ⓐ Ⓑ Ⓒ Ⓓ Ⓔ	37. Ⓐ Ⓑ Ⓒ Ⓓ Ⓔ	70. Ⓐ Ⓑ Ⓒ Ⓓ Ⓔ
4. Ⓐ Ⓑ Ⓒ Ⓓ Ⓔ	38. Ⓐ Ⓑ Ⓒ Ⓓ Ⓔ	71. Ⓐ Ⓑ Ⓒ Ⓓ Ⓔ
5. Ⓐ Ⓑ Ⓒ Ⓓ Ⓔ	39. Ⓐ Ⓑ Ⓒ Ⓓ Ⓔ	72. Ⓐ Ⓑ Ⓒ Ⓓ Ⓔ
6. Ⓐ Ⓑ Ⓒ Ⓓ Ⓔ	40. Ⓐ Ⓑ Ⓒ Ⓓ Ⓔ	73. Ⓐ Ⓑ Ⓒ Ⓓ Ⓔ
7. Ⓐ Ⓑ Ⓒ Ⓓ Ⓔ	41. Ⓐ Ⓑ Ⓒ Ⓓ Ⓔ	74. Ⓐ Ⓑ Ⓒ Ⓓ Ⓔ
8. Ⓐ Ⓑ Ⓒ Ⓓ Ⓔ	42. Ⓐ Ⓑ Ⓒ Ⓓ Ⓔ	75. Ⓐ Ⓑ Ⓒ Ⓓ Ⓔ
9. Ⓐ Ⓑ Ⓒ Ⓓ Ⓔ	43. Ⓐ Ⓑ Ⓒ Ⓓ Ⓔ	76. Ⓐ Ⓑ Ⓒ Ⓓ Ⓔ
10. Ⓐ Ⓑ Ⓒ Ⓓ Ⓔ	44. Ⓐ Ⓑ Ⓒ Ⓓ Ⓔ	77. Ⓐ Ⓑ Ⓒ Ⓓ Ⓔ
11. Ⓐ Ⓑ Ⓒ Ⓓ Ⓔ	45. Ⓐ Ⓑ Ⓒ Ⓓ Ⓔ	78. Ⓐ Ⓑ Ⓒ Ⓓ Ⓔ
12. Ⓐ Ⓑ Ⓒ Ⓓ Ⓔ	46. Ⓐ Ⓑ Ⓒ Ⓓ Ⓔ	79. Ⓐ Ⓑ Ⓒ Ⓓ Ⓔ
13. Ⓐ Ⓑ Ⓒ Ⓓ Ⓔ	47. Ⓐ Ⓑ Ⓒ Ⓓ Ⓔ	80. Ⓐ Ⓑ Ⓒ Ⓓ Ⓔ
14. Ⓐ Ⓑ Ⓒ Ⓓ Ⓔ	48. Ⓐ Ⓑ Ⓒ Ⓓ Ⓔ	81. Ⓐ Ⓑ Ⓒ Ⓓ Ⓔ
15. Ⓐ Ⓑ Ⓒ Ⓓ Ⓔ	49. Ⓐ Ⓑ Ⓒ Ⓓ Ⓔ	82. Ⓐ Ⓑ Ⓒ Ⓓ Ⓔ
16. Ⓐ Ⓑ Ⓒ Ⓓ Ⓔ	50. Ⓐ Ⓑ Ⓒ Ⓓ Ⓔ	83. Ⓐ Ⓑ Ⓒ Ⓓ Ⓔ
17. Ⓐ Ⓑ Ⓒ Ⓓ Ⓔ	51. Ⓐ Ⓑ Ⓒ Ⓓ Ⓔ	84. Ⓐ Ⓑ Ⓒ Ⓓ Ⓔ
18. Ⓐ Ⓑ Ⓒ Ⓓ Ⓔ	52. Ⓐ Ⓑ Ⓒ Ⓓ Ⓔ	85. Ⓐ Ⓑ Ⓒ Ⓓ Ⓔ
19. Ⓐ Ⓑ Ⓒ Ⓓ Ⓔ	53. Ⓐ Ⓑ Ⓒ Ⓓ Ⓔ	86. Ⓐ Ⓑ Ⓒ Ⓓ Ⓔ
20. Ⓐ Ⓑ Ⓒ Ⓓ Ⓔ	54. Ⓐ Ⓑ Ⓒ Ⓓ Ⓔ	87. Ⓐ Ⓑ Ⓒ Ⓓ Ⓔ
21. Ⓐ Ⓑ Ⓒ Ⓓ Ⓔ	55. Ⓐ Ⓑ Ⓒ Ⓓ Ⓔ	88. Ⓐ Ⓑ Ⓒ Ⓓ Ⓔ
22. Ⓐ Ⓑ Ⓒ Ⓓ Ⓔ	56. Ⓐ Ⓑ Ⓒ Ⓓ Ⓔ	89. Ⓐ Ⓑ Ⓒ Ⓓ Ⓔ
23. Ⓐ Ⓑ Ⓒ Ⓓ Ⓔ	57. Ⓐ Ⓑ Ⓒ Ⓓ Ⓔ	90. Ⓐ Ⓑ Ⓒ Ⓓ Ⓔ
24. Ⓐ Ⓑ Ⓒ Ⓓ Ⓔ	58. Ⓐ Ⓑ Ⓒ Ⓓ Ⓔ	91. Ⓐ Ⓑ Ⓒ Ⓓ Ⓔ
25. Ⓐ Ⓑ Ⓒ Ⓓ Ⓔ	59. Ⓐ Ⓑ Ⓒ Ⓓ Ⓔ	92. Ⓐ Ⓑ Ⓒ Ⓓ Ⓔ
26. Ⓐ Ⓑ Ⓒ Ⓓ Ⓔ	60. Ⓐ Ⓑ Ⓒ Ⓓ Ⓔ	93. Ⓐ Ⓑ Ⓒ Ⓓ Ⓔ
27. Ⓐ Ⓑ Ⓒ Ⓓ Ⓔ	61. Ⓐ Ⓑ Ⓒ Ⓓ Ⓔ	94. Ⓐ Ⓑ Ⓒ Ⓓ Ⓔ
28. Ⓐ Ⓑ Ⓒ Ⓓ Ⓔ	62. Ⓐ Ⓑ Ⓒ Ⓓ Ⓔ	95. Ⓐ Ⓑ Ⓒ Ⓓ Ⓔ
29. Ⓐ Ⓑ Ⓒ Ⓓ Ⓔ	63. Ⓐ Ⓑ Ⓒ Ⓓ Ⓔ	96. Ⓐ Ⓑ Ⓒ Ⓓ Ⓔ
30. Ⓐ Ⓑ Ⓒ Ⓓ Ⓔ	64. Ⓐ Ⓑ Ⓒ Ⓓ Ⓔ	97. Ⓐ Ⓑ Ⓒ Ⓓ Ⓔ
31. Ⓐ Ⓑ Ⓒ Ⓓ Ⓔ	65. Ⓐ Ⓑ Ⓒ Ⓓ Ⓔ	98. Ⓐ Ⓑ Ⓒ Ⓓ Ⓔ
32. Ⓐ Ⓑ Ⓒ Ⓓ Ⓔ	66. Ⓐ Ⓑ Ⓒ Ⓓ Ⓔ	99. Ⓐ Ⓑ Ⓒ Ⓓ Ⓔ
33. Ⓐ Ⓑ Ⓒ Ⓓ Ⓔ	67. Ⓐ Ⓑ Ⓒ Ⓓ Ⓔ	100. Ⓐ Ⓑ Ⓒ Ⓓ Ⓔ
34. Ⓐ Ⓑ Ⓒ Ⓓ Ⓔ		

Practice Test 2

CLEP American Government

Answer Sheet

1. Ⓐ Ⓑ Ⓒ Ⓓ Ⓔ
2. Ⓐ Ⓑ Ⓒ Ⓓ Ⓔ
3. Ⓐ Ⓑ Ⓒ Ⓓ Ⓔ
4. Ⓐ Ⓑ Ⓒ Ⓓ Ⓔ
5. Ⓐ Ⓑ Ⓒ Ⓓ Ⓔ
6. Ⓐ Ⓑ Ⓒ Ⓓ Ⓔ
7. Ⓐ Ⓑ Ⓒ Ⓓ Ⓔ
8. Ⓐ Ⓑ Ⓒ Ⓓ Ⓔ
9. Ⓐ Ⓑ Ⓒ Ⓓ Ⓔ
10. Ⓐ Ⓑ Ⓒ Ⓓ Ⓔ
11. Ⓐ Ⓑ Ⓒ Ⓓ Ⓔ
12. Ⓐ Ⓑ Ⓒ Ⓓ Ⓔ
13. Ⓐ Ⓑ Ⓒ Ⓓ Ⓔ
14. Ⓐ Ⓑ Ⓒ Ⓓ Ⓔ
15. Ⓐ Ⓑ Ⓒ Ⓓ Ⓔ
16. Ⓐ Ⓑ Ⓒ Ⓓ Ⓔ
17. Ⓐ Ⓑ Ⓒ Ⓓ Ⓔ
18. Ⓐ Ⓑ Ⓒ Ⓓ Ⓔ
19. Ⓐ Ⓑ Ⓒ Ⓓ Ⓔ
20. Ⓐ Ⓑ Ⓒ Ⓓ Ⓔ
21. Ⓐ Ⓑ Ⓒ Ⓓ Ⓔ
22. Ⓐ Ⓑ Ⓒ Ⓓ Ⓔ
23. Ⓐ Ⓑ Ⓒ Ⓓ Ⓔ
24. Ⓐ Ⓑ Ⓒ Ⓓ Ⓔ
25. Ⓐ Ⓑ Ⓒ Ⓓ Ⓔ
26. Ⓐ Ⓑ Ⓒ Ⓓ Ⓔ
27. Ⓐ Ⓑ Ⓒ Ⓓ Ⓔ
28. Ⓐ Ⓑ Ⓒ Ⓓ Ⓔ
29. Ⓐ Ⓑ Ⓒ Ⓓ Ⓔ
30. Ⓐ Ⓑ Ⓒ Ⓓ Ⓔ
31. Ⓐ Ⓑ Ⓒ Ⓓ Ⓔ
32. Ⓐ Ⓑ Ⓒ Ⓓ Ⓔ
33. Ⓐ Ⓑ Ⓒ Ⓓ Ⓔ
34. Ⓐ Ⓑ Ⓒ Ⓓ Ⓔ

35. Ⓐ Ⓑ Ⓒ Ⓓ Ⓔ
36. Ⓐ Ⓑ Ⓒ Ⓓ Ⓔ
37. Ⓐ Ⓑ Ⓒ Ⓓ Ⓔ
38. Ⓐ Ⓑ Ⓒ Ⓓ Ⓔ
39. Ⓐ Ⓑ Ⓒ Ⓓ Ⓔ
40. Ⓐ Ⓑ Ⓒ Ⓓ Ⓔ
41. Ⓐ Ⓑ Ⓒ Ⓓ Ⓔ
42. Ⓐ Ⓑ Ⓒ Ⓓ Ⓔ
43. Ⓐ Ⓑ Ⓒ Ⓓ Ⓔ
44. Ⓐ Ⓑ Ⓒ Ⓓ Ⓔ
45. Ⓐ Ⓑ Ⓒ Ⓓ Ⓔ
46. Ⓐ Ⓑ Ⓒ Ⓓ Ⓔ
47. Ⓐ Ⓑ Ⓒ Ⓓ Ⓔ
48. Ⓐ Ⓑ Ⓒ Ⓓ Ⓔ
49. Ⓐ Ⓑ Ⓒ Ⓓ Ⓔ
50. Ⓐ Ⓑ Ⓒ Ⓓ Ⓔ
51. Ⓐ Ⓑ Ⓒ Ⓓ Ⓔ
52. Ⓐ Ⓑ Ⓒ Ⓓ Ⓔ
53. Ⓐ Ⓑ Ⓒ Ⓓ Ⓔ
54. Ⓐ Ⓑ Ⓒ Ⓓ Ⓔ
55. Ⓐ Ⓑ Ⓒ Ⓓ Ⓔ
56. Ⓐ Ⓑ Ⓒ Ⓓ Ⓔ
57. Ⓐ Ⓑ Ⓒ Ⓓ Ⓔ
58. Ⓐ Ⓑ Ⓒ Ⓓ Ⓔ
59. Ⓐ Ⓑ Ⓒ Ⓓ Ⓔ
60. Ⓐ Ⓑ Ⓒ Ⓓ Ⓔ
61. Ⓐ Ⓑ Ⓒ Ⓓ Ⓔ
62. Ⓐ Ⓑ Ⓒ Ⓓ Ⓔ
63. Ⓐ Ⓑ Ⓒ Ⓓ Ⓔ
64. Ⓐ Ⓑ Ⓒ Ⓓ Ⓔ
65. Ⓐ Ⓑ Ⓒ Ⓓ Ⓔ
66. Ⓐ Ⓑ Ⓒ Ⓓ Ⓔ
67. Ⓐ Ⓑ Ⓒ Ⓓ Ⓔ

68. Ⓐ Ⓑ Ⓒ Ⓓ Ⓔ
69. Ⓐ Ⓑ Ⓒ Ⓓ Ⓔ
70. Ⓐ Ⓑ Ⓒ Ⓓ Ⓔ
71. Ⓐ Ⓑ Ⓒ Ⓓ Ⓔ
72. Ⓐ Ⓑ Ⓒ Ⓓ Ⓔ
73. Ⓐ Ⓑ Ⓒ Ⓓ Ⓔ
74. Ⓐ Ⓑ Ⓒ Ⓓ Ⓔ
75. Ⓐ Ⓑ Ⓒ Ⓓ Ⓔ
76. Ⓐ Ⓑ Ⓒ Ⓓ Ⓔ
77. Ⓐ Ⓑ Ⓒ Ⓓ Ⓔ
78. Ⓐ Ⓑ Ⓒ Ⓓ Ⓔ
79. Ⓐ Ⓑ Ⓒ Ⓓ Ⓔ
80. Ⓐ Ⓑ Ⓒ Ⓓ Ⓔ
81. Ⓐ Ⓑ Ⓒ Ⓓ Ⓔ
82. Ⓐ Ⓑ Ⓒ Ⓓ Ⓔ
83. Ⓐ Ⓑ Ⓒ Ⓓ Ⓔ
84. Ⓐ Ⓑ Ⓒ Ⓓ Ⓔ
85. Ⓐ Ⓑ Ⓒ Ⓓ Ⓔ
86. Ⓐ Ⓑ Ⓒ Ⓓ Ⓔ
87. Ⓐ Ⓑ Ⓒ Ⓓ Ⓔ
88. Ⓐ Ⓑ Ⓒ Ⓓ Ⓔ
89. Ⓐ Ⓑ Ⓒ Ⓓ Ⓔ
90. Ⓐ Ⓑ Ⓒ Ⓓ Ⓔ
91. Ⓐ Ⓑ Ⓒ Ⓓ Ⓔ
92. Ⓐ Ⓑ Ⓒ Ⓓ Ⓔ
93. Ⓐ Ⓑ Ⓒ Ⓓ Ⓔ
94. Ⓐ Ⓑ Ⓒ Ⓓ Ⓔ
95. Ⓐ Ⓑ Ⓒ Ⓓ Ⓔ
96. Ⓐ Ⓑ Ⓒ Ⓓ Ⓔ
97. Ⓐ Ⓑ Ⓒ Ⓓ Ⓔ
98. Ⓐ Ⓑ Ⓒ Ⓓ Ⓔ
99. Ⓐ Ⓑ Ⓒ Ⓓ Ⓔ
100. Ⓐ Ⓑ Ⓒ Ⓓ Ⓔ

Index

Notes

Notes

Notes

Notes

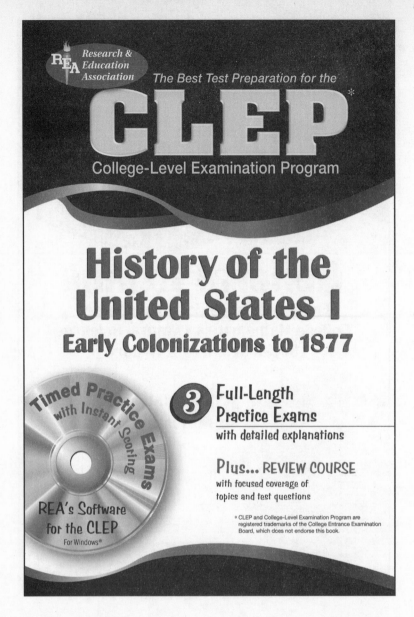

INSTALLING REA's TestWare®

SYSTEM REQUIREMENTS

Pentium 75 MHz (300 MHz recommended) or a higher or compatible processor; Microsoft Windows 98 or later; 64 MB Available RAM; Internet Explorer 5.5 or higher

INSTALLATION

1. Insert the CLEP American Government TestWare® CD-ROM into the CD-ROM drive.
2. If the installation doesn't begin automatically, from the Start Menu choose the RUN command. When the RUN dialog box appears, type d:\setup (where *d* is the letter of your CD-ROM drive) at the prompt and click OK.
3. The installation process will begin. A dialog box proposing the directory "Program Files\REA\CLEP_AmericanGovt" will appear. If the name and location are suitable, click OK. If you wish to specify a different name or location, type it in and click OK.
4. Start the CLEP American Government TestWare® application by double-clicking on the icon.

REA's CLEP American Government TestWare® is **EASY** to **LEARN AND USE**. To achieve maximum benefits, we recommend that you take a few minutes to go through the on-screen tutorial on your computer.

SSD ACCOMMODATIONS FOR STUDENTS WITH DISABILITIES

Many students qualify for extra time to take the CLEP American Government exam, and our TestWare® can be adapted to accommodate your time extension. This allows you to practice under the same extended-time accommodations that you will receive on the actual test day. To customize your TestWare® to suit the most common extensions, visit our website at *www.rea.com/ssd*.

TECHNICAL SUPPORT

REA's TestWare® is backed by customer and technical support. For questions about **installation or operation of your software**, contact us at:

> **Research & Education Association**
> **Phone: (732) 819-8880 (9 a.m. to 5 p.m. ET, Monday–Friday)**
> **Fax: (732) 819-8808**
> **Website: www.rea.com**
> **E-mail: info@rea.com**

Note to Windows XP Users: In order for the TestWare® to function properly, please install and run the application under the same computer administrator-level user account. Installing the TestWare® as one user and running it as another could cause file-access path conflicts.